Language Policy
and
Identity Politics
in the
United States

RONALD SCHMIDT, SR.

TEMPLE UNIVERSITY PRESS   Philadelphia

Temple University Press, Philadelphia 19122
Copyright © 2000 by Temple University
All rights reserved
Published 2000
Printed in the United States of America

Library of Congress Cataloging-in-Publication Data

Schmidt, Ronald, 1943–
    Language policy and identity politics in the United States / Ronald Schmidt, Sr.
      p.   cm. — (Mapping racisms)
    Includes bibliographical references and index.
    ISBN 1-56639-754-5 (cloth : alk. paper) — ISBN 1-56639-755-3 (paper : alk. paper)
      1. Language policy—United States.   2. Americanization.   3. Pluralism (Social
sciences)—United States.   I. Title.   II. Series.

P119.32.U6 S36 2000
306.44′973—dc21
                                            99-087484

For Rosemary

Contents

Acknowledgments   ix

Introduction: A Politics of Language in the United States?   1

I. THE ISSUES AND THE CONTEXT

1 Language Policies in Conflict: An Overview   11

2 Making Sense of Language Policy Conflict   37

3 The Social Foundations of U.S. Language Politics   69

II. THE ARGUMENTS

4 Historical Perspectives on U.S. Identity Politics and Ethnolinguistic Inequality   99

5 Language Policy and Equality: The Search for Justice   130

6 Language Policy and National Unity: The Search for the Common Good   163

III. CRITIQUE AND REFORM

7 Flaws at Every Turn: A Critique of Assimilationist, Pluralist, and Confederationist Alternatives   183

8 Pluralistic Integration: Toward Greater Justice and a More Common Good   221

Notes   251

References   257

Index   275

Acknowledgments

LIKE OTHER authors, I have looked forward to thanking the many people who helped me in writing this book. The frame of reference that informs my work germinated more than three decades ago in a series of in-depth conversations with Lorenza Calvillo Craig and Albert Molina. The initial occasion was our mutual effort to define and shape an adult education program for Spanish-speaking migrant farmworkers in California's San Joaquin Valley, and this was followed by equally illuminating discussions during Lorenza's subsequent years as a member of the California State Board of Education. For their important contributions to my education on these matters, I am deeply grateful to both of them. My doctoral mentor at the University of California at Riverside, Michael D. Reagan, taught me that it is possible to study public policy systematically while engaging the normative issues that undergird all important policy conflicts. By his example and by his encouragement, he has been a source of inspiration for more than thirty years.

The actual writing and production of this book have taken a decade, and the materials and ideas contained within have been shaped and reshaped through professional conference papers, seminars, published articles and multiple book manuscript drafts. Through this long process I have incurred debts to numerous individuals who read, commented on, and/or discussed the ideas and words that evolved into the present work. At the project's beginning in 1990, a National Endowment for the Humanities Summer Seminar for College Teachers at the University of Wisconsin, Madison, led by Professor Crawford Young, provided an indispensable comparative perspective to a scholar schooled within a U.S. frame of reference. To the NEH and to everyone involved in that seminar, many thanks are due. During the ensuing decade, numerous other colleagues and friends participated with me in professional conferences where they heard, read, and gave helpful criticisms, suggestions, and encouragement on the research papers through which my work has advanced. Among these are Tony Affigne, Manuel Avalos, Richard Bourhis, Raymond Breton, Joanne Bretzer, Max Castro, Fae Corsmo, Rodolfo de la Garza, Louis DeSipio, Luis Fraga, Patricia Gandara, F. Chris Garcia, Frank Gilliam, Fernando Guerra, Rodney Hero, Michael Jones-Correa, Jeff Lustig, Reynaldo Macias, Ben Marquez, David Marshall, Paula McClain, Dario Moreno, Noah Pickus, Jaime Regalado, Thomas Ricento, Wendy Sarvasy, Carol Schmid, Christine Sierra, Rogers Smith, Selma Sontagg, Raymond Tatalovich, and Terrence Wiley. Particular thanks are also due to the American Political Science Association and the Western Political Science Association for providing the institutional setting for most of these invaluable conferences.

Throughout my career as a scholar, I have been fortunate to have a faculty appointment at California State University, Long Beach. Although they are all members of a regional teaching institution suffering under an unconscionably heavy workload, my faculty, administrative, staff, and student colleagues at CSULB have succeeded against long odds in making our university a genuine learning community, and as such a continuing source of support and intellectual nourishment for my work. Numerous colleagues at CSULB have patiently supported my efforts by reading and commenting on papers and draft chapters, and/or by listening to my verbal attempts to refine the ideas that have now finally settled into print in this book. Among these are John Attinassi, Mary Caputi, Ken Curtis, Adela de la Torre, Larry George, Bob Gillespie, Maulana Karenga, Larry Martinez, Susan Luevano Molina, Federico Sanchez, George Scott, Christian Soe, Craig Stone, Terrence Wiley, and Terri Wright. I also owe special thanks to two other friends and colleagues at CSULB: Rodolfo Torres, who offered an unfailing support and encouragement throughout the book's long gestation, and then persuasively recruited the project for Temple University Press; and Charles Noble, who not only supported and advised me all along the way, but took time from a sabbatical to read the entire penultimate draft and make numerous helpful suggestions. Several other CSULB individuals and groups, moreover, supported the project, including my department chairs, Robert Delorme and Gerry Riposa, Dean Dorothy Abrahamse, Provost Karl Anatol, and members of the University Scholarly and Creative Activities Committee. CSULB President Robert Maxson, finally, has helped immeasurably by spreading his positive outlook and goodwill over this as well as all other faculty enterprises.

I also wish to thank Doris Braendel, Senior Acquisitions Editor at Temple University Press, for her support of this project. And I especially want to thank the two scholarly readers she recruited to review the manuscript, for both Luis Fraga and an anonymous reviewer provided strong encouragement for the book's publication, and offered insightful criticisms and helpful suggestions for improving the final product. Their hard work made this a better book.

Last, but by no means least, the members of my family have been my primary inspiration and support throughout the last decade. My son, Ron, Jr., who recently embarked on his own career in political science, read and commented on multiple papers and listened to my ideas with constant good cheer and sound critical judgment. My daughter, Rebecca Taylor, always willingly listened to my thoughts, providing steady encouragement, insightful ideas, and a helpful perspective from a very different intellectual frame of reference. And there is no way for me to adequately thank my wife, Rosemary. Through the years of its writing she has listened to and talked with me about virtually every idea contained in this book; an astute editor, she also has offered sound advice on how to improve more than a few of its pages. Among her many other gifts for which I am deeply thankful is the emotional foundation from which to engage in my life's work with joy and confidence; in that specific and deeply important sense, she has given me the voice with which to write. To her I have gratefully dedicated this book.

Language Policy and Identity Politics in the United States

Introduction

A Politics of Language in the United States?

IN THE United States, as in virtually every country in the world, multiple languages are spoken. We are, and always have been, a multilingual country. Nevertheless, throughout all of our history as an independent country, and including the present time, English has been our dominant language. Since the founding of the British colonies in North America, no other language has come close to challenging or displacing English as the *lingua franca* of the United States. English is almost the sole language of government and politics, it is the overwhelmingly dominant language of commerce and education, and it is spoken exclusively in the vast majority of homes and public spaces in civil society in every region of the country.

Moreover, since the end of World War I, demographers and sociolinguists have charted a steady pattern of linguistic assimilation, or "language shift," to English followed by virtually all newcomers to this country and their descendents: (1) most immigrants (the first generation) struggle to learn the dominant language and urge their children both to master English in order to be successful and to retain the home language as well; (2) the children of immigrants (the second generation) typically do retain an ability to speak and sometimes read and write their parents' language, even as English becomes the dominant tongue in their own homes and in their public lives at work and in the community; and (3) the grandchildren of the immigrants (the third generation) are English monolinguals, retaining very little, if any, ability to speak, read, or write the "old country" language.

Throughout most of this century, the process of Americanization has meant in part that we have become able to communicate in only one language—English—by the time our families' have been in the United States for three generations. There is considerable, although contested, evidence that this pattern continues today even among the relatively large number of new immigrants who have entered the United States since the 1960s (see, e.g., Veltman, 1983).

If all this is true, why write a book on political conflict over language in the United States? The reason is that, despite the truth of the above statements, language use, and especially public policy affecting language use, has become a highly emotional and volatile political issue in the United States over the past three decades. Consider the following incidents:

- In 1973 county commissioners in Dade County (Greater Miami), Florida, declared the county to be "bilingual and bicultural." Seven years later, in 1980, voters overwhelmingly approved a ballot initiative rescinding the 1973 ordinance and declaring Dade County to be officially monolingual and monocultural in English only. Then, in 1993, twenty years after the original ordinance was passed, a new majority of county commissioners reinstated official bilingualism in Dade County, despite the outraged cries of "official English" partisans. By 1998, with broad support from Miami's political and business leaders, Dade County's public schools officially adopted the goal of making every student in the metropolitan region bilingual in Spanish and English through a two-way bilingual education program.
- After hearing an appeal from lawyers on behalf of a Chinese-speaking student in San Francisco, the U.S. Supreme Court—in *Lau v. Nichols* (1974)—decided unanimously that unlawful discrimination has occurred, a violation of the Civil Rights Act of 1964, when public schools try to teach students only in a language they cannot understand (i.e., English).
- After hearing testimony from a parade of witnesses, most of them from Texas, the U.S. Congress declared in 1975 that "voting discrimination against citizens of language minorities is pervasive and national in scope, (U.S. Commission on Civil Rights, 1981:120)" and included language minorities as a protected group under the Voting Rights Act of 1965. Accordingly, Congress mandated that ballots and other election materials must be provided in languages other than English under certain circumstances.
- In California, the state with the largest number of non-English-speakers, voters in 1984 approved—by a 71 percent to 29 percent margin—a ballot initiative directing their governor to write a letter to the president expressing the state's opposition to Congress's mandate of multilingual ballots.

- In 1986, against the advice of the Republican governor and virtually all other top state officials, California voters adopted—this time by a margin of 73 percent to 27 percent—an amendment to the state's constitution declaring English to be the sole official language of the state. By 1998 twenty-one states had passed legislation making English their sole official language, and eighteen of these had done so *after* 1980.

- In 1987, against the advice of a bipartisan blue-ribbon commission he had helped to appoint, the same Republican governor of California vetoed—for the second year in a row—an extension of the state's mandatory bilingual education law, thus allowing it to "sunset." Despite the governor's veto, the state's department of education continued to enforce regulations that mandated bilingual education in most of the state's public schools until this was overruled by judicial action in early 1998.

- In 1990, a U.S. district court judge ruled that Arizona's "official English" constitutional amendment, adopted by voters in 1988 in a hotly contested election, violates the First Amendment of the U.S. Constitution and must not be enforced by the state. After this ruling was upheld by the Ninth District Court of Appeals the Supreme Court of the United States held in 1997 that both lower court decisions were invalid, requiring a new hearing of the issues at the trial court level. In 1998, the Arizona Supreme Court ruled the amendment was in violation of the U.S. Constitution.

- In 1996, after the Republican party won a majority in both houses of Congress, the U.S. House of Representatives passed (in a nearly party-line vote) the Emerson English-Language Empowerment Bill (H.R. 123), which would have made English the sole official language of the United States and abolished the language minority provisions of the Voting Rights Act of 1965. While the Senate did not act on the House bill, former Senate majority leader and Republican presidential candidate Robert Dole praised it and called for its passage. The Clinton White House, meanwhile, vowed to veto the bill if passed by the Senate.

- In 1998 California voters approved—by a 61 percent to 39 percent margin—an initiative that virtually outlawed all of the state's bilingual education programs, replacing them with a one-year English-immersion program. Organized and largely financed by Republican activist and computer software multimillionare Ron Unz, the initiative was immediately challenged in court and in classrooms by angered bilingual education teachers, who vowed to continue teaching students in their native languages.

These incidents are examples drawn from a complex conflict over language policy in the United States that many observers believe is spreading and growing in intensity. As a closer look will reveal, three types of issues have been predominant in this ongoing battle over language: (1) educational policy for language minority children and especially the place of bilingual education in their schooling; (2) linguistic access to political and civil rights (such as the right to vote) for non-English-speakers of all ages; and (3) the designation of English as the sole official language of the United States and its component states and local governments.

Most citizens of the United States undoubtedly remain unaware that language policy has become a politically contentious issue. Among the growing number of persons for whom this is a salient political issue, however, partisans tend to divide into two camps: *pluralists* and *assimilationists*. At the level of policy support, the conflict between these two groups is starkly clear: pluralists favor using the state to enhance the presence and status of minority languages in the United States, while assimilationists seek state policies that will ensure the status of English as the country's sole public language. Beyond this obvious division, however, the two groups of antagonists come to this political conflict with radically different understandings of what is at stake in the language policy debate.

Linguistic pluralists, for example, believe that the conflict is a question of justice involving the struggle of racialized language minorities for equality in a country that has dominated and suppressed them for over two hundred years. The pluralist narrative takes its bearings from the U.S. history of conquest, annexation, and oppression of peoples of color—including American Indians, African Americans, Mexican Americans, and Puerto Ricans—and the consequences of that history for these peoples. Pursuing justice, pluralists believe that the choices to be made in the language policy debate revolve around righting wrongs and removing culturally hegemonic obstacles to equality for long-oppressed groups. Moreover, because most language minority groups today are peoples of color (adding Asians and Pacific Islanders to those listed above), pluralists see this conflict as deeply linked to the struggle for racial equality in the United States. Since overt racism is no longer publicly acceptable in this country, they believe that linguistic prejudice and discrimination have become surrogates for the arguments and practices of white supremacy. Adopting policies of linguistic pluralism, then, is seen as a necessary step in the country's long struggle to purge itself of its racist heritage.

In contrast, linguistic assimilationists view this conflict in strikingly different ways. For them, the issue is not minority rights at all, but the socialization of immigrants and the common good. Assimilationists are especially preoccupied with their perception of an increasingly dangerous threat to national unity brought about by centrifugal forces of change in the late twentieth century. And they view the massive wave of immigration to the United States since the mid-1960s as one of two chief sources of this change. In itself, assimilationists believe, massive immigration always represents a serious challenge to national unity. In our time, however, this problem has been intensified by a second source of change—a politics of cultural pluralism that threatens to obstruct traditional processes of immigrant integration.

In their narrative of language policy conflict, assimilationists also appeal to U.S. history, but their focus is on the efforts of previous immigrant groups to become "Americanized" as quickly as possible. It is this historical tradition, they think, that minority activists and their allies threaten to undermine. In pursuing a vision of the common good, assimilationists believe that the English language is one of the few ties that hold this "nation of immigrants" together, and that recently enacted pluralistic language policies threaten to unleash an ethnic separatism that will tear apart the social fabric in highly destructive ways. Thus, while their language policy positions directly confront one another, the narratives employed by linguistic pluralists and assimilationists to make sense of and rationalize their positions are widely disparate.

The principal aims of this book are both descriptive and analytical. Descriptively, my goal is to provide a coherent overview of the contemporary U.S. conflict over language policy, and of the competing narratives and arguments offered by partisans in the debate. Analytically, my aim is to probe the partisans' positions more deeply in order to discern, articulate, and come to terms with the central issue in this conflict. For though the two sides' positions differ fundamentally, they do have an underlying common source that is rooted not in language per se but in a concern over identity and its consequences for individuals, groups and the country as a whole. Moreover, the analysis that follows will indicate that identity politics is deeply implicated in conflicts not only over symbolic recognition, but also over the allocation of substantive and material benefits to members of the society.

A NOTE ON METHOD

The method of analysis employed in this book was inspired early in my career by Martin Rein's (1971) call for "value-critical" policy analysis, which he distinguished from both "value-neutral" and "value-committed" approaches to public policy analysis. Guided by the canons of scientific research, the value-neutral approach takes as givens the value commitments toward which public policies aim and seeks to predict (through modeling and causal analysis) which of several alternative means of achieving a policy's goal is most likely to succeed and at what costs. Similarly, during and after a policy's implementation, value-neutral analysts attempt to describe the degree to which the policy succeeded or failed to achieve its aims and to explain why.

The value-committed approach to policy analysis has a long history. Here, the analysts attempt to justify a given policy in terms of values to which they are already committed by marshaling arguments and evidence that point in that direction (e.g., testimony presented by interest group representatives before legislative committees or ideologically grounded analyses made by scholars).

In contrast, Rein (1971) defined the value-critical approach as one that "subjects goals and values to critical review, that is, values themselves become the object of analysis; they are not merely accepted as a voluntary choice of the will, unamenable to further debate" (p. 13). Nor, on the other hand, does the value-critical analysis begin with an unexamined faith in an ideology, as in the case of the value-committed approach. Rather, on the assumption that values discourse can be conducted rationally, the value-critical analyst approaches public policy aims with a skeptical spirit, seeking to subject them to rigorous, but not cynical, analysis. The aim of a value-critical approach, then, is to contribute to the public discussion of policy conflicts by viewing the goals of that policy as subjects of analysis.

In keeping with the value-critical approach, this book will focus particularly on the aims or goals at stake in the U.S. language policy debate between assimilationists and pluralists. Having immersed myself in this issue, I became aware, on the one hand, that most value-committed policy analyses led to fruitless, value-smashing exercises between these partisans. On the other hand, however, I also came to believe that there is little hope that scientifically rigorous value-neutral policy analyses, no matter how well done, can lead to a deeper understanding of our language policy conflict, because what is really at stake in this division are strongly felt value differences. Critically engaging the hopes and dreams of conflicting language policy partisans, in contrast, offers the best chance of bringing us closer to resolving the language policy controversy in the United States in an appropriate and constructive fashion. It is not assumed that this analysis will put an end to the conflict but rather that it will shed greater light on the validity of the respective positions of the participants in the debate and provide a well-reasoned foundation for the conclusions reached at the book's end.

OUTLINE OF THE BOOK

Part I of this book traces the evolution of the U.S. language policy conflict over the past several decades (Chapter 1), and provides a broader comparative and theoretical perspective (Chapters 2 and 3) to help set the stage for what follows. Part II outlines in some detail the historical narratives of both sets of partisans (Chapter 4) and their discursive arguments on the value-conflict issues of equality for non-English-speakers (Chapter 5) and the relationship of language policy to national unity (Chapter 6). Part III (Chapters 7 and 8) offers my critical analysis of the debate and my own set of suggestions for how we can best resolve it in order to reach the goals of both greater justice for language minorities and a more common good. No language policy can resolve every aspect of the conflict to everyone's satisfaction. I argue, however, that a strengthened pluralistic language policy, supplemented by an engaged immigrant settlement policy and structural reforms aimed at reversing the growing economic inequality between U.S. ethnolinguistic groups, offers our best chance of meeting the criteria of justice and the common good.

We have a long distance to travel before reaching these conclusions, but I hope that the journey will lead to greater understanding of the reasons for a politics of language in the United States, the arguments in this volatile political conflict, and the goals at stake. We begin our journey in Chapter 1, with a narrative overview of the policy issues at the heart of the contemporary politics of language in the United States.

I. THE ISSUES AND THE CONTEXT

1   Language Policies in Conflict

An Overview

THE UNITED States has experienced heightened political conflict over language policy for the last three decades, as an ongoing disagreement between pluralists and assimilationists has engaged the attention of the media and policymakers in such a wide range of venues as radio talk shows, television debates, local school boards, PTA meetings, city councils, county governments, state legislatures, executive agencies, national political party nominating conventions, the Congress, and the Supreme Court of the United States. More specifically, this conflict has centered on three primary issues that are deeply intertwined in the minds of most of its partisans: (1) education policy for language minority children; (2) access to civil and political rights and government services by non-English-speakers; and (3) the establishment of English as the sole official language of the United States and its political subdivisions. This first chapter will introduce this subject by sketching a developmental narrative of this political debate that in turn will serve as the point of reference for the analysis to follow.

EDUCATION POLICY FOR LANGUAGE MINORITY STUDENTS

Contemporary language politics in the United States first emerged in the 1960s in reference to educational policy for language minority students in the public schools, especially Latino students. Initiated before the current wave of immigration to the United States took on large-scale proportions, the beginnings of the movement for an innovative approach to education for students from non-English-speaking homes was perceived by most policymakers as an equal opportunity program for "culturally disadvantaged" American minority students.

The first national legislation in this movement was the Bilingual Education Act of 1968, which amended the Elementary and Secondary Education Act of 1965 (ESEA) by adding Title VII. Arguing that poverty and

11

ignorance had denied millions of Americans an opportunity to live the American dream, by 1966 President Lyndon Johnson had pushed through Congress a sweeping series of domestic policy innovations known collectively as the "Great Society" program. The ESEA, by establishing the first large-scale federal program in support of local schools, was by far the most significant of its initiatives in the field of education (Sundquist, 1968: 155–220).

Present bilingual education policies had their origins in this Great Society quest for equal opportunity for the disadvantaged, especially racialized minorities. By the middle 1960s mounting evidence showed that non-English-speaking students in the public schools, particularly many Latinos in the Southwest, suffered unusually high dropout rates and progressively lower academic achievement scores compared to their English-speaking peers. The inability to speak English came to be viewed by many educators and activists as an important obstacle standing in the way of equal opportunity for these Americans. Among those taking this position was Senator Ralph Yarborough (D-Texas), who introduced the bilingual education amendment (Title VII) to ESEA in 1967. Senator Yarborough explained his motivation for sponsoring the bill as follows:

> The failure of our schools to educate Spanish-speaking students is reflected in comparative drop-out rates. In the five Southwestern States ..., Anglos 14 years of age and over have completed an average of 12 years of school compared with 8.1 years for Spanish-surnamed students. I regret to say that my own State of Texas ranks at the bottom, with a median of only 4.7 years of school completed by persons of Spanish surname. (Yarborough, 1992 [1967], p. 323).

While the Johnson administration did not initially support the bill, Senator Yarborough and several of his colleagues, together with widespread support from Latino political leaders and activists, managed to see it successfully through Congress.

As a relatively small demonstration grant program, Title VII was at first more symbolic than substantive. Political support for bilingual education continued to grow in the late 1960s and early 1970s, but the major impetus for its expansion came from the U.S. Supreme Court in its 1974 *Lau v. Nichols* decision. In that ruling on a class action suit brought against the San Francisco Unified School District on behalf of Chinese-speaking elementary school students, the Court held the 1964

Civil Rights Act to mean that failure by a school district to provide instruction in a language students can understand is unlawful discrimination that violates those students' civil rights. As Justice William O. Douglas wrote in the opinion of the Court, "there is no equality of treatment merely by providing students with the same facilities, textbooks, teachers and curriculum; for students who do not understand English are effectively foreclosed from any meaningful education" (U.S. Supreme Court, 1974).

While the Court did not mandate bilingual education as the remedy for these students, supporters of the Title VII program—both inside and outside government—seized upon the case as legitimation for its expansion. A subsequent task force convened by the U.S. Office of Education resulted in the so-called *Lau* Remedies, issued as guidelines to bring local school districts receiving federal funds into compliance with the *Lau* decision. Although the *Lau* Remedies also did not mandate bilingual education, they did place it in a preferred position: those schools desiring to use alternative pedagogical methods had to demonstrate that their approaches to educating non-English-speaking students were at least as effective as bilingual education.

Meanwhile, in the same year as the *Lau* decision, was handed down, Congress adopted the 1974 Equal Educational Opportunities Act, thereby codifying the language used by the Court. Section 1703(f) of the act prohibited "the failure by an educational agency to take appropriate action to overcome language barriers that impede equal participation by its students in its instructional program" (Salomone, 1986: 100). Thus, by the middle 1970s bilingual education had become a nationwide force for change in the public schools. In addition to the federal law, many states enacted legislation authorizing or mandating bilingual education in their public schools.

The original Bilingual Education Act did not specify the pedagogical methods involved in a bilingual approach to teaching non-English-speaking students. And by the early 1970s, controversy had erupted among educators and political activists over competing approaches. During the decade that followed the conflict came to center on a debate between transitional and maintenance approaches to bilingual education. The *transitional* approach uses the student's native language in subjects other than English only until the student masters the dominant language well enough to be mainstreamed into a monolingual English classroom. The orientation is remedial in that the child's home language is considered a crutch that should be dispensed with as quickly as possible.

The *maintenance* approach also seeks to enable students to master English and to move quickly into mainstream classrooms, but its orientation to their native languages is very different. Rather than seeing the home language as a crutch, the maintenance approach views it as a valuable resource—for the child, the community and the nation—that should be nurtured and developed along with other academic skills. Thus, maintenance programs continue to teach students in their native languages long after they have become proficient in English. The aim for them is mastery of *both* languages, not just English.

While educators and activists fought over these approaches (and a proliferation of subtypes within each), policymakers at all levels of government were making it increasingly clear that there was little support for the maintenance approach in legislative bodies. At the insistence of House conferees, for example, Congress stipulated in its 1974 amendments to the Bilingual Education Act that its expansion of the bilingual education program should "not be misinterpreted to indicate that an ultimate goal of the program is the establishment of a 'bilingual society'" (Schneider, 1976: 201). Further, Congress mandated that the native language of limited English-speaking (LES) children was to be used in bilingual programs only "to the extent necessary to allow children to progress effectively through the educational system" (Schneider, 1976: 215). By 1978 Congress became even less ambiguous: that year's amendments to the act stipulated that the native language could be used only ". . . to the extent necessary to allow a child to achieve competence in the English language" (Gray et al., 1981: 8).

State legislation followed a similar pattern. The Massachusetts law, for example, was titled the Transitional Bilingual Education Act. And California's 1980 bilingual education law, considered at the time one of the nation's strongest, stated that the "primary goal of all programs under this article is, as effectively and efficiently as possible, to develop in each child fluency in English," authorizing the use of students' primary languages only "when necessary" to attain that goal (Gray et al., 1981: 22).

By 1980 it seemed clear that the bilingual education movement, insofar as it was aimed at a bilingual citizenry, had peaked and was on the defensive. Indeed, within government in the 1980s the issue no longer centered around the "transitional versus maintenance" argument but on whether the requirements for bilingual instruction in federally funded programs for limited English-proficient (LEP) students would be maintained at all. Critics of the programs argued that this "expensive" method for the education of non-English-speaking students had not been able to prove itself in evaluation studies, and began to call for alternative approaches that would not employ the students' native languages in the classroom. School districts, hard-pressed to find qualified bilingual teachers, began to pressure legislators and federal education officials for permission to use their federal bilingual dollars to experiment with other approaches.

Among the favorite candidates for experimentation was an approach called "English-immersion." Loosely modeled after a French-immersion technique popular among Anglophone Canadians in Quebec, immersion involves placing non-English-speaking students in a structured English-only environment in which they are encouraged to rapidly switch to the dominant language without help from their native tongue. In turn, these moves toward experimentation were attacked immediately by bilingual education's supporters as a return to the pre-*Lau* days of "sink-or-swim English *submersion*," and the political conflict over language education policy continued (see California State Department of Education, 1984).

It did not take the Reagan administration very long to make it clear that it would side with those who argued against a maintenance approach and that it would favor loosening the requirements for bilingual education for LEP students. Shortly after taking office, for example, President Reagan made the following off-the-cuff remark to reporters: "It is absolutely wrong and against American concepts to have a bilingual education program that is now openly, admittedly dedicated to preserving their native language and never getting them adequate in English so they can go into the job market and participate" (quoted in Crawford, 1989: 43). In its first year in office, then, the new administration scuttled proposed U.S. Department of Education regulations developed at the end of the Carter years that would have strengthened the *Lau* Remedies issued in 1975 (Crawford, 1989: 42). Further, it also succeeded in 1981 in cutting back funding for the Bilingual Education Act (although not in consolidating the program into the education block grant of that year), and launched an effort in 1983 to end the privileged pedagogical status of bilingual education (Salomone, 1986: 92–97).

These efforts were stepped up very aggressively after Reagan appointed William C. Bennett as secretary of education in 1985 (General Accounting Office, 1987: 43–58). Indeed, Bennett became a leading national spokesperson for the campaign to "rescue" English as the sole national language from the forces of bilingualism and multiculturalism, and remained active in this campaign long after he left public office. Shortly after becoming secretary of education, Bennett delivered a widely noted speech in New York City in which he attacked his own department for having privileged (via the *Lau* Remedies) bilingual education "as virtually the only approved method of remedying discrimination," with the result that "we had lost sight of the goal of learning *English* as the key to equal educational opportunity" (quoted in Tatalovich, 1995: 19).

The Reagan administration was never fully successful in its efforts to derail bilingual education, however, due to stiff opposition from the program's supporters in Congress. In 1988 the administration was forced to accept a compromise in the reauthorization of the law, in which 75 percent of federal bilingual education funds were set aside for "transitional bilingual education programs," and the remaining 25 percent could be used for experimental programs at the local level (which could include both English-immersion and maintenance bilingual education).

Then came another shift in the beleaguered program's political fortunes. After Bennett was replaced as secretary of education by Lauro Cavazos in 1988, the orientation of the department became more positive toward the bilingual program. Indeed, shortly after President Bush reappointed Cavazos to head the department in 1989, the press began to write of a new revival of bilingual education in the country, spearheaded by the administration's educational administrators. In a 1990 *New York Times Magazine* article on Rita Esquivel, appointed by Cavazos as director of the Office of Bilingual Education and Minority Languages Affairs, Richard Bernstein described her as "an unequivocal advocate of bilingual education." Moreover, while reflecting the Republican administration's support for a decentralist version of federalism, Esquivel claimed to have President Bush's support for a maintenance approach to bilingual education, saying, "We certainly would like them to maintain their native languages. That's the President's point of view" (quoted in Bernstein, 1990: 48). Bill Clinton's election as president in 1992, meanwhile, continued executive-branch support for bilingual education at the federal level.

Despite these apparent successes in the defense of bilingual education, nevertheless, the program remained on the defensive in the 1990s. Federal funds never reached levels high enough to put more than a fraction of the eligible students into bilingual classrooms. And meanwhile, the number of LEP students in the nation had grown steadily for over two decades, largely as a result of continued high levels of immigration. As a consequence, the expense and difficulty of finding qualified teachers for bilingual classrooms made less stringent approaches to the education of language minority students ever more attractive to financially strapped and beleaguered school boards and administrators, and state and local elected officials. Moreover, the controversy over the effectiveness of bilingual education as a pedagogical method showed no signs of abating. Although support for bilingual education's relative effectiveness when fully implemented grew to near-consensus levels among professional educational researchers (see Ramírez et al., 1991), the program's ability to teach English to LEP students continued to be challenged by many educators and politicians, and attacks on its effectiveness were published in the press with ongoing regularity (see Chapter 5 for a more elaborate articulation of this point).

A major political test for bilingual education as federal policy came with the fifth reauthorization of the program in 1994. With the Democratic party controlling both Congress and the White House, an effort was made in that year to restructure federal educational policy in the Improving America's Schools Act (IASA), enacted in tandem with two other federal education laws, the Goals 2000: Educate America Act and the School-to-Work Opportunities Act. As a part of that education policy overhaul, the Bilingual Education Act was reauthorized as Title VII, Part A, of the IASA.

In integrating bilingual education into this federal educational reform effort, Congress stipulated several new goals for the program that have been interpreted by its supporters as major enhancements. In particular, the federal law first sought to ensure that language minority students are not left behind as the schools are pushed to demand ever higher standards of achievement for all U.S. public school students. Building on educational research, as James Crawford (1997) notes, the new law enacted the principle that "given access to challenging curriculum, language-minority and limited-English-Proficient (LEP) students can achieve to the same high standards as other students" (on-line article). And second, citing the research demonstrating bilingual education's effectiveness, federal law for the first time gave formal, legislative support to the goal of *maintaining* LEP students' native languages. Crawford (1997), described the legislation as follows:

> English proficiency has been and will remain a central goal of Title VII; but not the only goal. A coequal priority has been achievement in academic content areas. In 1994, Congress added yet another. It recognized the value of preserving, rather than replacing, a child's native language— first, as a foundation for learning, and second, as a source of valuable skills. Again, this policy is consistent with the latest research. Bilingualism is no longer considered a handicap to cognitive growth, but probably an advantage. In addition, it is seen as a job skill of increasing importance, a tool of cross-cultural understanding, and a vital resource in the global marketplace and international relations. (on-line article)

This third goal, of course, remains very controversial, and after the Republicans took control of both houses of Congress only a few months after the 1994 reauthorization, efforts were made to rescind it. As this book went to press, the five-year authorization of the Bilingual Education Act was due to expire at the end of 1999, and the Clinton administration had proposed its reauthorization to the Republican Congress. There was as yet, however, no indication of the proposed legislation's fate, although leading up to this decision, federal bilingual educational programs suffered a 38 percent budget cut from 1994 to 1996 (Crawford, 1997) despite continuing increases in the number of LEP children in U.S. public schools.

The controversy over bilingual education remains heated at the state and local levels of government as well. In California, which has nearly one-third of the nation's LEP students (Fleischman and Hopstock, 1993), voter adoption of Proposition 227 in June 1998 sought to replace virtually all of the state's bilingual education programs with one-year English-immersion classrooms. As of this writing, a legal challenge to the new policy had failed, and school districts up and down the state were engaged in an often contentious effort to implement the Unz initiative, with bilingual education advocates vowing not to give up the fight. The success of Proposition 227 in California, meanwhile, had already stimulated emulatory measures in other states.[1] Whatever the outcome of these specific battles, it is safe to assume that the controversy over native language instruction for minority language students is sure to continue into the foreseeable future.

LANGUAGE AND ACCESS TO POLITICAL AND CIVIL RIGHTS

A second area of contention over language policy emerged in the early 1970s, and has focused on the question of linguistic access to political and civil rights. In other words, should language minority persons have legally protected rights to participate in elections and more broadly to interact with their government in a language they understand? Or is knowledge of English a precondition for the exercise of these rights? Do the more general civil rights prohibitions against discrimination on the basis of national origin include language as a central marker of national origin? Much of the logic that has been used to justify bilingual education programs has also been applied to justify other rights for language minority persons in the United States. That is, if school districts are obligated to provide meaningful education to students in a language they can understand, should not other public institutions be required to ensure access to legitimate rights and services in a language understandable to members of the community? The issues in contention here can be grouped conveniently into linguistic access to three areas: electoral participation, governmental institutions and public services, and employment rights.

The most prominent and emotionally heated linguistic access issue has been that of providing ballots and other election materials in languages other than English. As was true to a greater extent for African Americans, several other racialized ethnic groups in the United States (e.g., Latinos, Asian Americans, and American Indians) had voting participation rates that were consistently below those of European-origin Americans throughout much of the twentieth century. Many political activists among these groups believed that discrimination was an important cause of this disparity in electoral participation. In the early 1970s, several minority political organizations (led principally by the Mexican American Legal Defense and Education Fund, or MALDEF) mounted a lobbying campaign aimed at gaining coverage for language minorities under the Voting Rights Act of 1965, which was seen as a potential vehicle for rectifying this disparity.

After initial resistance from several leading African American organizations (Thernstrom, 1987: 50), the coalition of civil rights lobbying groups known as the Leadership Conference on Civil Rights agreed to support the change. In 1975, moreover, the U.S. Civil Rights Commission issued an evaluation of the first ten years of the Voting Rights Act in which it urged the inclusion of language minorities under the act's protective umbrella (U.S. Commission on Civil Rights, 1975a: 356). Even the U.S. Justice Department submitted a state-by-state review of the issue to Congress, finding a "need to respond at the federal level to the problems of minority language groups" (Leibowitz, 1982: 5).

With little organized opposition, a parade of thirty-four witnesses testified before the House Judiciary Committee's hearings on the 1975 extension of the Voting Rights Act in support of the need for voting rights protections for members of language minority groups. The resulting statutory revisions included such strongly worded findings by Congress on the issue as the following, from Section 4(f):

> The Congress finds that voting discrimination against citizens of language minorities is pervasive and national in scope. Such minority citizens are from environments in which the dominant language is other than English. In addition they have been denied equal educational opportunities by State and local governments, resulting in severe disabilities and continuing illiteracy in the English language. The Congress further finds that, where State and local officials conduct elections only in English, language minority citizens are excluded from participating in the electoral process. In many areas of the country, this exclusion is aggravated by acts of physical, economic, and political intimidation. The Congress declares that, in order to enforce the guarantees of the fourteenth and fifteenth amendments to the United States Constitution, it is necessary to eliminate such discrimination by prohibiting English-only elections, and by prescribing other remedial devices. (U.S. Commission on Civil Rights, 1981a: 120)

Titles II and III of the Voting Rights Act, thus, were amended in 1975 to require that registration forms, ballots, and other election materials had to be provided in a language other than English if more than 5 percent of the voters in an election district spoke the same non-English language and if the English illiteracy rate in the district was greater than the national illiteracy rate (Leibowitz, 1982: 7–9). For purposes of this law, Congress defined "language minorities" or "language minority group" to include "persons who are American Indian, Asian American, Alaskan Natives or of Spanish heritage" (U.S. Commission on Civil Rights, 1981a: 129).

The rationale for this amendment was that no American citizen should lose the right to vote simply because she or he has a native language other than English. As with bilingual education, nevertheless, this law quickly became very controversial and was the subject of widespread opposition, particularly in areas with large numbers of non-English-speakers. As noted, for example, in California's November 1984 election voters overwhelmingly approved (by a margin of 71% to 29%) Proposition 38, which directed the governor to write a letter to President Reagan expressing the state's opposition to bilingual ballots. Among other things, the ballot initiative stated that

> the United States Government should foster similarities that unite our people, and the most important of which is the use of the English language.
> Multilingual ballots are divisive, costly and often delay or prevent our immigrant citizens from moving into the economic, political, educational and social mainstream of our country. (quoted in Pitt, 1985: 295)

The Reagan administration, however, needed little prompting from California voters, as it had already launched a campaign in 1982 to cut back on federal interventions in state government electoral practices through the Voting Rights Act. A compromise with congressional defenders of the act was eventually reached, in which the 1982 extension bill restricted the protections for language minority citizens, reducing the number of counties and subdivisions covered by the policy from 384 under the 1975 provisions to 197 under the 1982 bill (Rodriguez and Christman, 1988: 3).

When the Voting Rights Act came up for reauthorization again, in 1992, George Bush was president. As seen above, he had a much more positive perspective on linguistic diversity in the United States. Indeed, Bush's Latina daughter-in-law had delivered an address in Spanish at his 1988 Republican presidential nominating convention in an apparent effort to woo more Latino voters to support his candidacy. With Bush in the White House, language minority activists mounted a successful campaign in Congress to strengthen the language provisions of the Voting Rights Act in 1992. And this time Asian/Pacific Islander organizations and American Indian activists were much more prominent, along with Latinos, in the lobbying effort. The 1992 reauthorization of the law, then, expanded the language provisions beyond their original 1975 scope, which included jurisdictions in which 5 percent of the voting-age citizens were language minorities, to encompass jurisdictions (mostly counties) with ten thousand or more citizens of voting age who "are members of a single language minority and are limited-English proficient," (P.L. 102-344; H.R. 4312). The law was amended as well to expand the number of eligible American Indians living on reservations.

Proponents of linguistic access to elections placed special significance on the numerical criterion for coverage of a jurisdiction. The importance of this new criterion was that it brought a number of urban counties with multiple language minority groups under the federal mandate. With the 1982 Voting Rights Act reauthorization, for example, Los Angeles County was no longer required by federal mandate to provide multilingual ballots (although it continued to do so voluntarily). By contrast, with the 1992 reauthorization, Los Angeles County was required to provide these materials not only in Spanish (as under the original 1975 amendment), but in "Chinese, Filipino, Japanese, and Vietnamese" as well (Bureau of the Census, 1992). Congressional opponents of the law, however, continued to argue that the linguistic access provisions of the act were unnecessary, ineffective, and too costly, and would prove harmful both to their intended beneficiaries and to the national interest by impeding acquisition of English fluency.

A second front in the campaign for linguistic access is dedicated to breaking down language barriers to governmental institutions and public services more generally. The central rationale of this campaign, once again, is that government has an obligation to make itself understood to those whom it governs and serves, and that those who are governed and served should be able to communicate freely and effectively with their governors. Thus, for example, police dispatchers, hospital emergency room personnel, social workers, and school officials, should be able to communicate effectively with members of the community in order to fulfill their public responsibilities, even if their clients cannot understand English. Two Latino attorneys who were high-level public officials during California Governor Jerry Brown's administration put it this way in a 1980 essay:

Governmental laws and policies have simply failed to make provision for the non-English speaking. While the Court's and Congress' interest in protecting the fundamental interest of the right to vote has spawned protective legislation in voting, efforts have not gone so far as to recognize the needs of language minorities or to create affirmative obligations to provide government social services in a linguistically comprehensible manner. (Obledo and Alcala, 1980: 157)

Because Congress has not adopted legislation providing a clear statutory foundation for linguistic access to governmental institutions and public services, however, the primary venue for this aspect of language policy conflict has been the courts. And in this realm activists for language minorities have not been as successful in winning support for their claims. Pursuing a strategy of litigation, linguistic access activists have made claims founded on both the U.S. Constitution and on existing legislation, particularly the Civil Rights Act of 1964. Suits claiming a constitutional basis for linguistic access (via the Fourteenth Amendment's equal protection clause) have not been successful at the federal district court level, however, and the U.S. Supreme Court has declined to take up the issue on appeal (Piatt, 1990: 98–103).

Using the statutory basis of the Civil Rights Act of 1964, nevertheless, some activists have been able to make the claim that the prohibition against national origin discrimination requires linguistic access. In the cases of *Sanchez v. Norton* (1974) and *Pabon v. Levine* (1976), for example, federal district courts found on behalf of language minority plaintiffs who claimed that English-only unemployment insurance and welfare programs in areas with substantial numbers of non-English-speaking clients violates the 1964 Civil Rights Act (Leibowitz, 1982: 18). In California, a similar lawsuit (*Association Mixta Progresista v. H.E.W.*, 1974) resulted in a 1975 consent decree mandating bilingual hiring in the California Department of Payments (Obledo and Alcala, 1980: 158). In *Kuri v. Edelman* (1974), however, a federal circuit court ruled against minority language petitioners seeking linguistic access to welfare services (Leibowitz, 1982: 18). Political activists continue to press the issues, and many local governments in areas with large concentrations of non-English-speakers have in fact made provisions to communicate with their publics in those languages, although usually on a pragmatic basis and not as a matter of principle (see, e.g., Muir, 1990).

The courts and Congress have been generally more protective of linguistic access for minority language persons accused of crimes. In a 1970 case (*U.S. ex rel. Negron v. New York*), a federal circuit court of appeals ruled in favor of an appeal by a non-English-speaking man accused of murder, which was brought on the claim that he could not understand the trial court proceedings that had led to his conviction. The appeals court agreed with his contention that his Sixth Amendment right to "be confronted with the witnesses against him" was violated by the trial, which had been conducted in a language that he did not understand (Piatt, 1990: 81). In 1978, moreover, Congress passed the Court Interpreters Act, which "requires judges to utilize competent interpreters in criminal or civil actions initiated by the United States in a United States district court" (Piatt, 1990: 82). A number of state governments have enacted similar legislation applying to state courts (Piatt, 1990: 82–83).

In *Hernandez v. State of New York* (1991), however, the U.S. Supreme Court let stand a lower court decision upholding the exclusion of Spanish-speaking jurors in a case where all parties to the case spoke Spanish and most of the testimony was in Spanish. The prosecutors successfully barred the presence of any native Spanish-speakers from the jury by arguing that since they spoke Spanish, they were not bound by the translation provided by the court interpreter, unlike the prosecutor and the judge, who did not speak Spanish. The Supreme Court upheld this procedure by reasoning that the jurors were disqualified because of their language, not their race.[2]

The third linguistic access issue involves the question of language rights in the workplace under the Civil Rights Act of 1964. Here once again the courts—rather than legislative bodies or voter initiative campaigns—have been the primary arena of conflict, and two points have been the chief foci of contention. The first question concerns the degree to which English fluency may be used as a legitimate criterion in making employment decisions (e.g., hiring and promotion). For example, are there circumstances in which an unsuccessful employment applicant may legitimately charge a prospective employer with violating her civil rights because she was refused employment for not being literate in English or for not speaking English fluently? Similarly, are employers justified in refusing promotions to otherwise qualified employees on the grounds that they speak English with a "foreign" accent?

The second question considers the circumstances in which employers have the legitimate authority to require their employees to speak only in

English, even while conversing informally with each other. For example, can employers legitimately issue an edict requiring employees to speak only English at the workplace, even during lunch periods and other breaks, or when they are not interacting with the general public?

The leading federal advocate for language minorities in responding to both questions has been the Equal Employment Opportunities Commission (EEOC). The EEOC was established to implement parts of the 1964 Civil Rights Act, and early in its history the commission determined that the rights of language minorities would be an important part of its enforcement mission. Title VII of the Civil Rights Act prohibits employers (including state and local governments as well as private firms) from discriminating against potential or actual employees on grounds of "race, color, religion, sex, or national origin" (Leibowitz, 1982: 19).

Having decided that one's language is a core characteristic of national origin, the EEOC sought ways to prevent employers from using it to discriminate against employees and prospective employees in ways that violate the Civil Rights Act. For example, if an employer wishes to discriminate against an individual on the basis of his national origin or race but knows that this is illegal, she could use "lack of English fluency" as a substitute employment criterion, which would produce the same effect unless this criterion were subjected to critical scrutiny. By reasoning along lines such as this, the EEOC has sought to protect the employment rights of language minorities since at least 1970.

Procedurally, the EEOC built its language minority protections on the U.S. Supreme Court decision of *Griggs v. Duke Power Co.* (1971), which involved racial discrimination in employment. One of the key findings of the Court in *Griggs* was that employment practices involving "disparate treatment" and having an "adverse impact" on members of protected groups will be viewed as suspect by the courts, and must be justified by "business necessity" (i.e., that which is demonstrably necessary for business efficiency, employee safety, etc.). Thus, the employee or potential employee has the burden of proof to establish both "disparate treatment" and "adverse impact," but the employer has the burden of proof in establishing the "business necessity" of its employment practices. Using this reasoning, the EEOC's guidelines to employers on national origin discrimination have included caveats on language discrimination since 1973. The commission's 1980 revision of its guidelines put the matter this way:

The Commission has found that the use of the following selection procedures may be discriminatory on the basis of national origin. Therefore, it
will carefully investigate charges involving these selection procedures for
both disparate treatment and adverse impact on the basis of national origin. . . . (1) Fluency-in-English requirements, such as denying employment opportunities because of an individual's foreign accent, or inability
to communicate well in English. (quoted in Parliman and Shoeman, 1994:
559)[3]

In addition, the commission has been very consistent in its opposition to employer English-only work rules that prohibit employees from
speaking languages other than English. In a 1970 decision, for example,
the EEOC held that

the refusal to permit a Spanish-surnamed American to speak Spanish
adversely affects him with respect to terms and conditions of his employment because of his national origin. In the absence of a showing by
respondent that this policy is required by business considerations, the
policy is unlawful. (Leibowitz, 1982: 21)

By the time of the 1980 revisions to its *Guidelines on National Origin Discrimination,* the commission had elaborated a formula that was strongly
oriented toward the protection of language minority rights in the workplace:

Speak-English-only rules.
    (a) *When applied at all times.* A rule requiring employees to speak only
English at all times in the workplace is a burdensome term and condition
of employment. The primary language of an individual is often an essential national origin characteristic. Prohibiting employees at all times, in
the workplace, from speaking their primary language or the language
they speak most comfortably, disadvantages an individual's employment
opportunities on the basis of national origin. It may also create an atmo-
sphere of inferiority, isolation and intimidation based on national origin
which could result in a discriminatory working environment. Therefore,
the Commission will presume that such a rule violates title VII and will
scrutinize it.
    (b) *When applied only at certain times.* An employer may have a rule
requiring that employees speak only in English at certain times where the
employer can show that the rule is justified by business necessity.
    (c) *Notice of the rule.* It is common for individuals whose primary lan-
guage is not English to inadvertently change from speaking English to
their primary language. Therefore, if an employer believes it has a business necessity for a speak-English-only rule at certain times, the employer

should inform its employees of the general circumstances when speaking only in English is required and of the consequences of violating the rule. If an employer fails to effectively notify its employees of the rule and makes an adverse employment decision against an individual based on a violation of the rule, the Commission will consider the employer's application of the rule as evidence of discrimination on the basis of national origin. (quoted in Parliman and Shoeman, 1994: 556–58)

Despite this strong position by the EEOC, the federal courts have been much less consistent on the issue of linguistic employment rights. In two challenges to English-only work rules imposed by employers— *Frontera v. Sindell* (1975) and *Garcia v. Gloor* (1980)—federal courts of appeal ruled against the Spanish-speaking employees bringing suit, although both courts sought to carefully limit the application of their rulings (Leibowitz, 1982: 21–22). In the case of *Gutierrez v. Municipal Court* (1988), however, the U.S. Court of Appeals for the Ninth Circuit ruled in favor of a Los Angeles municipal court clerk who challenged the following rule imposed by her employers:

The English language shall be spoken by all court employees during regular working hours while attending to assigned work duties, unless an employee is translating for the non-English-speaking public. This rule does not apply to employees while on their lunch hour or work breaks. (Piatt, 1990: 69)

Contrary to the 1980 *Garcia* case, in *Gutierrez* the court did find that language is "an important aspect of national origin" (Piatt, 1990: 70). In 1989, the U.S. Supreme Court let stand the Ninth Circuit's decision (Mydans, 1990).

Revisiting the issue only five years later, however, the same federal appeals court appeared to reverse itself in *Garcia v. Spun Steak Co.* (1993), when "the Ninth Circuit adopted a diametrically opposed view of the EEOC speak-English-only guideline. In contrast to the deference usually given to EEOC interpretive guidelines, the [1993] Garcia court expressly rejected their use, finding that the EEOC guideline contravenes Title VII policy" (Parliman and Shoeman, 1994: 561). Finding that the Spanish-speaking bilingual employees who had brought the case had failed to demonstrate an adverse impact from their employer's prohibition of speaking non-English languages during working hours (but not during lunches or breaks), the Ninth Circuit's most significant ruling here was its rejection of "the EEOC guideline's presumption that across-the-board English-only policies are invalid" (Parliman and Shoeman, 1994: 566).

As of this writing, the legal status of the EEOC's attempts to protect language minority rights in the workplace remain in question and highly controversial. In *Garcia* the Ninth Circuit found that "Title VII was intended to strike a balance between preventing discrimination and preserving the independence of the employer" (Parliman and Shoeman, 1994: 566), but that the EEOC guidelines had threatened this balance by presuming the adverse impact of English-only workplace rules.[4]

Meanwhile, many workplaces experience growing tension over this issue as a result of the rapid increases in the numbers of employees for whom English is not a native language (see, e.g., Mydans, 1990; Locke, 1995). Indeed, one survey found that in June 1994 the EEOC was litigating 120 cases based on English-only workplace rules (Locke, 1995: 35). Typically, employers issue such rules based on complaints by monolingual English-speaking employees that other employees are "talking about them" in languages they do not understand (Mydans, 1990). As with bilingual education, then, controversy continues over the question of linguistic access to civil and political rights under the U.S. Constitituon and under several statutes passed by Congress during the last three decades. And this controversy has overlapped with that surrounding the third area of political conflict on language policy in the United States—the debate over making English our sole official language.

THE MOVEMENT FOR ENGLISH AS THE OFFICIAL LANGUAGE

The "official English" movement—known to its detractors and to some supporters as the "English-only" movement—formally began on a national level on April 27, 1981, when Senator S. I. Hayakawa (R-California) introduced into the Senate a proposed amendment to the Constitution that would have designated English as the sole official language of the United States. A similar proposed cnstitutional amendment has been introduced in each Congress since that time, although none has come to a vote on the floor of either house.

At the state and local levels, however, "official English" legislation has been much more successful,[5] as proponents have persuaded legislators and voters to adopt policies designating English as the official language in a number of states and localities. By 1999 the following twenty-two states had adopted English as their sole official language: Nebraska (1920), Illinois (1969), Virginia (1981), Indiana (1984), Kentucky (1984), Tennessee (1984), California (1986), Georgia (1986), Arkansas (1987), Mississippi (1987), North Carolina (1987), North Dakota (1987), South Carolina (1987), Arizona (1988), Colorado (1988), Florida (1988), Alabama (1990), New Hampshire (1995), Montana (1995), South Dakota (1995), Wyoming (1996), and Alaska (1998) (Crawford, 1999).[6] The most prominent local "official English" ordinances were adopted by voters in Miami (1980) and San Francisco (1984).

Some of these "official English" policies were adopted by statute in legislatures, while others—the most controversial, and those in states with the largest populations of non-English-speakers—were adopted as constitutional amendments by the voting public. The policies range from the purely symbolic to sanctioned restrictions on the behavior of public officials. At the symbolic level are those statutes, such as that signed by Governor Bill Clinton in Arkansas in 1987, which declares simply that "the English language shall be the official language of the State of Arkansas." As if underlining its symbolic intent, the remainder of the law stipulates that "this section shall not prohibit the public schools from performing their duty to provide equal educational opportunities for all children," an apparent reference to the *Lau* decision and the Equal Educational Opportunities Act of 1974.

At the other end of the spectrum is the constitutional amendment narrowly approved by Arizona voters in 1988, which sought to require that state's governments (including local governments and school districts) to operate *only* in the English language. Declaring first that "the English language is the language of the ballot, the public schools, and all government functions and actions," Section 1 of the Arizona amendment then described in great detail its applicability to every component part of Arizona government (e.g., branches, subdivisions, departments, agencies, statutes, rules, programs, policies, officials, and employees, among others listed). Section 2 imposed on each of the foregoing parties the obligation to "take all reasonable steps to preserve, protect and enhance the role of the English language as the official language of the State of Arizona." Section 3 further prohibited these parties from "using or requiring the use of languages other than English," the only exceptions being those required by federal law (e.g., "to assist students who are not proficient in the English language, to the extent necessary to comply with federal law," and "to protect the rights of criminal defendents or victims of crimes"), or those needed to teach students foreign languages as parts of the regular curriculum or to protect public health and safety. Finally, borrowing from California's "official English" amendment, Arizona's also gave to "any person who resides in or does business in this state" legal standing to sue the state to enforce its provisions (Section 4). Most other state-level policies are closer to those of Arkansas than to those of Arizona in being more symbolic than substantively coercive. However, several municipal "official English" ordinances adopted in the 1980s were also aimed at specific behavior, thereby attempting to restrict the use of "foreign" languages on commercial signs (Crawford, 1992: 186–94, 284–87).

Meanwhile, the fortunes of the "official English" campaign at the national level appeared to improve with the election of a Republican majority in both houses of Congress in 1994. For the first time, the 104th Congress witnessed serious committee hearings on several versions of "official English" policy. And in August 1996 the U.S. House of Representatives voted on and passed a bill (H.R. 123) that would have made English the sole official language of the U.S. government. In addition, it would have rescinded the language minority provisions of the Voting Rights Act, thus eliminating the "bilingual ballots" mandates that had been strengthened in 1992, as seen above. The Senate, however, did not act on the bill during the 104th Congress, which killed it for the time being. The issue did play a role in the 1996 presidential campaign, however, as "official English" was endorsed by Republican candidate Robert Dole and opposed by Democratic candidate Bill Clinton. While a number of "official English" bills were proposed to subsequent Congresses, none had been acted upon as of this writing.

What spurred this apparently growing movement for declaring English the sole official language of the United States and its political subdivisions? At the organizational level, the string of successes by the "official English" English-only forces is largely attributable to the 1983 formation of a nationwide lobbying group known as "U.S. English." Capitalizing on a growing mood of anger on the part of some segments of the population toward "the new bilingualism," U.S. English organized sweeping initiative campaign victories in several of the states cited above (see esp. Tatalovich, 1995). Headquartered in Washington, D.C., U.S. English claimed over 1.3 million members by 1999, and has included on its board of directors such American luminaries as Walter Annenberg, Jacques Barzun, Saul Bellow, Bruno Bettelheim, Alistair Cooke, Walter Cronkite, Norman Cousins, Angier Biddle Duke, George Gilder, Barry Goldwater, Sidney Hook, Norman Podhoretz, Arnold Schwarzenegger, and Karl Shapiro.

U.S. English was initiated by former Senator Hayakawa and Dr. John Tanton, an ophthalmologist who was previously president of Zero Population Growth and had also founded the Federation for American Immigration Reform (FAIR). The latter organization is one of the nation's leading lobbying groups supporting efforts to limit immigration to the United States. By 1986 another mass-membership lobbying organization had joined the "official English" movement, Virginia-based "English First." More stridently hard-line in its tone than U.S. English, English First was founded by Larry Pratt, president of Gun Owners of America, and is affiliated with the anti-abortion group Committee to Protect the Family (Henry, 1990: 32; Tatalovich, 1995: 10). Apparently in decline, English First claimed 250,000 active members in 1995, but its Web-site claim was down to 140,000 members by 1999.

At the level of policy, the program of U.S. English and its allies may be seen in large part as a reaction against the bilingual education and linguistic access initiatives described above. A 1990 promotional letter, for example, mailed to prospective members and contributors to U.S. English was accompanied by a copy of an undated column written by Guy Wright for the *San Francisco Sunday Examiner and Chronicle*, in which he described the group's program as consisting of three goals. In addition to adopting an "official English" constitutional amendment (the first goal), the group seeks to:

—Repeal laws mandating multilingual ballots and voting materials [and to]
—Restrict government funding for bilingual education to short-term transitional programs only (Wright, n.d.)

These policy changes are needed, Wright and U.S. English claim, because there is a grave danger that "this English-speaking nation [will be] turned into a poly-lingual babel." Despite the fact that there is

virtually no public support for the proposition that this country should conduct its affairs in foreign languages for the convenience of those who don't want to learn English, the ethnic leaders pressing that demand are highly organized and single-minded, and they have won every skirmish so far against the disorganized opposition of a general public with many other worries.

These ethnic leaders ("mostly Hispanic"), Wright continues, are motivated by an anti-assimilationist ideology that rejects the traditional American belief "that anyone who wanted to share in the benefits of American citizenship should learn English."

While opposed to the Voting Rights Act's mandates for language minorities and to any hint of maintenance bilingual education, U.S. English is eager to avoid being tagged with the label of nativist intolerance. Accordingly, the organization proclaims its pride in American ethnic diversity, and its commitment to the freedom of all Americans to be multilingual and to speak languages other than English in their homes. However, they argue, these latter freedoms must be seen as *private*, not public, rights. The role of government and language policy is to bring the country together in social harmony through the adoption of one official language, English. Other proponents of "official English" are not so energetic in their efforts to avoid being seen as restricting even the private language rights of others.

Despite its rapid growth, its impressive victories at the state and local levels, and its apparent increased strength in Congress, the movement for "official English" has suffered defeats as well and has stimulated organized resistance from its opponents. As noted, it has made little progress in convincing Congress to approve the proposed English Language Amendment to the Constitution. Further, legislative proposals for "official English" have failed in several states, including (as of 1999) Connecticut, Iowa, Louisiana, Maryland, Missouri, Nebraska, Oklahoma, Texas, Utah, and West Virginia (Crawford, 1999).

Also rankling to the "official English" English-only movement is the fact that two states are officially bilingual and show no signs of changing that fact: New Mexico, which has been officially bilingual in English and Spanish since adopting its first state constitution in 1912; and Hawaii, which adopted legislation in 1978 making both English and Hawaiian official languages of the state.

In 1987, moreover, a nationwide coalition of anti-English-only groups was formed to establish the English-Plus Information Clearinghouse (EPIC) in Washington, D.C. The groups supporting EPIC include Latino civil rights organizations (e.g., the Mexican American Legal Defense and Education Fund, the National Council of La Raza, and National Puerto Rican Coalition), other civil rights and civil liberties groups (e.g., the American Civil Liberties Union and the American Jewish Committee), and educator groups (e.g., the National Council of Teachers of English and the Joint National Committee for Languages). As denoted by its title, the aim of EPIC is to support the mastery of English by all residents of the U.S. *plus* the retention and/or learning of other languages (Henry, 1990: 32; Tatalovich, 1995: 16–18).

To support their goals and to regain the initiative on language policy, member organizations in the EPIC coalition have supported the English Proficiency Act, first introduced in the 100th Congress to "establish literacy programs for individuals of limited English proficiency." This act, renamed the English Literacy Grants Program, was signed into law by President Reagan on April 28, 1988 (Hornberger, 1990: 16). Members of the coalition have also supported the English-Plus Resolution, introduced into each Congress since 1987. In its 1997 form, introduced in the House of Representatives by Congressman Jose Serrano (D-New York), the proposed resolution acknowledges English as the country's language and declares that the U.S. government should provide the resources necessary to assist all non-English-speakers to gain proficiency in this language. At the same time, the resolution asks the government to (1) "conserve and develop the Nation's linguistic resources by encouraging all residents of this country to learn or maintain skills in a language other than English"; (2) to assist indigenous peoples "in their efforts to prevent the extinction of their languages and cultures"; and (3) to "continue to provide services in languages other than English as needed to facilitate access to essential functions of government, promote public health and safety, ensure due process, promote equal educational opportunity, and protect fundamental rights" (Serrano, 1997). No version of this resolution, however, has been voted upon in either house of Congress.

In 1988 U.S. English appeared to suffer a political setback when a journalist obtained and released a private memorandum, written by the group's co-founder, John Tanton, which expressed fears about the nature and character of Latin American immigrants, asking:

Will Latin American migrants bring with them the tradition of the *mordida* [bribe], the lack of involvement in public affairs? Will the present majority peaceably hand over its political power to a group that is simply more fertile?.... Perhaps this is the first instance in which those with their pants up are going to get caught by those with their pants down! (quoted in Henry, 1990: 28)

The release of Tanton's memo was widely reported in the press and elicited condemnations from many quarters. Critics pointed to it as evidence that Tanton and U.S. English are racist, and Tanton resigned from its board to try to limit the political damage to the group. To protest and to express their disgust at the memo's contents, Linda Chavez, U.S. English's second executive director, and Walter Cronkite, a member of the board of directors, also resigned.

Even after the resignations, new revelations continued to take the wind out of U.S. English's political sails. In reviewing funding sources for Tanton's various projects, investigative journalists disclosed that among his most generous contributors were two who were tainted with reputations for political extremism: Cordelia Scaife May, an heir to the Mellon fortune "who has also generously financed U.S. immigration and population control causes," and the Pioneer Fund, a New York–based foundation established in 1937 to support the study of eugenics, which more recently had "backed research in the 1970s purporting to prove that Blacks have lower IQs than Whites" (Henry, 1990: 30). These revelations fueled charges that U.S. English was a cover organization for anti-immigrant nativist and racist political forces in the U.S. (for a thorough examination of this episode, see Crawford, 1992: chap. 6).

Another setback to the "official English" movement occurred in February 1990, when Arizona's 1988 constitutional amendment was ruled unconstitutional by the U.S. District Court for the District of Arizona, ruling on *Yniguez and Gutierrez v. Mofford, Corbin, and Eden* (1990). The plaintiffs in the case, both officials of the state of Arizona, charged that the law denied their freedom of expression in violation of the First and Fourteenth Amendments to the U.S. Constitution. Both plaintiffs had routinely used Spanish to communicate with Spanish-speaking clients and constituents prior to the passage of the amendment (Yniguez worked for the Risk Management Division of Arizona's Department of Administration, and Gutierrez was a state senator).

The federal district court judge agreed, finding that the amendment is "so broad as to inhibit the constitutionally protected speech of third parties." This is so, he found, in that

> when read at its full literal breadth, Article XXVIII would force Arizona governmental officers and employees whose use of a non-English language in the performance of their official duties is protected by the First Amendment, such as state legislators speaking to constituents in a language other than English, state employees officially commenting on matters of public concern in a language other than English, and state judges performing marriage ceremonies in a language other than English, to either violate their sworn oaths to obey the state constitution, and thereby subject themselves to potential sanctions and private suits, or to curtail their free speech rights.

Accordingly, the judge enjoined the defendants and the State of Arizona from enforcing the amendment.

On appeal, a closely divided (6–5) U.S. Ninth Circuit Court of Appeals upheld the district court's ruling in 1995. In March 1997, however, a unanimous U.S. Supreme Court set aside the two lower court decisions without ruling on the merits of the case (titled, on appeal, *Arizonans for Official English v. State of Arizona*). The Court took the unusual step of issuing a thirty-five page decision to declare the case moot, since Yniguez had left her job with the state of Arizona (typically cases declared moot are dispatched in one or two sentences). The Court's decision had the effect of sending the case back to the Arizona Supreme Court, which ruled in April 1998 that portions of the initiative violated both the First and Fourteenth Amendments to the U.S. Constitution. Proponents appealed the state court's decision to the U.S. Supreme Court, but on January 11, 1999, the nation's highest court refused to hear the appeal, finally ending the lengthy legal career of Arizona's "official English" policy. Thus, as with the other policy issues described above, the controversy over making English the sole official language of the United States and its states and local governments shows little sign of abating.

There are, of course, other policies of government that affect language use and language maintenance in the United States besides those outlined above. In 1990, for example, Congress passed and President Bush signed the Native American Languages Act, which established a national goal of preserving and enhancing the indigenous languages of the country, a reversal of previous policies aimed at stamping out these same languages. The 1990 law, written by Senator Daniel Inouye (D-Hawaii), was essentially symbolic in that it authorized no actual programs; but a 1992 law, also written by Senator Inouye, authorized several programs to help implement the policy, and in 1994 the Clinton White House took the lead in the appropriation of the first federal dollars—$1 million—in support of the policy's aim (see Crawford, 1998; Hinton, 1994: chap. 18). Chapter 7 will discuss this legislation in greater detail.

Another area of U.S. language policy entails regulations concerning radio and television broadcasting in languages other than English, governed by the Federal Communications Commission (see Piatt, 1990). Still another issue of language policy erupted briefly onto the national stage in spring 1997, when the Oakland, California, school board decided to use Ebonics in bilingual education in an effort to improve the educational performance of African American students.

Still, while these and other issues of language policy gain public attention from time to time, the central concerns of language policy conflict in the United States are the three that have been surveyed in this chapter. Each of these remains highly volatile and unsettled, and each continues to erupt periodically in the nation's news media and in the arenas of public policy decision-making at all three levels of government. The aims of this book, as noted at the outset, are to gain greater understanding of the underlying political forces that motivate this conflict, and to sketch out an approach to language policy in the United States that would best meet the normative criteria of justice for language minority persons and the common good of the whole country. The first step toward greater understanding of the roots of our language policy conflict requires that we gain some theoretical and comparative perspective, a step taken in the next chapter.

2   Making Sense of Language
Policy Conflict

As DESCRIBED in Chapter 1, the United States has experienced a sharp increase in conflict over language policy. The first chapter provided an overview of the issues in this conflict, but it did not go below the surface to ask what is really at stake in the politics of language. What causes language to become a political issue of such emotional intensity? What are the root sources of this type of political conflict? How have political conflicts over language been dealt with in various contexts in the contemporary world?

This chapter will not answer these questions with finality, but rather aims to enable Americans to better understand their own conflict on this issue by placing it in a larger theoretical and comparative context. The chapter explores the preconditions for language policy conflict throughout many parts of the world, describes and explicates the most important fuels for these conflicts, and then sketches a way of understanding the most prevalent public policy responses to conflict over language.

This comparative and theoretical frame of reference will lay a foundation for understanding the nature and significance of our own language policy conflict, and for evaluating the claims made by partisans in the debate. The analytical framework developed in this chapter will be used in the remainder of the book to guide our understanding and analysis of these issues in the specific case of the United States.

PRECONDITIONS: LANGUAGE DIVERSITY
IN AN ACTIVIST STATE

How is it that language policy debate has erupted in many parts of the contemporary world, including the United States? The argument made here is that virtually everywhere language policy conflicts are fueled by a politics of identity in which competing rhetorical strategies are deployed on behalf of two competing public values: *national unity* and *equality.* These fuels can only ignite, however, in facilitative contexts, and this section of the chapter argues that the most conducive settings exist in countries where significant political actors expect the state to play an active role in relation to *language diversity, language contact* and *language competition.*

One of the primary preconditions of contemporary language policy conflict is the sheer fact of language diversity. Before a state can experience conflict over language policy, it must have multiple language groups within its jurisdiction. This condition is widespread in the contemporary world. Linguists estimate that there are between four thousand and eight thousand different languages spoken in the world today (Wardhaugh, 1987: 1). While about a hundred of these languages are used by some 95 percent of the world's people, it is a rare country that incorporates a unilingual population within its boundaries.

Most states have at least several significant linguistic groups, and many have populations speaking a wide range of written and unwritten languages. Indeed, it could hardly be otherwise. With only about 180 autonomous states in the world today, if we take the figure of 5,000 languages as a reasonable count, the result is about 28 active languages in the "average" state. An extreme case is represented by India, which recorded almost 800 languages and over 1,600 dialects in its 1961 and 1971 censuses. While many of these language groups are small, 33 had more than a million speakers each in 1971 (Apte, 1976: 141–42).

Another highly multilingual state is Nigeria, with nearly 400 recognized language groups (Akinnaso, 1989). The former Soviet Union's peoples speak over 130 different languages, and the USSR's 1989 census reported 22 nationality groups of more than a million people (Marshall, 1996: 9). Other well-known examples of multilingual states are Belgium, Canada, China, Malaysia, Paraguay, Peru, the Phillipines, Spain, South Africa, Switzerland, and Uganda. In many cases even states that do not immediately come to mind when thinking about multilingual countries (e.g., Australia, Finland, France, Great Britain, Norway, and Sweden) contain varied language groups within their populations. Thus, the fact that the United States—a self-proclaimed "nation of immigrants"—is also a multilingual state should occasion no surprise. And, in fact, as will be developed in greater detail in Chapter 3, the 1990 U.S. Census reported 18 different language groups with at least 200,000 members. Nearly 32 million people, or 15 percent of the

U.S. population, reported in 1990 that they usually spoke a language other than English in their homes.

In addition to linguistic diversity, language contact and competition are also omnipresent facts of life in many countries of the world. Through human mobility and technological advances, the people who use the multiple languages of the world are in ever-increasing contact with each other, requiring some degree of mutual adaptation to linguistic difference. Through contacts with members of other language groups, people incorporate new words and language rules into their own tongues and/or adopt other peoples' languages (in part or sometimes in whole) as their own. These adaptations result in changes to what linguists refer to as the *corpus* and the *status* of the affected languages (Weinstein, 1983: chap. 1). The corpus of a language refers to its "body" (i.e., vocabulary, spelling, meanings, pronunciation, rules of grammar, etc.), while its status is related to the language's prestige and prevalence of use in the various linguistic domains of a given society (Fishman, 1972).

The notion of a language's status is derived from the fact that linguistic change includes the birth and death of languages as well as their spread, growth, and decline. Most often the spread of one language involves the decline of another. Thus, Francophones around the world have invested considerable resources in recent decades in an attempt to halt the decline of the French language in the face of the seemingly irresistible march of Anglophone domination. From this point of view, then, languages—like states and empires—may be seen as being in competition with each other (Wardhaugh, 1987).

Finally, a third important precondition for language policy conflict is the expectation among political actors that the state should play an active role in doing something about the social facts of linguistic diversity, contact, and competition. This may seem obvious, but until the significant expansion of the role of the state occurred during the last several centuries, it was common to find multilingual states and empires in which it was not expected that language corpus and status should be the subjects of public policy.

The twentieth century has witnessed a dramatic growth of state power in virtually all countries. The states of the world have grown in respect to budgets, personnel, and scope of policy. A number of factors have contributed to this growth, including technological innovations (not least of which are the technologies of managing large numbers of people), increasing global communications and economic interdependence (made possible by technological developments), and ideological commitments placing progressively greater responsibility for the commonweal on state institutions. The increasing concentration of private power in the economic sphere—facilitated by these same technological developments—has played a major role in the growth of state power as well. In short, a greatly increased scale of interdependence has multiplied the number and scope of collective interactions in the contemporary world, creating greater demand for collective and authoritative means of conflict resolution. In some measure, states have acceded to this role and have made use of a wide range of technological innovations to develop the capacity to do so. The result is an expansive state, with ever greater interventions into the lives of the people it governs. In turn, the development and expansion of state policies and state institutions have spawned an explosion of politically active groups affected by and seeking to shape these policies and agencies.

Demands for state interventions (in the form of language policy) into the circumstances of language diversity and competition have increased in the context of this general growth of state power. While many participants in the politics of language seem to have mainly symbolic goals in mind, demands for state language policy have been accompanied by a developing technology known as "language planning" (Eastman, 1983). Language planning is based on the assumption that it is possible to understand and control the processes of linguistic adaptation and change. In order for the state to engage in this activity, it must have a set of language policy goals (derived from the political process), a body of knowledge about how language change occurs (derived from linguistics and sociolinguistics), and a technology of implementation (directed by state institutions and staffed by language-planning experts).

Language-planning goals have been set with respect to both the corpus and status of languages used within the territories of states, or in relation to competition between states (Weinstein, 1983: chap. 1). In many cases, experts have been employed to apply their knowledge of linguistics and/or sociolinguistics to develop programs designed to achieve the state's goals. And new state institutions have been created to implement these language policy programs, or old institutions have been charged with new language-planning responsibilities (e.g., public schools). Finally, the expansion of state language-planning institutions and policies has resulted in a tremendous growth of interest group organizations and activities related thereto. The point here, with respect to the state in general and to language policy in particular, is that the terrain for political conflict has greatly expanded in this century as a consequence of the development of new public policy aims and new technologies to achieve those aims. To summarize, then, before political conflict over language policy erupts, a state must have within its jurisdiction populations speaking multiple languages who are in some measure of contact and competition with each other, and political actors who expect the state to manage the terms of this contact and competition.

FUELS FOR THE FIRE: NATIONAL UNITY, THE QUEST FOR EQUALITY, AND THE POLITICS OF IDENTITY

Consideration of this challenge to the state brings us to the question of the fuels for language policy conflict. What is it that generates the heat of political conflict over language? Or, put differently, what are the stakes in these conflicts? What is to be gained or lost, and by whom, in the politics of language?

A clue to answering these questions lies in the fact that throughout the world there is a consistent pattern in the rhetoric of language policy conflicts, a pattern that pits the proponents of national unity against advocates of greater equality for ethnic minorities.[1] In virtually every documented case of political conflict over language policy, partisans speaking on behalf of minority language groups argue that a proposed or existing national language policy is unjust because it diminishes or suppresses the equal rights, opportunities, and/or well-being of members of these subordinated ethnolinguistic groups. The only just remedy, minority activists assert, is increased recognition, status, and opportunity for the minority language and its speakers.

Equally ubiquitous are the claims of opponents of minority-language status enhancement that such an elevation is certain to undermine national unity, bringing the nation-state unnecessary and destructive social and political conflict. The remedy for linguistic discord, therefore, is the adoption of a national language policy that will bring peace and harmony to the state. Advocates for minority language equality thus speak in the language of justice, while proponents of national unity speak in terms of the national good. One of the complexities of language policy conflict, in consequence, is that its partisans often appear to be speaking past each other—participating in parallel discourses—rather than to each other, seemingly motivated by differing concerns. The aim of this section of the chapter is to explicate the motivating forces behind each rhetorical strategy while seeking to uncover the common core that brings them into conflict with each other.

National Unity and Language Diversity

Proponents of language policies employing the rhetoric of national unity typically argue that the use of state policy to elevate the status of minority languages is dangerous because it is divisive, engenders political conflict, and threatens the stability of the national state. This line of reasoning derives from the modern project of nation-building, which is viewed here as continuous and ongoing rather than as a single, founding event. As used in this study, then, the nation-building concept refers not only to "new" states (such as those in Africa, Asia, and Eastern Europe released from formal imperial domination in the mid to late twentieth century), but to virtually all independent states. Beginning with the eighteenth century, the dominant ideal form of political association in the world has been the nation-state, and since such a structure does not exist in nature, it has had to be constructed and maintained through human agency. Almost everywhere in the modern world,[2] accordingly, state political elites have sought to bind their members into some form of consciousness of belonging to a "nation," membership in which is to be experienced as paramount in one's political identity.

   What, then, is a nation? It is at minimum a collection of people who share a sense of collective identity—as belonging together in some deep political sense—in distinction to the members of other national collectivities. The perceived uniqueness of each national group, in turn, is marked by boundaries that distinguish it from other equally unique national groups. These boundaries take many forms, typically one or several of the following: belief in a common natality expressed through narratives of formative collective experiences, perceived inherently distinctive characteristics (e.g., consanguinity or "race"), distinctive customs and traditions, rituals of collective commemoration, and other cultural traits including language. In the politics of modernity, in addition, national groups nearly always seek territorial boundaries, land of their own in which they can achieve self-determination (Ronen, 1979), usually through state sovereignty.

As Benedict Anderson (1983) depicted so well, every nation is an "imagined community" in the sense that it exists preeminently in the minds of its members. This is necessarily so, "because the members of even the smallest nation will never know most of their fellow members, meet them, or even hear of them, yet in the minds of each lives the image of their communion" (Anderson, 1983: 15). In the context of the present discussion, this serves to highlight the fact that all nations are constantly in the process of being built. Every nation is an ongoing and always unfinished project. Would-be political leaders must remember this fact, Rogers Smith (1997) has observed, because it confronts them with two constant challenges: "First, aspirants to power require a population to lead that imagines itself to be a 'people'; and, second, they need a people that imagines itself in ways that make leadership by those aspirants appropriate" (p. 6).

One of the always unfinished tasks of national political leaders, therefore, is to attend to the construction, repair, and renewal of the "image of their communion" in the minds of members of the nation. Furthermore, the process of nation-building must be attended to in the mind of every newcomer, whether that person enters the nation through birth or migration. To assist in this task, early in the modern era nationalist political elites discovered the potential power of nationalism as an ideology.

"Fundamentally," Anthony D. Smith (1983) has noted, "nationalism fuses three ideals: collective self-determination of the people, the expression of national character and individuality, and finally the vertical division of the world into unique nations each contributing its special genius to the common fund of humanity" (p. 23). Through widespread belief in the convergence of these ideals, nationalism is thought to aid political elites in shaping and motivating "a people" who can be effectively led by these particular leaders. Thus, the typical claim of nationalist leaders is remarkably consistent: "Our people have a unique contribution to make to the world, but since that world is one of inherently scarce resources for which we must compete, our harmonious unity is necessary both internally and externally." *Internally,* division and conflict undermine the common national good by wasting valuable resources (e.g., time, energy, material goods, and good will) on destructive rather than productive enterprise, and externally, division and internal conflicts weaken the collective ability to respond effectively in the face of competition and threats posed by others.

In this context, language has often been conceived as a key medium for achieving national unity and for expressing the "special genius," the core identity, of particular nations. The German Romantics are especially credited with having spread the idea that language is essential in defining and expressing a nation's spirit. Johann Herder, for example, won a top prize of the Berlin Academy of Sciences in 1770 with his essay "On the Origin of Speech," in which he asked:

> Has a nationality anything dearer than the speech of its fathers? In its speech resides its whole thought domain, its tradition, history, religion and basis of life, all its heart and soul. To deprive a people of its speech is to deprive it of its one eternal good. . . . With language is created the heart of a people." (quoted in Wardhaugh, 1987: 54)

Seen in the light of this Romantic hue, one of the special roles for language policy in the modern era is to help build a national identity and national unity through the elevation of the status of the nation's language and/or through the standardization of its corpus. From this perspective, linguistic diversity is often viewed as a corruption of the nation that must be repressed or eradicated as expeditiously as possible.

And indeed, history is replete with examples of attempts at nation-building through language policy in the last several centuries. Leaders of national unity in the United Kingdom, for example, worked vigorously for several centuries to achieve linguistic standardization of English in areas that had previously spoken several Irish, Welsh, and Scottish languages (see, e.g., Phillipson, 1992; Wardhaugh, 1987). Similarly, modern France was partially constructed through forceful efforts at linguistic unification, a project that continues in the present (see, e.g., Wardhaugh, 1987).

These efforts at national identity construction through language policy have been complicated, however, by the nearly universal existence of multilingualism in contemporary states, which brings into focus the fact that the process of nation-building described above is presented solely from the perspective of nationalist elites bent on nor-

Don't scandals of US English undermine this alleged "natl. good" goal?

malizing their own languages as the languages of the state and of the country.

But from the perspective of speakers of other languages, these efforts may be seen as moves to establish hegemonic languages to aid in the domination of minority language groups by the elites of dominant groups. Accordingly, efforts to unify nations through the repression and/or elimination of linguistic differences have nearly everywhere been resisted by the speakers of minority languages. What nationalist leaders see as a clear question of national unity, minority ethnic activists may see equally clearly as an effort by a dominant ethnic group (that controls the state) to advance its own interests at the expense of other groups.

Ethnic Equality and Language Diversity

This problematization of the process of nation-building directs our attention to the virtually worldwide phenomenon of *ethnic* revival. Contrary to the expectations of most modern intellectuals (e.g., liberals, Marxists, humanists, nationalists, and other Enlightenment universalists), one of the most striking developments of the second half of the twentieth century has been an upsurge of ethnic solidarity and political mobilization throughout the world (for overviews, see Horowitz, 1985; Smith, 1981; Young, 1976, 1993). On every settled continent of the globe, ethnic groups have made it clear that they do not intend to self-destruct by being absorbed into larger national or universalistic groupings, and that they will resist the subordination of their interests to those of other groups.

The distinction between *national* and *ethnic* groupings has been the subject of considerable intellectual discussion in recent decades (see, e.g., Connor, 1994: esp. chap. 4). As used in this study, however, the difference to be emphasized is that ethnic groups do not aspire to sovereign statehood for themselves. If an ethnic group develops a clear goal that it should achieve collective independence, with effective and separate control over its own territory, it becomes by virtue of that goal a nationalist group. Apart from this distinction, ethnic groups share many of the same sociological characteristics as national groups. That is, they are recognized—by their own members and by outsiders— through boundaries that may take one or more of a variety of forms very similar to the boundaries of national groups outlined above, including, of course, language. And ethnic groups, like nations, are "imagined communities" whose "images of communion" are constructed and maintained through human agency.

Twentieth-century ethnic mobilizations have been inspired in no small measure by the fact of systematic ethnic inequality. Nearly all societies are multiethnic, and multiethnic societies are usually stratified along ethnic lines; that is, membership in minority ethnic groups is systematically associated with lower-than-average amounts of many of the goods that people struggle for in those societies, such as income, wealth, status, education, political power, and recognition. Some scholars, indeed, believe that the primary function of ethnic identities is to create and perpetuate structures of social inequality (see, e.g., Wilmsen and McAllister, 1996). In any case, the rhetorical strategies of ethnic mobilizations in the twentieth century have usually been articulated in the language of equality (Horowitz, 1985). Since equality has been one of the central public values of the modern age,[3] leaders of subordinated ethnic communities have been able to mobilize their followers and to challenge state political elites by pointing to these systematic patterns of inequality as being derived from unjust oppression by dominant groups in violation of widely shared egalitarian norms.

As a key boundary of many ethnic groups, language sometimes plays a critical role in the struggle over ethnic inequality. Indeed, in multilingual societies prestige and power are typically stratified along ethnolinguistic lines (Wolfson and Manes, 1985). In such societies, the life chances of any given individual are deeply affected by that individual's membership in a given ethnolinguistic community. Members of powerful and affluent ethnolinguistic communities have a broad range of advantages over members of weak and subordinate groups.

In this context, the language policy of the state plainly affects the interests of members of differing language groups in different ways. Unlike the case of religion, the state cannot claim to be neutral in respect to language. There can be no wall of separation between the state and language because the state must employ language to function at all. As Hannah Arendt (1958) reminded us, the essential and central medium of political life is speech. Thus, if the state chooses to use not *my* language but some other group's language as the medium for its authority, my interests will have been negatively affected. The same is true of nonstate institutions and arenas in civil society (e.g., economic, religious, and cultural institutions). Given the normative power of egalitarianism in the modern world, it is easy to see how differential patterns of language use and policy may become key elements in the mobilization of ethnic identities and conflict in the political arena.

Identity Politics and Language: Another Take on the Stakes

By exploring these broad patterns of political rhetoric in language policy conflicts, it is possible to uncover some of what is at stake in these struggles. Still, the fundamental issue that pits partisans mobilized for national unity against those having a vital interest in ethnolinguistic equality is not yet in focus. I shall argue that language policy conflicts can be understood best in terms of the politics of identity. In other words, the dispute between nationalist and ethnic minority activists is essentially a disagreement over the meanings and uses of group identity in the public life of the nation-state, and not language as such.

Still an evolving concept in social scientific analysis, identity politics involves the increasing contention over several aspects of group membership in nation-states today. For example, should the state use identity group designations in making public policy? What are the consequences of the answer to this question for the group members themselves? For those who are not members of designated groups? For the society as a whole? A steadily increasing array of social groups have been connected to the politics of identity in relation to these issues (e.g., women and men, homosexuals and bisexuals, and the physically challenged), but among the most important politically are ethnic and nationalist groups.

How can we understand what is at stake in the politics of identity? Why should anyone care, for example, if ethnic identity seems centrally important to some people, while others argue for the preeminence of national identity? More specifically, how do we answer this question when the subject in dispute is language policy? In what follows, it is suggested that there are three key aspects to understanding the importance of group identity for individual human beings: group identity is central (1) to the constitution of the self and (2) to the self's relationships with other selves; and (3) group identity is of great significance in the structuring and allocation of goods through the decision-making processes of the society. Further, language can play a key role in each of these facets of identity.

Identity as Constitutive and Relational   One of the deepest and most perplexing questions confronting any of us is, "Who am I?" As a beginning point, identity is the basis for meaning, coherence, and achievement in our lives. Building on the work of Erik Erikson, Kenneth Hoover (1991) argues that successful identity formation is the indispensable foundation for human competence, integrity, and mutuality. Without the formation of an identity, indeed, we cannot be "selves" at all. The price we pay for identity, however, is difference, for without boundaries between ourselves and others, there is no self and no identity (Connolly, 1991).

Despite, or perhaps because of, this need for boundaries, our identities are not constructed by ourselves alone, but in dialectically intertwined relationships with others. All personal identities are social constructions in which others play a part. The communitarian philosopher Alisdair MacIntyre (1984) captured this notion well in noting that our "story" as individuals is already partly told before we are born, and that while we are the "co-authors" of our lives, we must remember that we are *only* the co-authors: "We enter upon a stage which we did not design and we find ourselves part of an action that was not of our making. Each of us being a main character in his own drama plays subordinate parts in the dramas of others, and each drama constrains the others" (p. 213).

This interactive foundation means that each identity is constructed both from the inside (by us) and from the outside (by them). From the perspective of the inward-facing, constitutive side of our selves, we experience our lives as having a core that resides in our consciousness, and that seems to have a more or less fixed and continuous character ("I" am myself and no other, and I remember being myself at earlier times in my life). Further, I experience my self as being—to some degree—a reflection and product of characteristics and efforts unique to my own person (I participate in being/becoming myself). Yet when I seek to specify and articulate the core characteristics of my identity, I am forced to acknowledge that many of them are derived from outside myself. My identity as a person was formed through myriad relationships involving multiple individuals and social groups in which I have participated. It seems to be impossible, therefore, to articulate even to myself certain aspects of who "I" am without also referring to some parts of the world outside the physical boundaries of my body. Thus,

"I" am a political scientist, a professor, an American, a husband, a father, an "Anglo" or Euro-American, and a Californian, and each of these aspects of my identity is constituted by relationships with persons or groups of people outside myself. In short, my identity is not only constitutive of myself, but also inherently relational in nature.

Despite the relational nature of identity, it is nevertheless impossible for me to conceive of myself without having a constitutive core that is my unique self. But because of its relational nature, the characteristics of that constitutive core are the result of influences from outside my physical boundaries. Reflecting this dialogic reality, individuals may be deeply attached to ethnonational groups at the level of personal identity. The fact that I am an American can be experienced as a core aspect of my personal identity. This relational reality has led some scholars (sometimes described as essentialists) to articulate group identity as being primordial (see, e.g., Geertz, 1973: 260; Young, 1993: 22–23), because group membership aspects of our core identities seem "natural" to us, or given by nature. But even those who do not use the primordialist language can make a similar point. Borrowing from Martin Heidegger, for example, Iris Marion Young (1990) has noted that membership in social identity groups is constituted by a certain *"thrownness,"* as "one *finds oneself* as a member of a group, which one experiences as always already having been" (p. 46 [emphasis in original]). And Young (1990) argues that the experience of membership in such groups is fundamentally different from that of membership in voluntary "associations" or in "aggregates" of people with statistically similar characteristics (pp. 42–48).

This foray into the constitutive and relational nature of personal identity is helpful in understanding how language becomes perceived as an important issue in the politics of identity. For while it is possible for me to change my language and my language loyalties, it is also possible—depending on the circumstances—that I will experience my language as a fundamental and constitutive part of who I am. Although I did not invent my own language, I may experience it as constitutive of my core identity, so that any attack on my language is experienced as an attack on my very being. This understanding of the constitutive nature of language has been given one of its most evocative articulations by the political scientist Harold R. Isaacs (1975) in his now-classic primordialist treatment of the ethnic revival:

That first learned language is, to begin with, the *mother's* tongue, with all that conveys and contributes to the forming of the self and the development of the individual personality. It opens into every aspect of life. . . .

"The world of communicable facts" is the world as it is seen by the family, the group, the culture in which the child enters. It is the world as named and described in the group's language, the tongue in which the child learns what the world is and how it came to be, the words and tones in which the group describes itself, spins its tales of the past, sings its songs of joy or sorrow, celebrates the beauties of its land, the greatness of its heroes, the power of its myths. It is the language in which he learns, absorbs, repeats, and passes on all the group's given truths, its system of beliefs, its answers to the mysteries of creation, life, and death, its ethics, aesthetics, and its conventional wisdom. The mother's tongue serves to connect the child to a whole universe of others now living or long dead. It thus extends to all who share or have shared this tongue, as Herbert Kelman has put it, "some of the emotional intensity and irreducible quality" attached to "those primordial bonds that tie the child to his mother and immediate kin." (pp. 94–95)

Although his formulation was perhaps hyperbolic, Isaacs's depiction may go a long way toward explaining the intense emotions often expressed in the political conflict over language policy. And if, through the social context of my life, my core identity is closely linked to what I see as a national language, while the core identity of another in my society has been linked by equally powerful circumstances with an ethnic group's language, the conditions have been set to motivate us toward deeply felt political conflict.

This formulation of the foundations for language policy conflict as identity politics, however, contains a further complication that involves references to social context and circumstances. While each of us is constituted through membership in an array of social groups ranging among family, kin, neighborhood, village, district, region, school ties, class, occupation, gender, religion, ethnicity, nationality, and the like, the significance of any one of these formative influences in our identities depends on the context of the occasion. This is inherent in the relational nature of personal identity. Thus, in one context our family membership is likely to be preeminent in defining our identity, while in another it is our occupational membership that is most important. Similarly, in some contexts individuals may seem to easily give up their native language, shifting from one language to another, while in other contexts people are prepared to defend their "mother's tongue" to the death.

A further complication of our understanding of identity politics comes with the realization that our identities are not only constitutive and relational, contextual and therefore mutable, but inherently contestable as well. This is particularly true for our identities as members in "imagined communities" such as ethnic and national groups. Because they are "imagined communities," it is always possible that they may be imagined differently, with different characteristics, boundaries, and historical memories. The fact that they are contestable, further, means that identities always involve power relations as well. Those able to bring the most effective and compelling resources to bear on the boundary definition process of any individual or group will to that degree be successful in defining the boundaries of any particular identity. At the individual level, you and I will differ to some degree about exactly who I am, and the outcome of this dispute involves a relationship in which we each have resources to bring to bear. You may assert, for example, that I am obviously a Latino, whereas I may firmly insist that I am "simply an American." Who is correct? In a very important sense, the "correct" answer will depend on the power resources each of us is able to mobilize in our relationship.

In summary, then, personal identity is the product of a complex set of interactions between individuals and their environments, which means that identity must be understood as having multiple facets: It is constitutive and relational, contextual and mutable, ambiguous and contestable. Because language is sometimes experienced as a core aspect of personal identity, it can become a highly explosive fuel motivating political conflict in struggles over collective identity. But a deeper understanding of which circumstances lend themselves to enhancing the significance of a factor such as language in identity politics is necessary, and examining the nature of the goods under dispute in the politics of identity may shed some light on this important question.

Identity and the Quest for Goods Political conflict derives ultimately from the coexistence of human interdependence and difference. We need each other for certain goods, but we differ from each other in our interests in relation to these goods, and in our views of how these goods should be understood, structured, and allocated. As seen above, identities themselves are constituted out of both interdependence and difference, and hence are susceptible to being incorporated into political conflict. When people engage in political conflict over language, they are expressing the view (at least implicitly) that language is connected to some sort of good that they desire or believe they need. What sorts of goods are at stake in political conflicts over identity in which language is an important political terrain? How can political disputes over identity and language affect the well-being of individuals, groups, and societies?

A recent spate of political theorizing on identity politics (see, e.g., Benhabib, 1996; Connolly, 1991, 1995; Fraser, 1997; Kymlicka, 1989, 1995; Lash and Friedman, 1992; Norton, 1988; Taylor, 1994; Young, 1990) has produced several clarifying discussions that may prove useful in answering this question. In particular, I want to argue that two key forms of goods are helpful in understanding how language becomes an important terrain for the politics of identity. These go by various names, each of which contributes an understanding of what is at stake, but I will use the terms *symbolic recognition* and *material interests* to signify them.

Symbolic recognition refers to the acknowledgment, acceptance, and respect by others of the legitimacy and value of particular identity formations and communities. Because personal and group identities are constituted relationally, as we saw above, they cannot be constructed from the inside alone. We need others to recognize us, and the manner in which they do so has profound implications for our well-being as individuals and as groups. The two chief evils in relation to symbolic recognition, as Charles Taylor (1994) has pointed out, are *misrecognition* (in which we are represented in inaccurate, hurtful, and/or harmful ways) and *nonrecognition* (in which our identities are ignored, or rendered invisible by the deficiencies or maliciousness of others).[4] The central thrust of the contemporary movement for multiculturalism, accordingly, is described by Taylor (1994) as follows:

> The thesis is that our identity is partly shaped by recognition or its absence, often by the *mis*representation of others, and so a person or group of people can suffer real damage, real distortion, if the people or society around them mirror back to them a confining or demeaning or contemptible picture of themselves. Nonrecognition or misrecognition can inflict harm, can be a form of oppression, imprisoning someone in a false, distorted, and reduced mode of being. (p. 25, emphasis in original)

This misrecognition and/or nonrecognition has figured prominently in the mobilization of the ethnic revival of the late twentieth century.

The struggle for ethnic equality has aimed, in part, at winning greater acknowlegment, acceptance, and respect for the boundary-marking characteristics and ways of life of subordinated or despised ethnic minorities. Therefore, if language, for example, becomes an important marker of ethnic identity, then language policy represents one avenue through which to gain greater public recognition and respect for a particular ethnic community. By gaining public recognition for my language, I enhance the status not only of my language, but of my ethnic community and myself. Insofar as my language infuses and represents my way of life,[5] the latter is given public validation and respect through a status-enhancing language policy. Conversely, language policy may be used by a state's political elites to demean or deny recognition to an ethnic community, thus contributing to its continuing subordination in the larger society (Weinstein, 1983).[6]

This explication of the role of symbolic recognition in identity politics emphasizes the significance of gaining appropriate and enhancing affirmation from those outside ourselves (individually or as a group). Another aspect of symbolic recognition that needs to be outlined, however, derives from the fact that our memberships in significant identity groups renders our personal identities vulnerable to the behaviors and characteristics of those within our group as well. That is, the need for mutual recognition of our identity's characteristics applies not only to outsiders but to insiders as well. Thus, for example, if I believe that my personal identity is centrally associated with being an American, and I further believe that being American entails speaking English as our national language, then my personal identity is vulnerable to the recognition that this is the case by others both within and outside my "imagined community." The same dynamic, of course, works for the recognition and maintenance of boundary markers for ethnic minority identities. If being Quebecois means speaking French, then seeing one of us conversing publically in English represents a threat to our (and therefore my) identity. It is easy to see, then, how symbolic recognition functions as a central dynamic and motivating force for the politics of identity, and how language can function as a key signifier in this process. Under these circumstances, it should be clear that two incompatible claims for symbolic recognition of language as identity signifier can serve to pit the holders of these claims in deep political conflict.

This discussion deepens and enriches our understanding of the rhetorical conflicts outlined above in relation to national unity and ethnic equality. Those who express strong concerns about the threat of multiple languages to national unity may be motivated, at least in part, by concerns for the unity of their own personal identities (on this point, see Connolly, 1991). Further, if my language has been successfully installed as a hegemonic[7] national language signifying a core part of a national identity, efforts to reimagine (re-cognize) that national identity as multilingual and multicultural will represent a direct threat to my personal identity. By the same token, the very existence of a hegemonic language in a multilingual society represents and expresses a subordination of the minority language(s) and language group(s) in that society.

Material interests constitute the second form of goods at stake in identity politics. The most common referents to material goods are wealth, income, property, and office or position, but the concept is also used to refer to other objective social indicators of status (e.g., educational attainment) and to access to services thought to promote people's material well-being (e.g., health care, electronic communications, and recreational opportunities).

Material interests become intertwined with identity politics when the distribution of material goods becomes systematically linked with group identities. And, as noted, every multiethnic society for which information is available has been characterized by the systematic inequality of material goods and, more generally, life chances, along ethnic lines. Thus, one's group identity is nearly always linked in important ways to one's material interests. This linkage has led some social scientists (usually described as instrumentalists or circumstantialists) to explain the attachment to ethnic identity in terms of the competition for material resources. A good example is the following generalization by Susan Olzak and Joane Nagel (1986):

> Competition theories of ethnic relations ... are based on the premise that mobilization along ethnic lines surfaces (or resurfaces) as ethnically distinct groups come to compete in the same labor, housing, marriage, or other kinds of markets. ... The central task of competition theories of ethnic relations is to explain the conditions under which ethnic mobilization and ethnic identity surpersede other potential loyalties and political cleavages (pp. 2–3, emphasis in original).

Group identities matter to people, in short, because they are usually directly connected to their material well-being.

Moreover, there is also an important link between the symbolic recognition aspect of identity politics and the distribution of material resources. That is, recognition is important not only because it has symbolic meaning, but also because it functions to facilitate or inhibit access to material goods. Due to the relational nature of identity, this operates—once again—both internally and externally. Externally, recognition of group identity is used as a cue for making the myriad qualitative judgments about others that either open or close doors to opportunity and material well-being. A familiar example is the social science research demonstrating that teachers' expectations about the capacities of students (filtered through the lenses of group identity) greatly influence the nature and quality of their work with those students and of the students' performance.

In addition, self-identity—formed in part through the internalization of external symbolic recognition—creates self-expectations and patterns of behavior that can greatly influence one's capacity for effective agency in the pursuit of material goods. Indeed, this is one of the ways in which misrecognition and nonrecognition can operate as forms of oppression, as Taylor noted. If I am convinced that "my kind of people" have no chance of success in the dominant avenues leading to relative material abundance (e.g., professional education), that conviction will influence my capacity to pursue those directions. In this sense, negative forms of group recognition serve to create internal—in addition to external—obstacles to social mobility.

Once again, language policy can figure importantly in these processes influencing the distribution of material goods. As noted, if the state (and other institutions in civil society and in the economic sector) uses not my language but that of others to conduct its business, I will be directly disadvantaged as a result. Along these lines Brian Weinstein has written that language policy is important in several ways because it can be used to facilitate or deny access to valued goods and services in the political economy. For example, he says there are ". . . at least four forms of deprivation dependent on language choices":

1. Refusal to allow certain groups to learn or use a language—their own mother tongue, the official language of the country, or a world language.

2. Refusal to allow certain people to participate because they are identified as speakers of a certain language just as members of a certain racial category might be excluded once they are identified.
3. Arbitrary requirement of certain languages for access to employment, professions, or licensing even though the language has little or nothing to do with competence in the job or profession.
4. Affairs of the community—the government, the media, the courts, and the schools—conducted in languages which large groups of people do not know. (Weinstein, 1983: 83)

Of course, these same policies that deny access to members of some language groups serve to advantage the members of other groups.

And language functions not only instrumentally, as a gatekeeping device, but also symbolically. Even those who are fluent in the dominant language of a society may be marked by an accent, which is then used as an ethnic identifier for purposes of invidious comparison and discrimination. This is the social dynamic underlying political conflict over corpus language planning.

This discussion of the material interests at stake in identity politics should once again facilitate understanding of the rhetorical competition in language policy conflicts between those motivated by considerations of national unity and those most concerned about ethnic equality. There are not only important symbolic goods at stake, but material interests as well.

It should no longer be a mystery that language policy has emerged as a point of political contention in the contemporary world. The preconditions of language diversity, contact, and competition are widespread throughout the world. Moreover, political conflicts in our era are preeminently managed by nation-states, which are increasingly activist but which also characteristically are troubled by the problematic character of the nation in a time of widespread identity politics. Because of its own characteristics and potential importance in the constitution of identities (individual, ethnic, national), language has the capacity to engage people's interests and political imaginations on a deeply emotional level. The question remaining for this chapter is how those engaged in language policy conflict aim to resolve it. What are the policy solutions to the politics of language envisioned by its partisans? It is to this question that we now turn.

RESOLVING LANGUAGE POLICY CONFLICTS: A TYPOLOGY

Given the complexity of the forces motivating language policy conflict, generalization is obviously a risky enterprise. This risk is exacerbated in the realm of identity politics in that one of the principal boundaries of ethnonational groups is a unique historical experience maintained through vigilant protection of the group's memory.

Nevertheless, it is possible and helpful to group language policy approaches into four types. The four cells in the typology depicted in Figure 2.1 are derived from the connections between two primary questions that must be addressed to develop a language policy: (1) What will be the status of the languages in use in the society? and (2) what relationship is envisioned between the ethnolinguistic groups affected by the policy? Thus, the two axes of Figure 2.1 have the following meanings:

1. *Linguistic/cultural status equality:* The vertical axis classifies language policies in terms of the extent to which they are intended to equalize the status of languages and cultures within the state's jurisdiction.
2. *Social integration of ethnolinguistic groups:* The horizontal axis classifies language policies in terms of the degree to which they aim to integrate the members of distinct ethnolinguistic groups into the same public spaces of the society.

Figure 2.1

Typology of Language Policy Approaches

High	*Confederation* (e.g., Switzerland; Belgium; India)	*Pluralism* (e.g., Canadian federal government; Austria)
Low	*Domination/exclusion* (e.g., ante-bellum, American South; apartheid South Africa)	*Assimilation* (e.g., Franco's Spain; France; United Kingdom; United States in the 1920s)
	Low	**High**

Language/ Cultural Status/ Equality labels the vertical axis.

Social Integration of Ethnolinguistic Groups

The result of this mapping process is four cells containing distinct approaches to resolving political conflict over language diversity: domination/exclusion, assimilation, pluralism, and confederation. Virtually all public policy proposals in response to linguistic diversity can be fit meaningfully into one of these categories. Outlining and explicating these policy approaches will help to put the language policy debate in the United States into a larger, comparative perspective. This perspective, in turn, yields greater understanding of the relative depth and seriousness of our own politics of language.

Domination/Exclusion

Weinstein alludes to the first policy approach of domination/exclusion in his discussion of linguistic deprivation mechanisms quoted above. Sometimes dominant ethnolinguistic groups have sought to maintain their privileged position in the society by using language to exclude the members of subordinate groups from effective participation and power in the public domains of the society. Members of subordinated groups are denied access to the dominant linguistic domains, and their language is designated (either formally or informally) as being of low status. Here participation in the language of power—that is, the language of public discourse in the dominant cultural, economic, and political institutions of the society—is reserved exclusively for members of the dominant ethnolinguistic groups. Members of subordinated groups, except for those few who are needed as a buffer to facilitate necessary exchanges between dominant and subordinate groups, are effectively kept in a private linguistic shadow world outside the realms of civil society and public life.

This policy approach has been widely practiced by colonial powers throughout recorded history. The British, for example, practiced a version of this approach in their African and Asian colonies, as did the Dutch (Akinnaso, 1989; O'Barr and O'Barr, 1976; Das Gupta, 1985). Sometimes the elites of deeply divided societies may employ this approach to publicly symbolize the maintenance of their explicit domination over a subordinated group. After stripping the slaves of any knowledge of their African languages, for example, a number of states in the pre–Civil War American South made it a crime to teach the slaves how to read and write in English (although they were expected, of course, to be able to speak a kind of Pidgin English in order to do their work). More recently, South Africa's predemocratic "mother tongue principle," in which blacks were educated in their own languages while the languages of power were Afrikaans and English, was criticized by some as a policy intended to keep the blacks in a subordinate and excluded position, as well as internally divided.

The policy of domination/exclusion is, of course, a frankly inegalitarian approach and therefore suffers from a high degree of political illegitimacy in the contemporary world. For that very reason, it also tends to undermine efforts toward national unity. Consequently, it is difficult to find any state today that openly admits to practicing this approach. Nevertheless, advocates for subordinated ethnolinguistic groups in many countries, including the United States, have charged that this policy still may be found in the state's neglect of the educational needs of minority group members.

Assimilation

Assimilation, the second approach to language policy, aims to eliminate linguistic controversy by inducing a shift toward the dominant language in the society. Individual members of subordinate language groups may be assimilated into the dominant group insofar as they adopt the dominant group's culture and become fluent in the dominant language. Because subordinate language groups are to be integrated into the dominant society, the status of their native tongues and cultures is low.

A number of states have pursued this policy approach over time with greater or lesser degrees of intensity. For example, the British attempted linguistic assimilation in Ireland, Scotland, and Wales (Wardhaugh, 1987), although, as noted, they did not attempt to assimilate most of their colonial subjects in Africa or Asia. Both Spain and France (Wardhaugh, 1987; Beer and Jacob, 1985; Cérron-Palomino, 1989), on the other hand, have at times pursued very vigorous assimilative policies toward subordinate linguistic groups in both their national territories and in their colonial possessions. Similarly, Pakistan's strong policy of linguistic assimilation provoked the Bangladesh succession in the 1960s (Das Gupta, 1985).

While the stated aim of assimilative policies remains the same, the policy instruments employed by the state may range from very coercive to very permissive. Among the most coercive paths taken in recent

European history was that of Generalissimo Francisco Franco in Spain. In both Catalonia and the Basque country, he

> set out to destroy the local vernaculars. He mandated Castilian as the language of the press, radio, television, eventually, and even most books. Institutes for the study of regional culture were either downgraded or destroyed outright. Perhaps most importantly, instruction in local languages was outlawed. Teachers required their students to "hablar cristiano," speak like Christians, a particularly ironic injunction in light of the Basque's traditional piety. Indeed, in Catalonia and the Basque Country the police refused to permit use of regional languages outside the home. (Rial, 1985: 100)

Other regimes—including the United States—have taken a more permissive line, relying primarily on social pressures, marketplace incentives, and public education for encouraging a shift to the dominant tongue (Weinstein, 1983: chap. 8).

Everywhere assimilative policies have been justified in terms of both egalitarian and national unity goals. This approach is said to promote equality by providing an avenue of advancement for members of subordinate groups, and to foster national unity by purging the society of the very diversity that is the basis for ethnolinguistic conflict. Critics everywhere, on the other hand, argue that assimilation is a destructive policy aimed against the languages and cultures of subordinate groups, and therefore is highly inegalitarian by definition. Its very destructiveness, further, generates a defensive reaction by subordinate ethnolinguistic groups that undermines national unity rather than promoting it.

Pluralism

A third approach to language policy is pluralistic in that it aims to support the use of more than one language within common territories of the state. Pluralist policies attempt to elevate the status of subordinate languages and cultures, and to integrate the speakers of those languages into the mainstream public arenas of civil society. Generally speaking, pluralist policies recognize and affirm the multilingual nature of the society, declare that multiple languages (and ethnolinguistic groups) are national resources to be nurtured as a collective asset, grant equal language rights to individuals and/or groups to retain their "mother's tongue," and stipulate a policy goal of facilitating native language retention and maintenance, most commonly through the educational system.

An excellent contemporary example of a pluralist language policy is Canada's Official Languages Act, adopted by the federal government in 1969, and then revised and strengthened in 1988 (Ricento and Burnaby, 1998). After declaring both English and French to be official languages with equal status in Canada, the act sought to guarantee the language rights of individual members of both groups by stipulating that "every citizen in his or her private capacity has the right to speak any language," and that "where official language minority groups exist in Canada, they will be assisted and encouraged by public authorities to retain and preserve their language." To this end, "wherever numbers warrant, . . . Canadians have a right to have their children educated in the official language of their choice" (Canada, Government of, 1977: 43).

Further, Canada's federal government sought to encourage bilingualism in the country's citizens, declaring that learning both official languages "is desirable as a personal and national asset so that members of the two official language groups may be able to communicate with each other, understand and cherish each other's diverse ways of life, and serve as a natural link between the two linguistic communities." Finally, the act attempted to ensure that each individual Francophone and Anglophone would be able to interact with the federal government with equal ease and status, and have equal access to federal government employment opportunities in either official language (Canada, Government of, 1977: 45).

In addition to Canada, a number of other states have implemented public policies officially aimed at encouraging the sharing by two or more languages of at least some of the public domains of the society. Australia, for example, has been moving toward official pluralism for several decades. It adopted a national policy on languages in 1987 that set "a national goal that every child in Australia should learn a second language. For those who do not speak English natively, this means learning English while maintaining the first language. But, reciprocally, Anglo-Australians will all be encouraged to learn a language other than English" (Guy, 1989: 50). Similarly, several states in India have pluralistic language policies (O'Barr and O'Barr, 1976; Das Gupta, 1985), as do Paraguay (Rubin, 1968) and Peru (Hornberger, 1988; Cérron-Palomino, 1989). Also, the former Soviet Union (Pool, 1978; Marshall, 1996) had and China (Lee, 1986; Tseng, 1985) has official policies of encouraging the retention of native languages while trying as well to ensure that minority peoples learn the dominant language. And, although predemocratic South Africa was accused by some critics of pursuing a kind of domination/exclusion approach toward its native peoples, it had a type of pluralistic policy toward its European-origin peoples, recognizing both English and Afrikaans as languages of government since 1925 (Kloss, 1978; Regan, 1986).

Not surprisingly given its nearly four hundred languages, Nigeria has attempted a complicated form of the pluralist approach. Under this nation's educational policy, students are required to be educated in one of the three major languages (Hausa, Igbo, and Yoruba) in addition to their mother tongue, but English is widely taught as well at the secondary and postsecondary levels. Further, the official languages of government are the three major Nigerian languages plus English (which comes closest to being the de facto lingua franca countrywide, especially in the upper reaches of society). State governments (Nigeria has a federal system) must use English and one or more of the three major Nigerian languages. French and Arabic are also spoken widely, the latter especially in the linguistic domain of religion. The Nigerian policy, in short, is an attempt to promote national unity and integration while at the same time trying to instill respect for its great linguistic diversity and support for the language rights of its various ethnolinguistic groups (Akinnaso, 1989).

To reiterate, the essence of the pluralist approach is that it attempts to bring the speakers of multiple languages together as members of the same nation, while respecting their native languages and attempting to ensure that people are not disadvantaged by virtue of their ethnolinguistic memberships. The motto of this approach might well be "unity and equality through mutual respect for diversity." In terms of identity politics, it makes the linguistic assumption that individuals can make use of multiple languages in various domains (reflecting their active membership in multiple social groups), and that multiple language groups can live together in the same territory in relative harmony and without engendering a sense of unjust domination of one group by another, at least on the ethnic marker of language. Pluralists also argue that individual bilingualism is not only possible but desirable in that it facilitates cultural enrichment and cross-cultural understanding. By combatting distrust and intolerance toward linguistic diversity, pluralists hope to create a climate of acceptance that will promote greater status equality between ethnolinguistic groups and therefore a higher level of national unity. In comparative perspective, it seems evident that it is this pluralist approach toward which U.S. proponents of bilingual education and linguistic access measures have been aiming.

Critics of pluralistic language policies attack the approach from two directions. Assimilationists everywhere argue that linguistic pluralism, rather than promoting harmony, leads to the retention of separate ethnic enclaves that ultimately maintains inequalities between groups and fosters ethnic conflict in the society. Only linguistic assimilation will ensure the genuine social, political, and economic integration necessary for equality of opportunity and political harmony.

Others, the linguistic confederationists to be described below, argue that the pluralist approach is futile in that it does not serve to maintain minority language use. This is particularly the case, these critics assert, in contexts of ethnic stratification, where there inevitably are large status differences between languages in a society. Where individual members of ethnolinguistic groups have the choice, and where another language is associated with power, wealth, and prestige, the tendency of individuals is to choose the language of success. Over time, therefore, language shift will tend to threaten the very survival of the less powerful language groups rather than work toward their equalization in status. This is the rationale used by Quebec, as we will see in greater detail below, in its insistence that some minority language rights of Anglophones and immigrants must be curtailed in order to assure the survival and equality of French-speaking Canada.

Confederation

Confederation, the last policy approach to be outlined here, is based on the assumption that although equality between languages and ethnolinguistic groups should be achieved in the polity, the only way for this to occur is to give each language group its own territory in which it can be dominant. Thus, a kind of federal or confederal state is organized according to a linguistic "territorial principle" (McRae, 1975). Here the state aims at status equality between languages, but they are separated into different political territories dominated by single ethnolinguistic groups.

This approach to conflict resolution is nearly always associated with multilingual polities in which different language groups are dominant in distinct geopolitical regions. Generally such states have been created through the conquest of one language territory by another (e.g., China, the Soviet Union, and Canada), through post colonial sovereignty for multilingual areas unified by former imperial powers (e.g., India and Nigeria), or through the voluntary union of formerly independent states speaking different languages (e.g., Switzerland). Other well-known examples of territorially based multilingual states include Canada, Belgium, Spain, France, and the former Yugoslavia. Less clearcut or more disputed examples might include South Africa, Malaysia, Finland, and Great Britain. Versions of confederationist language policies have been worked out in several of these states, including Belgium, Switzerland, Spain, Finland, India, and the former Yugoslavia.

The confederal approach shares with assimilation the assumption that there can be only one language of success in a given geographic area. That is, one language or another seems inevitably to dominate in such arenas of power as the state itself, the marketplace, industrial enterprises, the educational system, and religious institutions. That being so, federal political structures can be used to implement a territorial principle so that political jurisdictions (and language policies) coincide as far as possible with the geographic boundaries of the several language groups within the larger state. Language policies within political subdivisions are typically monolingual in the dominant language of the region, unless the confederal policy is supplemented by a pluralist policy approach, as in several Indian states and Nigeria.

Confederal policies are also justified in terms of their contributions to national unity and egalitarianism. National unity is facilitated in that the population is so divided ethnolinguistically that any effort to assimilate one group to another would be highly divisive politically. When it is possible to federate state institutions to coincide with linguistic territories, enough harmony may be purchased thereby that the various language groups will remain loyal to the national state as a whole. Such has been the strategy of national elites in Belgium, Switzerland, and more recently, Spain. This has also been the argument of Quebec's federalist leaders since the mid-1970s, although they have been unable thus far to achieve a countrywide consensus on this position among Canada's political elites.

The confederal approach may also be seen as egalitarian in that each language may be declared formally and officially equal to the others, with each language group being given control over a political subdivision of equal authority (e.g., province, autonomous territory, etc.). In order for this policy to be credible as egalitarian, however, the central state institutions must themselves operate multilingually. That is, each language group must be able to communicate with the central government in its own language in order to experience the state as equally theirs.

Canada's political conflicts over language again offer a nearby example for Americans. Canada's Francophones have rejected elements of that country's federal pluralist policy for nearly three decades, arguing for a version of linguistic confederation instead. And indeed, Quebec adopted a kind of confederationist policy in its 1977 Charter of the French Language (Bill 101), which was "designed to make Quebec both institutionally and socially a unilingual French state [and] . . . to curb the growth of the English-speaking community and to diminish its status" (d'Anglejan, 1984: 40).

Quebec's Bill 101 departed from the federal government's pluralist language policy in several respects. In addition to reiterating that French is the only official language of the province, it (1) restricted the right of parents moving into Quebec to have their children educated in English rather than French (although a Canadian Supreme Court decision subsequently restored that right for Anglophone Canadian citizens), (2) imposed a series of sanctions designed to advantage Francophones in economic and professional activities (e.g., through "Francisation" programs designed to ensure that French is the dominant language used in business and the professions); and (3) provided measures designed to ensure a French *visage* in the province (e.g., monolingual French outdoor commercial signs and billboards, and the "Francisation" of geographic names). Quebec's government also adopted several additional programs aimed at ensuring the integration of adult immigrants into the Francophone community of the province.

The rationale of Quebec's political leaders for these seemingly restrictive measures involved considerations of both material interest and symbolic recognition, as will be detailed in Chapter 7. Here it need only be emphasized that Quebecois nationalists believe that genuinely egalitarian multiculturalism is an impossibility for both individuals and societies. That being so, the only fair way to resolve linguistic diversity in multilingual countries is through a policy of confederation in which each member language and cultural group will have its own territory in which to be dominant.

However, Canada's conflict between advocates of pluralism and confederation may eventually be resolved, the confederal approach to language policy does seem to be quite succesful in Switzerland (Wardhaugh, 1987: chap. 9) and Finland (Allardt, 1985), where relatively high degrees of political harmony prevail, and where none of the federated language groups appear to feel unjustly dominated by the others. Despite these positive examples, however, the confederal approach is viewed with skepticism by many.

The major problem, critics argue, stems from the difficulty of defining and maintaining equality between the languages and language groups. Official proclamations of equality do not necessarily mean that members of language groups feel that they are being treated equally in the political economy or by the state. Opportunities for invidious comparisons abound in the behaviors of central states, political subdivisions, and other public institutions. Indeed, dividing the institutions of the state along ethnolinguistic lines seems to invite comparisons along these very lines.

Similarly, the typically monolingual (and assimilative) language policies of political subdivisions within federated multilingual states often stimulate smoldering resentments by minority language group members (e.g., Anglophones and native peoples in Quebec), who themselves may or may not have access to their own linguistic territories. Consequently, multilingual states pursuing confederal policies may find little national unity or consensus that the ambiguous norm of equality prevails under those policies. Spain and Sri Lanka offer examples of contemporary confederated states whose ethnolinguistic conflicts provide unhappy contrasts with the more successful examples of Finland and Switzerland. Despite these cases of severe political instability, however, given the conditions creating language conflict in multilingual countries with regions dominated by one ethnolinguistic group, there often seems little alternative to a confederal approach if the country is to be governed by a single sovereign state.

SUMMARY

This chapter has employed theoretical and comparative perspectives to investigate the origins and causes of language policy conflict in the contemporary polity, as well as to survey the approaches used in trying to resolve such conflicts. As we have seen, political conflict over language policy stems from linguistic diversity in countries with activist states and in contexts where language use and language loyalty are intertwined with identity politics and contested ethnic stratification. Moreover, four types of policy approaches were outlined, based upon the interplay between two variables: the extent to which the policy tries to equalize the status of languages and cultures within the state, and the degree to which the policy attempts to integrate ethnolinguistic groups in the polity.

This discussion has made broad generalizations that appear to hold true at a relatively high level of abstraction and over a wide range of cases in the contemporary world. Given the complexity of the sources of political conflict over language, it should be obvious that the most appropriate language policy for a given country will vary depending on a great variety of factors. Nevertheless, the analytical framework outlined above should point us in the right direction as we seek to understand and evaluate the debate over language policy in the United States. Indeed, the frame of reference delineated in this chapter will structure the description and analysis of language policy conflict in the chapters that follow.

THE PLAN OF THE BOOK

How does the United States fit into the patterns of language policy conflict outlined above? How are we to use this analytical framework to understand our own conflict about language policy? As noted in Chapter 1, contemporary language policy conflict in the United States centers on a debate between the advocates of linguistic pluralism and the supporters of a policy of assimilation. In Part II we will examine and analyze in some detail the arguments made by the advocates of each of these policy alternatives.

Our examination of these matters will make clear that many of the generalizations described above hold true for the United States as well. That is, as predicted by the analytical framework, the language policy debate in the United States was occasioned by an expansion of state activities in social arenas (e.g., education and employment opportunity) closely connected to language use and cultural practice, during a political era (the 1960s) in which ethnic competition and conflict had reemerged with particular force.

Further, the central political values around which the U.S. debate over language policy has swirled are precisely those of national unity and equality in a context of heightened conflict over identity politics. What sort of language policy will best ensure that members of language minority groups can achieve equality within the United States? Can a policy that seeks to achieve equality for language minorities also preserve and enhance our unity as a nation? These are the questions that serve as focal points for fundamental disagreement between the partisans in our own national debate on this subject, and they will serve as the organizing basis for the explication to follow in Part II. Before taking up the description and analysis of the U.S. argument on these questions, however, Chapter 3 will outline the social and political foundations for the conflict in relation to the contextual factors highlighted in the preceding analysis in this chapter.

3 The Social Foundations of U.S. Language Politics

IN CHAPTER 2, it was argued that language policy conflicts tend to emerge in countries where there is linguistic diversity, where ethnolinguistic contact and competition take place, and where political actors—motivated by concerns over group identity, national unity, and/or ethnolinguistic inequality—push the state to do something about these facts. In Chapter 1, we saw that a significant conflict of expectations exists among some political actors over language policy in the United States. The purpose of this chapter is to examine the extent to which the other conditions outlined in Chapter 2 exist in the United States, fanning the flames of language policy conflict in the contemporary era.

The pages that follow will describe some of the social and political foundations for language policy conflict in the United States. The first section of the chapter provides some background information on the United States regarding the preconditions for political conflict: language diversity, contact, and competition. Since the remaining chapters of the book are devoted to an elaboration and critical analysis of the partisans' specific arguments on the questions of group identity, national unity, and ethnolinguistic equality in relation to language policy, the second part of this chapter will provide only a brief overview of the U.S. discussion of national identity and national unity, as well as its structure of ethnic stratification in relation to language. This will set out additional background for understanding the U.S. debate over language policy in the contemporary period.

PRECONDITIONS: LANGUAGE DIVERSITY, CONTACT, AND COMPETITION IN THE UNITED STATES

To what extent is the United States a linguistically diverse country? What social forces maintain or diminish that diversity? What are the long-term trends? The patterns are not always clear, as demographic change is highly characteristic of our country's historical development. The first and overwhelming linguistic fact in the United States, nevertheless, is the long-term dominance of English as the language of power. English has been the language of the country's political rulers, and of its economic and social elites, from its inception as a sovereign nation-state in the late eighteenth century. No other language group has even attempted a challenge to the dominance of English in the political, economic, or social spheres, much less come close to succeeding.

At the same time, the United States is not a monolingual English-speaking country. According to the most recent Census, in 1990 some 15 percent of the country's population over age five spoke a language other than English in the home (see Table 3.1), a percentage that has almost certainly increased since that date. This represents a sizable number of people, nearly 32 million. Spanish-speakers (17.3 million people over age five) have become overwhelmingly the largest non-English-language (NEL) group in the United States, making up over half of those who usually speak a language other than English in the home. This is a significant change in that throughout much of the country's history, until 1950, German-speakers made up the largest non-English group. In part as a consequence of anti-German hostility during and after World War I, however, German-speakers engaged in a massive language shift to English during the early twentieth century, and this shift was not countered by large-scale immigration from Germany during the postwar periods (see Wiley, 1998). By 1980 German-speakers had dropped to third place among non-English-speakers. Eighteen language groups listed in the 1990 Census had more than 200,000 speakers, with an overall 38 percent increase in the 1980s among those speaking languages other than English at home (Table 3.1). Among the speakers of non-English languages, further, the Census found some 332,000 speakers of American Indian and Alaska languages, of whom 148,000 Navajo-speakers constitute the largest (44.8%) group (Waggoner, 1993a: 2). In short, the 1990 Census indicated that the United States continues to be among the world's multilingual countries.

Perhaps more important to language politics than the sheer numbers of speakers are the patterns of growth. Which language groups are growing in numbers? Here there are some striking patterns. Spanish-speakers experienced a 56 percent growth-rate during the 1980s, as indicated in Table 3.1, adding over 6.2 million new members during that

Table 3.1

Number of Those Age Five and Over Speaking Non-English Language at Home, 1980 and 1990, and Percent Change, by Selected Language or Group of Languages

Language(s)	1980	1990	Percent Change
Total, all languages	23,060,000	31,845,000	+38.1
Arabic	218,000	355,000	+63.3
Armenian	101,000	150,000	+48.8
Asian Indian languages	243,000	644,000	+164.8
Chinese languages	631,000	1,319,000	+109.2
Czech	122,000	92,000	−24.4
Dutch and Afrikaans	148,000	148,000	+0.1
Farsi	107,000	202,000	+88.7
Filipino languages	474,000	899,000	+89.5
French	1,551,000	1,702,000	+9.8
German	1,587,000	1,547,000	−2.4
Greek	401,000	388,000	−3.3
Hungarian	179,000	148,000	−17.4
Italian	1,618,000	1,309,000	−19.1
Japanese	336,000	428,000	+27.2
Korean	266,000	626,000	+135.3
Native American and Alaska Native languages	333,000	332,000	−0.4
Norwegian	112,000	81,000	−28.2
Polish	821,000	723,000	−11.8
Portuguese	352,000	430,000	+22.4
Russian	173,000	243,000	+39.6
Serbo-Croatian	150,000	142,000	−5.4
Spanish	11,116,000	17,340,000	+56.0
Swedish	100,000	78,000	−22.5
Thai and Laotian	85,000	206,000	+142.8
Ukrainian	121,000	97,000	−20.4
Vietnamese	195,000	507,000	+160.6
Yiddish	316,000	213,000	−32.6

Source: Waggoner 1993a, 1993b.

decade. In percentage terms, the largest increases were marked by several Asian language groups that had more than 100 percent increases in one decade: Asian Indian languages (+164.8 percent), Vietnamese (+160.6 percent), Thai and Laotian (+142.8 percent), Korean (+135.3 percent), and Chinese languages (+109.2 percent). These growth rates are not surprising in that the largest sources of immigration to the United States during the 1980s were Latin American and Asian countries. Nevertheless, the 1990 Census found that "native-born people still constitute half of the people in the United States, aged 5 and older, who speak languages other than English in their homes . . . , [and that] native-born people also make up at least a third of the home speakers of non-English languages who have difficulty speaking English" (Waggoner, 1993: 1).

Helping to fuel the language policy debate was a continued growth in the number of school-aged children who not only come from NEL homes, but have difficulty speaking English. Waggoner's analysis of the 1990 Census indicates a 39 percent increase from 1980 to 1990 of U.S. school-age youngsters living in NEL homes, and an 83 percent increase among youths age five to seventeen who were reported not to speak English very well (Waggoner, 1993c: 2). Combining Census data with studies of language proficiency among U.S. students, Waggoner estimates that the number of language minority school-age children jumped from 8 million in 1980 to as many as 11 million in 1990. Further, she found that the number of limited English proficient (LEP) students in the United States may have increased from an estimated 3.6 to 5.4 million in 1980 to some 5 to 7.5 million in 1990 (Waggoner, 1993c: 2).[1] Among English-language learners in school, moreover, Spanish-speakers are again overwhelmingly dominant in numbers, making up some 73 percent of the national total in 1991, with Vietnamese speakers being the next-largest group at 3.9 percent nationally (August and Hakuta, 1997). Based upon continued high rates of immigration, there is no reason to believe that these growth rates have slowed in the 1990s.

A third question that lies near the heart of language policy conflict in the United States is that of the relationships between patterns of monolingualism, bilingualism, and language shift. Three different patterns are at issue for any given language group. First, in *non-English-language monolingualism,* members of the language minority group retain their non-English language without learning the dominant language of the country. In the second pattern, *bilingualism,* group members retain their native language and master English as well. The third pattern, a *shift to English monolingualism,* involves losing the group's original language and becoming fluent only in English.

On this question the data are much less clear and subject to contention. As noted in Chapter 1, the prototypical pattern reported by linguists is that of a three-generational shift to English, with the first generation after settlement here being predominantly monolingual in a language other than English, the second generation being bilingual, and the third generation being monolingual in English. The underlying assumption of this pattern, of course, is that non-English languages exist in the United States primarily because of immigration and not because non-English language groups are native to this country, a question to which we will return.

To what extent do these patterns fit the contemporary United States? Strangely enough, the U.S. Census has not asked respondents whether they are bilingual as such. However, in addition to asking which language was usually spoken in the home, the Census did ask how well respondents could speak English, so that it is possible to estimate some aspects of the question at issue. Waggoner's (1993a) report of this data indicates a high degree of bilingualism among the 1990 Census respondents from NEL households:

> Four out of five . . . reported to speak English at least well, most of them very well, according to the census responses. In 1990, 17.9 million of the total of 31.8 million home speakers of non-English languages were reported to speak English very well and 7.3 million, well. Non-English speakers constituted about 5.8% of the total. (p. 3)

Among the relatively few who reported not being able to speak English at all, there was a comparatively high concentration in certain language groups. Thus Spanish-speakers, making up a little over 50 percent of NEL speakers, were nearly 80 percent of 1990 Census respondents who could not speak English at all. Nevertheless, speakers of eight other languages or language groups—Hmong, Mon-Khmer, Chinese languages, Korean, Vietnamese, Thai and Laotian, Russian, and Armenian—reported even higher rates of difficulty in speaking English than did Spanish speakers (Waggoner, September 1993a: 3).

A more recent study by Macias (1995) has generated 1992 data on U.S. bilingualism and biliteracy, classified according to U.S. Census Bureau racial/ethnic group categories. Focusing only on adults over the age of sixteen in 1992, and using performance test scores rather than self-reporting,[2] Macias found that bilingualism is much higher among Asian/Pacific Islander and Latino groups, than among whites and blacks, as indicated in Table 3.2.

Table 3.2

Bilingualism by Race/Ethnicity for Adults, Age Sixteen and Older, in the United States, 1992

Race/Ethnicity	Bilingual	English Monolingual	NEL Monolingual	Total
Whites	4.9%	94.9%	0.2%	100.0%
Blacks	2.9%	96.9%	0.2%	100.0%
Asian/Pacific Islanders	58.9%	26.4%	14.5%	100.0%
American Indians and Alaskan Natives	22.9%	76.7%	0.3%	100.0%
Other	41.9%	37.9%	20.2%	100.0%
Latinos				
Mexicans	47.8%	24.8%	26.5%	100.0%
Puerto Ricans	66.1%	20.4%	12.4%	100.0%
Cubans	54.6%	3.5%	41.9%	100.0%
Central and South Americans	48.6%	17.3%	31.6%	100.0%
Other Latinos	41.1%	46.3%	12.4%	100.0%

Source: Macias, 1995.

Macias's data indicate, as well, that significant numbers of Asian/ Pacific Islander and Latino adults are monolingual in their non-English languages. His data on adult literacy is generally congruent with that on bilingualism/monolingualism (see Macias, 1995: Table 2). What is most significant to the language policy debate in the United States, however, is that both sets of data—that of the U.S. Census and that of Macias—indicate that high percentages of speakers of non-English languages are fairly proficient in the English language as well.

Related to this question is the issue of language loyalty versus language shift over time. That is, to what extent are non-English languages being maintained beyond the second generation in the United States? Here the data are even less clear and subject to even more contention among scholars. The question is often posed this way: If all migration to the United States stopped today, which—if any—languages other than English would remain vital into the future? Veltman (1983), Fishman (1985), and others have argued that only the Navajo language would be likely to survive into the long-term future without the influx and influence of new immigrants speaking the "mother's tongue." Others dispute this claim, citing data showing that Spanish-English bilingualism is not uncommon among third and later generation Latinos (Waggoner, 1994; Macias, 1995).

Another source of data on this question is emerging from sociological studies of the adaptation of second-generation immigrants to contemporary U.S. life. Portes and Schauffler (1994) report, for example, that the most important findings in their ongoing study of language-use patterns among second-generation immigrant youths in South Florida were "the overwhelming dominance of English knowledge among children of immigrants and its strong positive association with length of residence in the United States" (p. 650). They found, further, that over 80 percent of the youths in their study expressed a preference for speaking English over the language of their parents, and among Cuban American students attending private, bilingual schools (who had the highest percentage of Spanish-proficient respondents), an even higher percentage—over 93 percent—preferred speaking English to Spanish (Portes and Schauffler, 1994: 648–49). In any case, it is not my purpose to resolve this issue here, but the long-term answer may well depend on the future shape of language policy in the United States, the subject of this book.

Language Contact and Competition in the United States

To what extent is there contact between language groups in the contemporary United States? To what extent does this contact result in linguistic competition? While no quantitative data could be found on these questions, it seems fair to assume that nearly everyone in the country has some daily contact with the English language through the media of mass communications and commerce, if not through personal usage. With 15 percent of the U.S. population over age five speaking a language other than English in the home, moreover, it is evident that a considerable number of contemporary Americans, including those who are monolingual English-speakers, may have contact with non-English languages in their daily lives as well.

From a political perspective, however, it is important to note that the United States does not have large political territories, such as Quebec in Canada, in which a minority language group greatly outnumbers the country's majority language group. The only U.S. exception to this generalization is the Commonwealth of Puerto Rico, an island some distance from the U.S. mainland.

At the same time, language minority groups are not randomly spread around the country. Rather, for both historical and socioeconomic reasons, non-English languages tend to be concentrated in certain regions. Although becoming more diffuse over time, for example, Spanish-speakers remain concentrated in the Southwest (particularly those of Mexican origin), Florida (particularly those from Cuba), the Northeast (particularly those from Puerto Rico), and certain cities of the Midwest. Speakers of Asian languages, too, are highly concentrated in Northeastern, Midwestern, and especially Western cities. Thus, against the benchmark of 15 percent nationally, the 1990 Census found that 41 percent of New York City's population spoke a language other than English in the home, up from 35 percent in 1980. In Miami, three-quarters of the population lived in NEL households, and 67 percent of these reported they did not speak English well. Most strikingly, the Census reported that the NEL population of Los Angeles grew from 35.1 percent in 1980 to 49.9 percent in 1990. Statewide, nearly 32 percent of 1990 California residents reported speaking a language other than English in the home. Other cities with large concentrations of NEL speakers according to the 1990 Census, included Paterson, New Jersey, (50%); Santa Fe, New Mexico (40%); Hartford, Connecticut (nearly 40%); Providence, Rhode Island (30%); and Boston (26%) (Vobejda, 1992). In short, the level of contact between English-speakers and the speakers of other languages varies in different areas of the United States, being most likely to occur in cities along the eastern seaboard and in the Southwest. The fact that the intensity of language policy political conflict has been greatest in these areas, then, seems unlikely to be a random coincidence.

To what extent has this language diversity and contact resulted in linguistic competition in the United States? Here differing perceptions and definitions of linguistic competition become very important. On one level, it is certainly true that no other language is close to challenging the hegemony of English in the public domains of the United States. Indeed, sociolinguists throughout the world are busily charting the growing hegemony of English on a world wide scale, especially in the train of the exploding globalization of science, commerce, and communications (see, e.g., Phillipson, 1992). And among sociolinguists, as we saw above, the question is not whether English is being displaced in this country, but whether other languages would be able to *survive* in the

United States if large-scale immigration were cut off. At this level of analysis, then, there is little competition between languages in the United States.

In political life, nevertheless, demands for policy change emerge from perceptions that yield discontent, and language policy conflict in the United States has emerged from changes—or the threat of changes—that have been perceived as linguistic competition. As will be outlined in greater detail below, activists promoting the two dominant policy positions in U.S. language politics—assimilationism and pluralism—have very different perceptions of the nature and meaning of this linguistic competition. Put very briefly, linguistic pluralists see recently adopted pluralistic language policies as long-overdue efforts to ameliorate injustices stemming from the hegemony of the English language in a country that has never been monolingual. Pluralists view English language hegemony, in short, as the unjust result of a very unequal competition between different language groups.

Assimilationists, on the other hand, view the long-time dominance of English in the United States as being threatened by new linguistic competition from immigrants who are being encouraged by public policy to retain their home languages rather than shifting to English in the most efficient manner possible. Consequently and more specifically, they feel their English-language "public space" has been encroached upon by other languages on the streets, in commercial settings, on the airwaves, in the workplace, in the schools, and in some arenas of politics and government.

To what extent are these conflicting political activist perceptions of linguistic competition reflected in rank-and-file public opinion? The question has not been posed in this way by survey researchers, but we can summarize several public opinion studies indicating some level of division along ethnic lines among the general public over language issues.

In reviewing public opinion data on this subject, it is important to note at the outset that most Americans do not perceive language issues as highly significant to the public welfare. When asked which public policy issues are critical to the future of the country or to themselves and their families, very few Americans of any ethnic background offer language policy (or the specific language issues described in Chapter 1) as among the most important. Most of the time, then, language policy has low salience as a political issue for the general public (see, e.g., Sonntag, 1990).

Nevertheless, when Americans are directly confronted with language issues, there are some important differences between Anglo Americans[3] and Latinos[4] that provide possible foundations for political conflict.[5] The primacy of the English language in the United States, however, is *not* one of the issues that divides Americans along ethnic lines. Public opinion surveys of both the general public and of Latinos in particular show strong consistency of support for those who are not proficient in the language to learn English (see, e.g., Citrin, Reingold, and Green, 1990; Citrin et al., 1994; Huddy and Sears, 1990; Schmidt, 1997; Tatalovich, 1995: chap 6). To emphasize, there is no empirical evidence to support the often-expressed view that contemporary non-English-speaking groups—and particularly Latino immigrants—are resistant to learning or using the English language (see Table 3.3). U.S. immigrants—including Latinos—display consistent support for policies that provide access to English-language acquisition, and seek to use such policies in numbers far exceeding the capacity of English-language educational programs.

There does appear to be an important division of opinion, however,

Table 3.3

Support For U.S. Citizens and Residents Learning English, by National Origin

"U.S. Citizens and Residents Should Learn English"	Mexican	Puerto Rican	Cuban
Strongly agree	251	142	79
	29.1%	25.0%	25.6%
Agree	537	386	206
	62.3%	67.7%	66.8%
Disagree	62	32	19
	7.2%	5.6%	6.1%
Strongly disagree	12	10	5
	1.4%	1.7%	1.6%
Total	862	569	309
	100.0%	100.0%	100.0%

Source: de la Garza et al. 1992: 98

on the appropriate role of non-English languages in U.S. public policy and civic life. That is, to say that Latinos and other language minorities are eager to master the English language is not to say that they are not also eager to retain and use their native tongues. An analysis of data from the largest available survey of Latino public opinion to date, the Latino National Political Survey (LNPS) of 1989, showed strong support across the board among members of the three largest Latino national-origin groups (i.e., Mexican Americans, Puerto Ricans, and Cubans) for a pluralistic, bilingual approach to U.S. language policy (Schmidt and Garcia, 1996; Schmidt, 1997). And this support is sharply divergent from the more assimilationist bent of the general public as reported in several public opinion studies.

Latinos interviewed for the 1989 LNPS, for example, were highly supportive of bilingual education programs, to the extent of being willing to pay more taxes for them. Further, they understood the appropriate purpose of bilingual education as learning *both* English and Spanish, not as providing a temporary transition to English-only classrooms. These observations are supported by the data in Tables 3.4–3.6.

More recent surveys show that these positive evaluations of bilingual education have not changed since the LNPS data was collected in 1989.

Table 3.4

Attitude Toward Bilingual Education, by National Origin

	Mexican	Puerto Rican	Cuban
Strongly support	321 37.1%	232 39.7%	100 32.3%
Support	368 42.5%	278 47.5%	174 56.1%
Feel uncertain	113 13.0%	42 7.2%	19 6.1%
Oppose	46 5.3%	23 3.9%	6 1.9%
Strongly oppose	18 2.1%	10 1.7%	11 3.5%
Total	866 100.0%	585 100.0%	310 100.0%

Source: de la Garza et al. 1992: 99.

Table 3.5

Willingness to be Taxed for Bilingual Education,
by National Origin

	Mexican	Puerto Rican	Cuban
No	266	174	142
	31.0%	30.0%	45.9%
Yes	592	406	167
	69.0%	70.0%	54.1%
Total	858	580	309
	100.0%	100.0%	100.0%

Source: de la Garza et al. 1992: 99.

In 1998, for example, a national survey of Latino opinion commissioned by the Spanish-language television network Univision[6] found similarly high levels of support for a bilingual, bicultural approach to public policy. The poll found that 83 percent of Latinos polled supported bilingual education, and that 64 percent believe it has been effective (Roth, 1998). Similarly, a *Los Angeles Times*/CNN exit poll from the June 2, 1998, pri-

Table 3.6

Objective of Bilingual Education, by National Origin

	Mexican	Puerto Rican	Cuban
To learn English	119	67	32
	14.7%	11.9%	10.3%
To learn two languages	569	415	240
	70.3%	73.65%	77.3%
To maintain Spanish language and culture	74	45	15
	9.1%	7.9%	4.9%
Other	48	37	23
	5.9%	6.6%	7.5%
Total	809	564	310
	100.0%	100.0%	100.0%

Source: de la Garza et al. 1992: 99.

mary election in California, found that Latinos voted nearly two to one (37% to 63%) against Proposition 227, which was aimed at eliminating nearly all bilingual education classes in the state's public schools, while white voters favored the measure by 67 percent to 33 percent (*Los Angeles Times*, 1998).[7]

The Latino National Political Survey found other measures of Latino public support for a pluralistic, bilingual approach to language policy, including strong majority backing for public services in the Spanish language, and majority opposition to "official English" legislation and to employer restrictions on the use of languages other than English in the workplace. These findings are summarized in Tables 3.7–3.9.

In contrast to these demonstrations of Latino public support for a pluralistic language policy, studies of general (mostly Anglo) U.S. public opinion seem to indicate a consistent pattern of support for an assimilative approach to language policy. Huddy and Sears's 1990 report on a national survey of Anglo attitudes toward bilingual education, for example, found qualified support for bilingual education only to the extent that it is limited to the aim of mastery in English. That is, the Anglo public supported only transitional forms of bilingual education

Table 3.7

Attitude Toward Providing Public Services in Spanish, by National Origin

"Public Services Should Be Provided in Spanish"	Mexican	Puerto Rican	Cuban	Anglo
Strongly agree	197	154	85	59
	22.9%	26.5%	28.1%	13.7%
Agree	579	390	202	244
	67.3%	67.2%	66.4%	56.9%
Disagree	71	31	15	85
	8.3%	5.4%	5.0%	19.8%
Strongly disagree	14	5	2	41
	1.6%	0.9%	0.5%	9.6%
Total	861	580	304	429
	100.0%	100.0%	100.0%	100.0%

Source: de la Garza et al. 1992: 97.

Table 3.8

Attitude Toward English as the Official Language,
by National Origin

"English Should Be the Official Language"	Mexican	Puerto Rican	Cuban	Anglo
Strongly agree	116	66	33	198
	13.7%	12.1%	10.7%	45.6%
Agree	262	200	89	147
	30.7%	36.8%	29.3%	33.7%
Disagree	334	223	145	75
	39.2%	41.2%	47.5%	17.3%
Strongly disagree	140	54	38	15
	16.4%	10.0%	12.4%	3.4%
Total	852	543	304	435
	100.0%	100.0%	100.0%	100.0%

Source: de la Garza et al. 1992: 97.

and, according to Huddy and Sears, was quite hostile to maintenance versions of the program.

Similarly, analyzing a 1988 California poll, Citrin, Reingold, and Green (1990) reported that "64% of the Anglos surveyed believed that 'citizens who can't read English should not be allowed to vote,'" and that "73% of the Anglos in California were unwilling to pay any more taxes so the public schools could teach Hispanic and Asian children in their native tongue 'if they don't know English well'" (pp. 1142–43). More recently, analyzing the 1992 National Election Survey, Citrin et al. (1994) reported that "only 18%" of the survey's respondents "favored the multiculturalists' goal of continuous instruction in both languages 'so that children can keep up their native languages and culture if they choose'" (p. 19). And virtually every general public opinion survey this author has seen reported shows strong Anglo support—when asked— for the proposition that English should be the sole official language of the United States and its political subdivisions (for a good overview of the surveys, see Tatalovich, 1995).

In short, while there are broad areas of agreement on the primacy of the English language in U.S. life and in public policy, there is some level of

Table 3.9

Attitudes Toward Requiring English in the Workplace, by National Origin

"Businesses Can Require English During Working Hours"	Mexican	Puerto Rican	Cuban	Anglo
Strongly agree	58	19	18	84
	6.7%	3.4%	5.8%	19.4%
Agree	198	122	65	150
	23.1%	21.8%	21.3%	34.6%
Disagree	459	332	166	155
	53.5%	59.1%	54.2%	35.8%
Strongly disagree	144	88	57	44
	16.7%	15.7%	18.8%	10.2%
Total	859	561	306	433
	100.0%	100.0%	100.0%	100.0%

Source: de la Garza et al. 1992: 98.

disagreement on the appropriate role for additional languages, and especially the Spanish language. In this sense, there is some evidence of linguistic competition in American public life in the late twentieth century.

FUELS FOR THE FIRE: IDENTITY POLITICS AND ETHNOLINGUISTIC INEQUALITY IN THE UNITED STATES

In Chapter 2 it was argued that political conflict over language policy requires more than the preconditions of language diversity, contact, and perceived competition. Language policy conflict erupts most forcefully when competing concerns over the relationship between language and group identity, fueled by anxieties over national unity and drives for greater ethnic equality, are expressed politically in the form of demands for state action. Because every country's historical experience is unique, each has a singular (albeit contested) understanding of its national identity and its internal ethnic composition. The United States is no exception, having its own particular tradition of discourse on these matters that has helped to set the stage for the recent debates over language policy in this country. Those debates will be described in some detail in the chapters that follow. The remainder of this chapter will provide further background for these debates by sketching some of the terms of our discourses on national and ethnic identity, and on the structure of ethnic inequality in the United States.

National and Ethnic Identity in the United States

At least since the war for independence from Great Britain in the eighteenth century, there has been near unanimity among U.S. political elites—and among foreign commentators on the United States as well—that there is a distinctively *American* national identity. Few have doubted that Americans have a character unto themselves, constituting a national community unique in the world.

At the same time the substantive content of what exactly constitutes the American national identity has been contested throughout our history. This is hardly surprising since, as noted in Chapter 2, nationalism is an ideology and the terms of any particular version are inherently contestable. The debates over what constitutes the American national character have proceeded along many tributaries during our history, and it is impossible and unnecessary to summarize them here. Since the conflict over national versus ethnic identity is a central preoccupation of this book, moreover, we will return to this issue many times in the chapters that follow. At this point, it will suffice to present some basic facts about the origins of the American people and the terms of several debates over the core of U.S. national identity that are signficant for the language policy conflict.

The intricacy of U.S. debates over the national character is attributable, in part, to the complexity of the country's origins. Americans can trace their roots to a uniquely diverse range of ancestors. There is virtually no place on earth that has not contributed to the flow of people who eventually became citizens of the United States. And the diversity of means to becoming American may be uniquely complex as well. While our dominant myth is surely that we are a nation of immigrants, immigration is only the most common among several ways in which we have become a people. In addition to voluntary immigration and colonization by several European powers (Great Britain, Spain, France, the Netherlands, Sweden, and Russia), some peoples became part of the United States not by choice but by purchase (e.g., through the Louisiana Purchase in 1803) or by violence (e.g., through the infamous Middle Passage from Africa to enslavement; and through the military conquest and annexation of native peoples' lands, nearly one-half of Mexico's territory in 1846–48, and Puerto Rico in 1898). As will be seen in chapters to follow, these divergent paths to becoming American continue to reverberate in our understandings of both the stakes and the appropriate course of action to follow in relation to our linguistic diversity.

A second source of complexity in understanding the American national character is attributable to the fact that the United States became an independent country through a series of contested political acts by a particular set of political actors. Most of the political actors who gave birth to an independent United States had British roots, and understood their political actions in terms of English political beliefs that have been characterized by recent scholars as either "liberal" or "republican," or a unique combination of both. Among the consequences is that one of the most powerful claimants for core status in the American national identity is a kind of political volunteerism that remains unusual in the contemporary world. From the beginning of our national independence, that is, Americans have been asked to choose their nationality through a political act. This, in turn, gives rise to a kind of universalism that makes it possible for any human being—no matter what her or his original nationality—to be an American through an act of choice. But this has also made possible a kind of political exclusivity rarely found in other countries, symbolized in the mid-twentieth century by legislative committees established to investigate "*un*American" activities and beliefs. Thus while it is possible for anyone in the world to become an American, it is also possible for one's fellow citizens to declare that—based on your actions and beliefs—you are not really an "American" after all. Another example could be found in popular automobile bumper stickers of the late 1960s/early 1970s that read, "America—love it or leave it!" This was understood by all to signify that if one did not support the U.S. war effort in Vietnam, one should—by rights—forfeit one's citizenship and go elsewhere. Few other countries, if any, understand their national identities in this way.

At the same time that this ideological tension between universalism and exclusivity has operated on one plane, another tension, between the potential universalism of American political beliefs and their decidedly British roots, has existed on a different plane. That is, the fact that nearly all the political elites who founded the United States as an independent country were British in origin has given to the American national identity a strong ethno-ascriptive character of Anglo origin that has existed in tension with the universalism of the country's official political ideology. While all might become Americans, some have been perceived as more "American" than others, by virtue not of their political beliefs and actions but of their blood roots. The word "nation", after all, has its origins in the Latin *natal*, or "birth".

The result of these complex and conflicting realities is what Rogers Smith (1997) has aptly termed "multiple traditions" of membership in the American political community. One tradition strains toward the volunteeristic universalism of a political definition of American national identity, while another stands firmly rooted in an ascriptive hierarchy of ethno-Americanism.

Within that ascriptive hierarchy of Americanism exist a myriad of ever-changing, but never absent, ethnic groupings. As noted in Chapter 2, ethnic identities—like national identities—are socially constructed through the delineation of boundaries, using comparisons of origin narratives, cultural practices and beliefs, religious traditions, beliefs in inherently distinctive or biological characteristics (e.g., race), and the like. In the United States, some of the ethnic boundaries that matter most have changed dramatically over time. Prior to the 1960s, for example, religious affiliation was a centrally important ethnic boundary, with certain branches of Protestantism at the top of the hierarchy as the norm against which all others were measured, with Roman Catholicism marked as decidedly inferior, and Judaism even more severely marked. A half-century later, these distinctions matter much less to the life chances and social standing of most Americans.

Similarly, national-origin distinctions between European Americans were once much more important in American life than they are at present. The prospect of a marriage between the daughter of English-origin parents and the son of an Italian American couple once brought a level of dismay almost incomprehensible to Americans who have come of age since the 1960s. Both national-origin and religious identities remain extant in the United States at the end of the twentieth century, but these boundaries are far less rigid and pronounced than they were several generations ago.

Nevertheless, one ethnic boundary that has remained highly significant in American life, from the country's origins to the present, is that of race. As noted, the concept of race is based on perceived distinctions understood as inherent or essential to the nature of different peoples (i.e., as biological). As such, the concept of race challenges the assertion made above that all ethnic boundaries are socially constructed. Because these perceived essential differences, moreover, are used to establish a hierarchy of worth and values among peoples, race becomes a "sign of privilege and honor" on one side, and a sign of eligibility for "policies of discrimination and control" on the other (Montejano, 1987: 4–5).

Belying their own assumptions, however, racial boundaries have assumed a variety of forms, as those making the racial categorizations have relied upon an ever-changing multiplicity of characteristics signifying essentially different peoples (e.g., cultural beliefs and practices, national origins, skin color and other physical characteristics, languages, and so on). It was common, for example, for early twentieth-century writers to discourse with great confidence about the inherent differences between the English, French, and German "races". Nevertheless, these inconsistencies, together with the denial by most social and physical scientists of any natural or biological foundations for the ethnic boundaries creating the racial groupings of the United States, have had little effect on the reality of these boundaries in the experienced lives of most contemporary Americans. Indeed, racial groupings continue to be the most important ethnic boundaries in American public life.

In recent decades, in virtually all arenas of life (e.g., among academicians, the media, political actors, and government officials, as well as in the civil and private niches of daily living), most Americans have come to understand their most significant ethnic divisions in terms of five primary groups—each of which has a racial connotation. The largest group is composed (for the most part)[8] of European-origin Americans, variously termed "white," "Anglo," and "Euro-American." The second largest of these racialized groupings is that of African-origin Americans, described as "black," "Afro-American," and "African American." Third, and rapidly growing toward becoming the second largest of the groups, are those of Latin American origin (including those from Spanish-speaking Caribbean islands), most frequently designated as "Latinos" or "Hispanics." The fourth-largest group comprises those Americans with roots in Asia and the Pacific Islands, typically called "Asian Americans" or "Asian/Pacific Islanders." The smallest group, finally, is composed of those whose ancestors were most native to the territory of the United States, who did not migrate to the "New World" following the "Age of

Discovery," and who include those described as "Native Americans," "American Indians," "Inuits," "Aleuts," "Eskimos," and "Native Hawaiians." As well as having geographic origins, each of these racialized groups has been color-coded in U.S. cultural discourse: white, black, brown, yellow, or red.

As social constructs, each of these groups is subject to boundary-definition controversies and to internal division. Each of them is an "imagined community" not existing in nature, and each is a meta-ethnic grouping composed of highly diverse peoples sometimes characterized by long-standing conflicts with each other. Many Irish-, French-, or German-origin Americans, for example, find it extremely offensive to be called "Anglo" (with its so clearly British roots). Similar internal divisions can be found among members of each of the other U.S. meta-ethnic communities (e.g., descendants of African American slaves versus recent migrants from Africa or the Caribbean; Chinese versus Japanese versus Filipino versus Vietnamese versus Cambodian versus Indian Americans; Mexican versus Cuban versus Puerto Rican versus Nicaraguan Americans; Navajo versus Hopi versus Lakota Sioux versus Hawaiian Natives).

Despite this range of diversity and the problematic nature of each group's boundaries,[9] American public and private life in the late twentieth century has been suffused with these racialized ethnic groupings. In informal social discourse, as well as in more formal public discussion, Americans habitually take cognizance of and refer to each other's ethnic identities in terms of these five primary categories. And yet it also remains true that there is widespread agreement around the globe and within the country that there is a distinctively "American" national character.

As noted, the significance of our ethnic group memberships in relation to language policy is highly contested and will be a central focus for the remainder of this book. What remains to be sketched here in terms of the context for the language policy debate in the United States are the facts that (1) the problematic relationship between national and ethnic group identities has given rise to a set of debates often termed "culture wars" among the country's intellectual and political elites in recent years, and (2) this politics of identity in the United States is also fueled by long-standing inequalities between our racialized ethnic groups.

Ethnicity, Nationality, and the U.S. "Culture Wars"

To understand language policy conflict in the United States, it is important to recognize that these debates over language have become intertwined with a larger set of conflicts often described as "culture wars." The core of the debate, while raging along many fronts, has been over how to appropriately understand the relationship between culture and our identity as a national people. And the central terms of the debate have been set by the question of whether the United States is best understood as a multicultural nation or as a country with one singular and unifying American culture. Its battle fields have included preschools, postgraduate schools, college and university campuses, academic professional associations, a large number of published books, academic journals as well as more popular journals of public affairs and news magazines, national political conventions, legislative bodies at all levels of government, and, of course, the expansive air waves of radio, television, and cyberspace.

The most prominent supporters of a multicultural understanding of the United States in these debates have been college professors and teachers, as well as some political activists from among peoples of color. The Reverend Jesse Jackson, for example, has frequently spoken out in favor of a "rainbow coalition" that will promote a multicultural understanding of American society. Similarly, opponents have included both intellectuals and political leaders, from all parts of the political spectrum, including conservative Republicans (e.g., Patrick Buchanan and William Bennett), liberal Democrats (e.g., Arthur Schlesinger), and those farther left (e.g., Todd Gitlin).

It is not necessary or desirable to summarize this debate in any detail here, but several points deserve articulation. First, this debate is highly symbolic in nature, being centrally concerned with the symbols through which Americans understand themselves to be a people. A good metaphor for understanding this is the Latin phrase enshrined on our money—"*E pluribus unum*"—which translates as "Out of many, one." An ambiguous phrase, it can be understood—and has been defended in the culture wars—as either supporting or opposing a multicultural understanding of the American people. What is often forgotten, however, is that the phrase is purely symbolic, a talisman of no material signficance in that the value of the money on which it is emblazoned is not affected by its interpretation.

Second, as David A. Hollinger (1995) has rightly pointed out, it is important to understand that these often vitriolic "culture wars" are not really about a multicultural understanding of American life at all. They *are* about "culture" to be sure, in that their subject is most frequently the appropriate cultural education for Americans. Virtually no proponent of multicultural education, however, has argued that American education should import and incorporate as its own a non-American cultural edifice from another country. Rather, the debate concerns the national educational significance of cultural contributions by Americans whose origins are not European, and especially not Anglo European. Should we understand our national cultural heritage as one that has developed from British roots, elaborated and dialectically expanded by Americans, but still an extension of an inherited British culture to which all previous newcomers have adapted? Or should American culture be understood, in addition, in terms of oppositions and tensions emanating from the fact that the British colonization of, and subsequent U.S. expansion over, much of the North American continent had opponents and victims who drew upon a vast array of cultural materials (including, sometimes, British and other European materials) to fashion and articulate their own understanding of what it meant—for them—to be Americans and human beings? Until recently, U.S. education at all levels has been unaware of the very existence of this wide range of American voices and cultural contributions, much less attempting to incorporate it in the teaching of who we are as a people. Put differently, then, the "culture wars" debates are most centrally about the national cultural significance of the voices of those who have been excluded from elite status and high-level power positions by virtue of their ascribed characteristics (e.g., race, gender, religion, national origin, etc.).

Seen in this way, the "culture wars" of the late twentieth century are best understood as a debate over the significance of our meta-ethnic identities in relation to our national identity. Are we a people with one, coherent European-origin (especially Anglo-origin) culture that should be passed along as a precious heritage to all Americans as their own; or, should the racialized ethnic experiences and the multiple articulations of the American experience deriving from our often violent history of ethnic conflicts be prominently incorporated into our understanding of our national identity and culture? More personally, should all Americans understand their past and culture from the point of view of, say, George Washington and Thomas Jefferson; or should they understand themselves as including also the experiences and worldviews of Nat Turner, Sojourner Truth, and César Chávez—*in addition to* those of Washington and Jefferson? And more tritely, the question is often formulated as: Should we understand ourselves in terms of a melting pot or a stew pot or a salad bowl? As might be self-evident by now, these questions are closely intertwined with the debates over language policy, as the identity politics concerns of both sets of political argument are virtually identical. In that sense, the analysis in this book should contribute to a better understanding of these other "culture wars" as well as to the debate over language policy.

Racialized Ethnicity and Social Inequality

As outlined in Chapter 2, the quest for equality between ethnolinguistic groups is one of the two primary fuels driving language policy conflict around the world. In the United States, moreover, our history of racialized ethnicity and discrimination on the basis of ascribed ethnic identities forms an important backdrop for the language policy debate. As a closer look at the non-English-language data from the 1990 Census reveals, many of the persons making up the largest and fastest-growing minority language groups are categorized as members of the non-white, non-European-origin racialized ethnic groups outlined above (e.g., Latinos or Hispanics, or Asian/Pacific Islander peoples). As such, they are members of minority ethnic communities with long histories of exclusion and domination in the United States. This confluence of memberships in U.S. language minorities and racial minorities has given particular impetus to the argument for a pluralist language policy in this country, as will be seen in the pages that follow, particularly in Chapters 4 and 5. Both this argument and the response by assimilationist leaders, in turn, place the debate firmly in the territory of identity politics.

Helping to fuel the debate of both the "culture wars" and of language policy is the persistent social stratification among the primary U.S. ethnic communities, and therefore among ethnolinguistic communities as well. This is not the place to explain the origins or consequences of U.S. ethnic inequalities. Those aspects of this issue intertwined with the U.S. language policy debate will be prominently discussed in chapters to come. Here, rather, the discussion and tables that follow simply illustrate that on several quantitative measures of social well-being, the United States can be characterized as having a pattern of social inequality along ethnic lines.

In particular, the United States, as well as virtually every other country in the contemporary world, is ethnically stratified in relation to wealth, income, occupational status, educational attainment, and social prestige. And, with few exceptions, status on the lower rungs of this stratification system is disproportionately related to membership in U.S. racial minority groups. Thus, Latinos, Native Americans, African Americans, and members of some Asian/Pacific American groups have a greater chance of being poor, underemployed, undereducated, and socially despised than do European-origin Americans or members of certain other Asian American communities, as demonstrated in Tables 3.10–3.13, each of which is based on analysis of the 1990 U.S. Census.

A 1996 Census Bureau update of the figures on those living in poverty revealed minor changes, but the overall pattern remained the same: The poverty rate among non-Latino whites was 8.6 percent; among blacks, 28.4 percent; among Asian Americans, 14.5 percent; among Latinos, 30.3 percent; and among American Indians, 31.2 percent (McClain and Stewart, 1998: Tables 2.1, 2.2).

Each of these U.S. ethnic groups has considerable internal variation, but in view of the widespread perception of Asian/Pacific Americans as a "model minority," it is especially important to note that this category includes groups that are experiencing considerable poverty and low social and educational mobility. This is particularly true among certain refugee populations from Southeast Asia (e.g., Cambodians and the Hmong) and some Pacific Islander groups. Paul Ong (1993), for example, reported 1990 Census data for Southern California indicating a 25 percent poverty rate for Vietnamese Americans and 45 percent rate for other Southeast Asian-origin peoples (p. 15). Paula D. McClain and

Table 3.10

Education Attainment of Young Adults by Race and Ethnicity, 1992

Ethnic Group	Percent High School Graduates	Percent with Some College	Percent College Graduates
Anglo/white	91	27	28
African American	81	26	14
Latino	60	20	10
Asian	92	20	47
American Indian	78	30	11

Source: O'Hare, 1992: 29.

Table 3.11

Median Household Income by Race and Ethnicity,
1979 and 1989

Ethnic Group	1979 Household Income	1989 Household Income
Anglo/white	$30,200	$31,400
African American	$18,700	$19,800
Latino	$23,100	$24,200
Asian	$34,100	$34,800

Source: O'Hare, p. 34.

Joseph Stewart, Jr. (1998), moreover, cite 1990 Census data indicating that 14 percent of Chinese-origin Americans and 13.7 percent of Korean-origin Americans live in poverty (p. 32).

Placement on these vertical rungs on the U.S. status structure, it should be noted, is not just a function of educational attainment, despite the general correlation between educational level and social and occupational standing. Rather, when educational levels are controlled for analysis, European-origin Americans (especially males) still enjoy quite favorable occupational placement, wealth, and income in comparison with African Americans, Latinos, and Asian/Pacific Americans. Even highly educated Asian Americans, for example, appear to experience a "glass ceiling" that limits their proportionate representation among higher levels of the U.S. managerial and techno-institutional social structure (Hubler and Silverstein, 1993).

What role, if any, does language play in the construction and main-

Table 3.12

Median Net Worth of Households by Race and Ethnicity, 1988

Household Type	White	African American	Latino
All households	$44,400	$3,800	$5,500
Married-couple households	$61,400	$14,900	$12,300
Female households	$25,500	$700	$500

Source: O'Hare, 1992: 36.

Table 3.13

Poverty and Welfare Receipt by Race and Ethnicity, 1991

Income Category	Anglo/ White	African American	Asian	American Indian	Latino
Percent in poverty	9	33	14	32	29
Percent in deep poverty	3	16	7	14	10
Percent receiving welfare	13	47	19	51	44
Percent of poor receiving welfare	61	85	62	87	79
Numbers (in 1,000s)	188,667	30,758	7,065	1,730	22,039

Source: O'Hare, 1992: 38.

tenance of this ethnic stratification system? The argument over this question will be treated at length in Chapter 5, but two points may be made here. First, the ability to use English is highly correlated with occupational standing, wealth, and income in the United States. That is, those individuals who are unable to use English at all are disproportionately found at the lower end of the U.S. social structure. Second, however, the use of a language other than English is *not* correlated with low economic standing, provided that the individuals are able to speak English fluently. In other words, non-English monolinguals in the United States do pay a price for not being able to use the dominant language. Bilinguals who know English well, however, are not penalized in the occupational structure for their knowledge and use of a language other than English (see, Tienda and Neidert, 1985). In any case, there is ample fuel for the conflict over language policy in the United States in the convergence of our highly racialized ethnic stratification system and the immigration-fed growth of NEL monolingualism.

SUMMARY AND CONCLUSION

To summarize, then, it is evident that the U.S. political conflict over language policy does have social foundations. Multiple language groups coexist in the country, and there are contact and some sense of competition among them. The two principal fuels igniting language policy conflict throughout the world—ethnolinguistic inequality and an identity politics that is connected with language diversity and is centered on the relationship between national and ethnic identities—also exist to some degree in U.S. society. Activists and political leaders involved in U.S. language politics, moreover, have made conflicting claims upon the state for public policies addressing certain aspects of this linguistic diversity, contact, and competition. The particular claims made by these political activists in relation to both identity politics and U.S. ethnolinguistic stratification remain to be discussed. Chapters 5 and 6, in turn, will outline more specifically the claims upon the state being made by both pluralists and assimilationists in regard to language policy and ethnolinguistic equality, and language policy and the contested relationship between ethnic and national identities in the United States. Before turning to that exposition, however, Chapter 4 will explore the competing perspectives of linguistic assimilationists and pluralists on the relationship between language diversity, identity politics, and ethnolinguistic inequality in U.S. history.

II. THE ARGUMENTS

4 Historical Perspectives on U.S. Identity Politics and Ethnolinguistic Inequality

TWO ARGUMENTS have dominated the U.S. conflict over language policy in recent years. One concerns the relationships between language policy and ethnic equality, the other those between language policy, ethnic identity, and national unity. Before outlining and assessing the protagonists' arguments in these two disputes, it is important that we examine their competing historical narratives. Indeed, one of the most divisive of issues in the present conflict over language policy in this country is how we understand the origins of both our linguistic diversity and our ethnolinguistic stratification. The two sides in the U.S. debate—pluralists and assimilationists—are as deeply divided over these questions as on any other, and their dispute over historical memory undergirds and informs their conflicts on all other issues in the language policy debate.

Why is this question of origins so important to the current debate? As indicated in Chapter 2, both national and ethnic group boundaries are maintained in part by the construction and maintenance of historical memories—narratives of the past—through which group members obtain a sense of who they are and why they are different from others. Thus, history is at the very center of identity politics: It is central to our understanding of who "we" are and, equally important, who "we" are *not*.

In addition to the role it plays in defining group identity, historical memory is also important in the political conflict over the patterns of racialized ethnic inequality that figure so prominently in language policy conflict. This is so because our understanding of why some ethnic groups are relatively prosperous and powerful while others are not is shaped in no small measure by our understandings of what has happened in the past. Both dominant and subordinate groups look to the past for explanations of where they have been and how they got to be where they are now. In view of the importance of historical viewpoint to understanding our present-day conflict over language policy, then, it will be useful to outline the competing perspectives of pluralists and assimilationists on how the United States has come to be both multilingual and characterized by systematic ethnolinguistic inequalities.

LEGACIES OF CONQUEST AND IMPERIALISM: THE PLURALIST HISTORICAL NARRATIVE

Because pluralist policy innovations of the last three decades (e.g., bilingual education and multilingual public access policies) initiated the contemporary U.S. language policy debate, it seems most instructive to begin with the historical frame of reference that has informed much of the support for these recent policies. And that narrative makes the most sense when viewed through the prism of racialized ethnic political activism in the 1960s, which most shaped the current drive for pluralistic language policies.

What came to be known as the "ethnic revival" of cultural pluralism in the 1960s and 1970s began in the crucible of the African American civil rights movement in the U.S. South. Out of that movement came a strong assertion of rights to equality and social justice that were understood in terms of historical racialization, an assertion that, in turn, revitalized political efforts by other peoples of color throughout the country. And from the outset of this revitalization, language and culture played a central role in defining the policy agendas of Latinos, American Indians, and some Asian/Pacific American groups.

As the politics of these decades evolved, pluralist scholars and political activists came to articulate the view that both linguistic diversity in the United States *and* this country's long-standing pattern of racialized ethnic inequality are best understood in terms of European imperialism and conquest, along with the patterns of racial domination and exclusion, as well as the resistance to oppression, that followed in their wake. This view of our history challenges the self-interpretation of the United States as a "nation of immigrants," a view favored by assimilationists and outlined below.

The linguistic pluralists' narrative of U.S. history emphasizes three key points: *first*, that most peoples of color—including American Indians, Latinos, and some Asian American groups, along with African

Americans—did not originally become members of U.S. society through voluntary individual immigration; *second*, that having come involuntarily under U.S. jurisdiction, peoples of color have experienced racialized oppression—domination/exclusion along racial lines—for much of the country's history; and *third*, that this systematic oppression has included specific efforts to disparage and/or exterminate the cultural forms—including language—giving meaning to the lives of those so oppressed. Each point will require some elaboration here.

Becoming Americans

The United States has long understood itself as a "nation of immigrants," and our dominant national narrative has stressed the inducements that this country offered to the poor, huddled masses of other countries as memorialized in Emma Lazarus's famous poem inscribed on the Statue of Liberty in New York harbor. In fact, however, the American people has evolved into being from a complex, many-faceted series of processes. In addition to immigration in search of individual freedom, the American people derives from processes of colonization, an international slave trade, military conquest, territorial purchase from European powers, imperialist aspirations in the Western Hemisphere and in Asia, and other foreign policy interventions resulting in political refugees claiming special access to U.S. protection.

To take the most obvious case first, Native Americans did not immigrate to the United States in search of freedom. Quite the opposite, as the original "Americans," their lands were invaded by European colonists and conquerers, whose diseases and military technology killed huge numbers of their members and ultimately drove most of those remaining onto reservations that became ever-smaller, more remote, and depleted of the resources that had sustained their traditional ways of life.

Relatedly, in 1803 the United States purchased the Louisiana Territory from France, a vast tract of land stretching from the Mississippi Basin to the Pacific Ocean. The purchase resulted in U.S. jurisdiction over a large number of Native Americans and many non-English speaking European-origin settlers (including the French-speaking Acadians, who had been forcibly resettled by the British following the conquest of New France in 1767). None of these newly incorporated "Americans," of course, had voluntarily immigrated to the United

States, nor had they been consulted about their own national or linguistic loyalties.

As is well known, further, most African Americans are descendants of diverse peoples who were captured in western Africa by slave traders, imprisoned and put into chains, transported via the horrific Middle Passage to the Western Hemisphere, and sold as chattel into hereditary slavery to European-origin Americans. These too were not immigrants who came to America in search of freedom.

Like Native Americans, Mexican Americans first became part of the United States through military conquest and annexation. In 1846 the United States declared war on Mexico, moving to shield U.S.–origin Texans who had declared their independence after defeating forces led by Mexico's president, General Santa Ana.[1] The two-year war of the United States against Mexico resulted in the 1848 Treaty of Guadalupe Hidalgo in which Mexico was forced to sell nearly half of its territory to the United States (including present-day Texas, New Mexico, Arizona, California, Nevada, Utah, most of Colorado, and small parts of Oklahoma, Kansas, and Wyoming). The Mexican citizens who lived in this vast territory were given the option of pulling up their roots and moving "back" to Mexico—or becoming "Americans."

Near the end of the nineteenth century, the Spanish-American War resulted in the forcible acquisition of other populations of new Americans when Spain ceded Puerto Rico, the Philippine Islands, and other Pacific islands to the United States. While the Philippines was granted independence in 1946, its nearly half-century as a colonial possession of the United States continues to shape the special ties between its peoples and this country. Meanwhile, Puerto Ricans and Pacific Islanders remain U.S. citizens, although not as a result of voluntary immigration.

Finally, the coming of other Asian Americans into the fold cannot be understood accurately in terms of the dominant voluntary-immigration-in-search-of-freedom narrative. In the first place, Asians were singled out for coercive exclusion from the United States for seventy years. Under pressure from Californians in particular, Congress adopted the Chinese Exclusion Act in 1882, the first of several anti-Asian measures that virtually precluded immigration from most Asian countries until 1952. And second, especially prevalent among contemporary Asian-origin immigrants are people from countries (e.g., the Philippines, Korea, Vietnam, and Cambodia) in which U.S. foreign policy interventions have created special relationships and obligations that are not best understood in terms of the traditional individual immigration model. The same may be said about most Cuban and many Central American immigrants in the contemporary period.[2]

The point that pluralists want to emphasize is that many of the groups comprising the American people did not become members of this society as voluntary immigrants in search of America's much-vaunted freedom. Rather, many were coerced into U.S. jurisdiction, which meant theirs was a kind of second-class, subservient membership that had little to do with democratic freedom. Others sharing many of the same racialized identities became part of the American people as a result of U.S. foreign policy interventions over which they had no influence or control. As will be seen, the implications of this understanding of how some of us became Americans is an important point of contention between contemporary linguistic pluralists and their assimilationist opponents.

Racialized Domination/Exclusion

The second theme emphasized in the pluralist historical narrative is that the same peoples who became Americans through force have been subjected to a long history of racialized domination and exclusion in this country. That is, once made a part of the United States population, these peoples of color were excluded from full participation as equal members of the society and were kept in subordinate positions through a variety of ideological, social, economic, and political mechanisms. And, while a number of European-origin groups experienced similar discrimination for at least a time, the ethnic boundary of race has been the most consistent and far-reaching in its long-term consequences for peoples of color.

A variety of practices were employed to maintain the system of racialized domination/exclusion that has characterized much of U.S. history. The historical relationships between Native Americans and European-origin Americans are very complex, but their dominant realities are that American Indian societies were overwhelmed by the coming of European colonizers, and that Native Americans were placed in a subordinate position—socially, culturally, economically, politically, legally—to their European-origin rulers, a position in which Indian country remains today. American Indians were subjected to a variety of policies, including: colonial invasion; military conquest; the "trail of tears" to Indian Territory; treaties guaranteeing their sovereignty on reservations "for as long as the grass grows and the water flows"; forced assimilation via the Dawes Act, BIA operated Indian Schools, and relocation programs in the mid-twentieth century; a New Deal under John Collier's tutelage; and the more recent "self-determination" program. In each case, however, native Americans have struggled, and continue to struggle, to find an equal place for themselves within the territorial boundaries of the United States (see, e.g., Chaudhuri, 1982; Deloria, 1969 [1988]; Gonzalez and Cook-Lynn, 1999; Prucha, 1985; U.S. Commission on Civil Rights, 1981; Washburn, 1988; Wilkinson, 1987).

The systems of chattel slavery and post-Reconstruction Jim Crow segregation, moreover, were carefully designed and implemented to maintain African Americans in subordinate positions in the U.S. political economy as well. Nationwide, a whole legal and extralegal structure of domination was erected and maintained by European Americans to ensure the subordination of African Americans in the social, economic, political, and legal arenas of American society (see, e.g., Bennett, 1962 [1987]; Harding, 1983; Huggins, 1977; Karenga, 1982; Smith, 1997; Woodward, 1957).

The treatment of annexed *Mexicanos* by Anglo Americans also followed patterns of racial exclusion and domination in the years following their conquest by the United States. The particular pattern varied according to local circumstances, but within a couple of decades following the annexation the main features of a new, racially segmented system were in place wherever *Mexicanos* lived, principally in Texas, California, and the New Mexico territory (see, e.g., Acuña, 1988; Barrera, 1979; Camarillo, 1984; Deutsch, 1987; Montejano, 1987).

The first step in the process of transformation was the Anglo acquisition of Mexican-held land. Through a variety of devices—such as legal subterfuge, tax policies incompatible with Mexican material culture, and direct violence—most of the large tracts of land that had been held by *Mexicanos* passed into the hands of Anglo Americans in the entire annexed region of the Southwest (Acuña, 1988; Barrera, 1979; Deutsch, 1987).

The second step in the transformation process was the incorporation of *Mexicanos* into what Mario Barrera (1979) has called a "colonial labor system" (34). Underpinned by the railroads, the main initial ingredients of the southwestern economy in the late nineteenth century were ranching, agriculture, and mineral extraction. In all four economic activities Chicanos became important sources of wage labor, and the labor system that was developed included the following racially segmented features: (1) *"labor repression, . . .* the use of non-market sanctions such as coercion and legal restrictions to limit the degree of freedom of Chicanos as compared to non-minority [sic] workers"; (2) *"the dual wage system,"* which "consists of paying one wage to minority workers and another to nonminority workers who perform the same task"; (3) *"occupational stratification, . . .* the practice of classifying certain kinds of jobs as suited for minorities [e.g., low-paying field labor] and others as suited for nonminorities [e.g., higher-paying skilled work]"; and (4) the use of Chicanos as a *"reserved labor force,"* in which employers made strenuous efforts to recruit potential workers far in excess of the number to be offered full-time employment, a practice particularly common among agricultural employers (Barrera, 1979: 41–48, emphasis in original). More generally, as Barrera (1979) concludes:

> The system of colonial labor appears to have been based on racial rather than ethnic distinctions. On the subordinate side were all the racial minorities in the Southwest at that time: Native Americans, Asians, Blacks, and Chicanos and other Latinos. On the other side were all the White groups, regardless of ethnicity. (p. 49)

In addition to this segmented labor system, social and residential segregation was the dominant pattern for Chicanos throughout the Southwest until well after World War II.

A similar process of racial segregation, legal discrimination, and labor segmentation occured in relation to Asian Americans. Prior to their complete exclusion from the United States in the 1880s, the patterns were set in relation to the Chinese and then applied to groups arriving later from other parts of Asia (e.g., Japan, the Philippines, Korea, and South Asia). As historian Ronald T. Takaki (1982, 1989) has described, these patterns of domination and exclusion involved forced segregation in housing and social patterns, racially segmented labor practices similar to those applied to other peoples of color, and—under the legal category of "aliens ineligible for citizenship," based on the Naturalization Act of 1790—denial of the right to own property in virtually every state in the West and Southwest and several others in the Midwest and South.

From the pluralist perspective, it is important to emphasize that the structures of racial domination and exclusion outlined above were buttressed by public policies as well as by the actions of private citizens.[3] Far too numerous and various to be described here, such governmental actions supported and validated private actions by such parties as slave owners, employers, merchants, bankers, home sellers, rentiers, Ku Klux Klan terrorists, and many others.

Finally, undergirding this entire public/private structure of racial oppression was an ideology of racialism that has been documented and described by Reginald Horsman (1981) and others (see, e.g., Omi and Winant, 1994: chap. 4). In Horsman's telling, Europeans widely applied evaluations of innate inferiority toward both Indians and Africans at the beginning of the country's history. Prior to the nineteenth century, however, these beliefs were not fully developed into an ideology, and they competed with Christian and Enlightenment views that all human beings are capable of being "civilized" into members of the same community.

By 1850, however, the inchoate but powerful beliefs of European superiority had congealed into a highly developed and increasingly dominant ideology of Anglo-Saxonism that derived from several streams of British, American, and Western European thought. As summarized by Horsman (1981):

> From their own successful past as Puritan colonists, Revolutionary patriots, conquerers of the wilderness, and creators of an immense material prosperity, the Americans had evidence plain before them that they were a chosen people; from the English they had learned that the Anglo-Saxons had always been peculiarly gifted in the arts of government; from the scientists and ethnologists they were learning that they were of a distinct Caucasian race, innately endowed with abilities that placed them above other races; from the philologists, often through literary sources, they were learning that they were the descendants of those Aryans who followed the sun to carry civilization to the whole world. (p. 5)

This racialist ideology provided intellectual justification for the expansionist Manifest Destiny doctrine propelling the war of conquest against Mexico as well as the U.S. interventions in Latin America and Asia at the end of the nineteenth century. Internally, the ideology was "used to force new immigrants to conform to the prevailing . . . system, and . . . to justify the sufferings or deaths of blacks, Indians, or Mexicans" (Horsman, 1981: 5). For pluralists, the research of Horsman and other scholars leaves little doubt that the racialist ideology of exclusion and domination was applied to all peoples of color and not just to African Americans.

Cultural Oppression

Part and parcel of the system of racial oppression described above, contemporary pluralists emphasize, was the devaluation and attempted destruction of the cultural practices—including language—that made up the way of life of the peoples so dominated. The mention of "philologists" in the quote from Horsman above is a reference to an important linguistic plank in the nineteenth-century ideology of Anglo-Saxonism:

> The identity of race and language was taken for granted, and race was exalted as the basis of a nation. . . .
> In little more than fifty years a whole scholarly base had been created for the affinity between language and race, and what was best in Europe and the world was increasingly ascribed to that people, soon generally to be called Aryan, who had pressed westward out of central Asia to revitalize the Roman Empire and eventually dominate Europe and the world. (Horsman, 1981: 35–36)

Since these "Aryans" were thought to have developed and perfected their race-based language as they moved west, British philologists of the time concluded that through this process of purification "the Saxons became the elite of an elite" (Horsman, 1981: 38). One can imagine the attractiveness of this new "science" to many Anglo American readers, who were located even further to the west than the British Isles.

Anglo Americans, however, did not have to wait for the arrival of philology to begin systematic practices of cultural domination. American Indians were subjected to a wide variety of attempts to destroy their material and symbolic cultures, including their languages, from very early points in their history of contact with European-origin Americans. Military conquests of resisting tribes typically included systematic efforts to obliterate all belongings of the defeated Indians, thereby decimating their cultures. President Thomas Jefferson supported a policy of assimilating the Five Civilized Tribes in several southern states, but his efforts were rebuffed by land-hungry white settlers and eventually gave way to the "trail of tears" that resulted from the Indian relocation policy implemented by Andrew Jackson.

The most systematic efforts at cultural and linguistic destruction, however, occurred later in the nineteenth century, when Christian missionaries were given semiofficial "civilizing" roles on Indian reservations, which meant that Indian youngsters were forcibly removed from their families and communities to undergo a process aimed at their linguistic and cultural assimilation into Anglo society. The Dawes Act of 1871 started the integrally related process of "Indian allotment," under which Indian reservations were carved up into individual and family farm plots, with the remainder sold to white settlers (the proceeds went into a fund for educating the Indians).

An even more destructive system of cultural decimation was aimed at Africans brought here for enslavement. Indeed, the institution of slavery as a whole has been described by one scholar as "cultural genocide against Africans," defined as "the wholesale intentional destruction of a people's culture and cultural identity and their capacity to produce, reproduce and expand themselves" (Karenga, 1982: 85). More specifically, Nathan Irwin Huggins (1977) showed that while American English came to embody many Africanisms (particularly in the South), control over language use was an integral part of the system of racial domination that developed in and from slavery:

> White people . . . were anxious to keep their language to themselves. They wanted it as an emblem of the social superiority they felt to blacks and the lower orders. They wanted to talk to one another, among blacks, and not have their meaning understood. They wanted language to serve in limited ways to communicate between themselves and slaves, but they also wanted it to remain enigmatic. Language to them was a mark of civilization as well as a tool of communication, and they needed a sense of security a monopoly of good speech and literacy gave them. Furthermore, they knew that language transported ideas, and ideas could be weapons against established order. So, rather than finding a prideful, missionizing achievement in the acculturation of Afro-Americans into English, the Anglo-Americans were protective and jealous. Above all, as far as it was possible, slaves were to be kept ignorant of the written word. (p. 67)

Partly as a result, the slave codes of the Old South made learning written English a crime for slaves, and teaching literacy to slaves was a crime for all southerners, black or white (see, e.g., Stampp, 1956; Bennett, 1975). Not only were the slaves prevented from mastering the dominant language of their new land, however, but they were also typically punished severely for speaking African languages, practicing their native religions, or following other cultural traditions of their fore-bears.

While specific practices varied according to time and place, the most typical cultural pattern by the end of the nineteenth century was that the spatially and socially segregated peoples of color were expected to learn enough English to take orders in the racially segmented jobs through which they were integrated into the economy. Beyond that level of cultural acquisition, though, they were not expected to accul-turate—nor allowed to assimilate—into the dominant society, as were most European-origin immigrants. Believing that members of these racialized "lower orders" were fundamentally unassimilable, most Anglo Americans seemed to assume that Indians and Mexicans would be "outbred" into extinction and that Asians could be no more than tem-porary sojourners here (see, e.g., Higham, 1984: chap. 8; Horsman, 1981: 243; Dinnerstein and Reimers, 1988: 64; Takaki, 1989).

The pattern is most instructive with respect to education policy. Each of the racialized peoples of color was subjected to educational discrim-ination in several ways. First, each group was extended the benefits of public education more slowly and more grudgingly than were Euro-pean Americans. Second, when education was extended to them, it was within segregated and inferior schools. Third, the groups' cultures and languages were disparaged and suppressed by public educators and other community leaders, and the public schools accordingly denied them the opportunity to maintain and perpetuate their cultural her-itages. And fourth, even in the face of these visible forms of rejection and exclusion by the dominant groups in the society, the curriculum that *was* offered was exclusively assimilationist or Anglo-conformist in orientation (Weinberg, 1977; Stein, 1986: chap. 1; Baron, 1990: 164–66; Gonzalez, 1997).

The net effect of these social and educational practices was to provide a cultural basis for the continued domination of these racialized minor-ity peoples. That is, in the larger context of the racialized domination described above, the simultaneous provision of inferior, truncated, and segregated public education in the dominant culture and language, *and* the disparagement and denial of their own heritage cultures and lan-guages, was a combination well designed to perpetuate their exclusion and subordination in U.S. society. The triple message delivered to minority youths (and their parents) was clear: "You are a member of an 'inferior' race, which has provided you with an 'inferior' culture; if you want to 'better' yourself, you will learn our culture and language; still, because you are 'inferior' by nature, we don't expect you to do as well as one of 'our own,' nor will we allow you to integrate too closely with 'our own.' " Anthropologist John U. Ogbu (1978) has described this system of education as "caste-like" in its assumptions and effects.

There is evidence that the dominant economic interests in communities where these minority populations played an important and subordinate role in the labor force were very much aware of these effects. In the early 1930s, for example, economist Paul Taylor quoted an onion grower in Dimmit County, Texas, on the subject of the education of Mexican American children:

> The little education they get in schools here spoils them, and makes them trifling. They become peddlars or bootleggers, or seek some easy way of making a living. They don't want to do this [onion clipping] or other work. . . . But the more ignorant they are, the better laborers they are. (quoted in San Miguel, 1987: 51)

In sum, then, as pluralists look into the mists of the past, they see the present campaign for linguistic pluralism as having evolved out of a long-term struggle for racial equality. It was a struggle, moreover, that sought to overcome a highly developed system of oppression founded on coercive incorporation into the society and an ideology of racialization, practicing systematic methods of group domination and exclusion that maintained peoples of color in subordinate positions in the political economy, and that decimated their cultures while simultaneously limiting their access to the dominant culture.

History, Resistance, and Cultural Pluralism:
The Other American Tradition

Domination and destruction, however, are not the only lessons pluralists want us to learn from American history. In addition, they view the past as a storehouse of examples of resistance and positive pluralism that form an alternative tradition in U.S. history. Peoples of color, who were pressured to assimilate culturally even while being subjugated and excluded, as seen above, resisted the destruction of their own cultural traditions and practices by employing a variety of resistance strategies.

Many European-origin Americans, pressured as well to assimilate as quickly as possible, also resisted the loss of their traditions and sought ways to exercise and reproduce their languages and cultural practices. Indeed, pluralists emphasize that virtually all non-Anglo groups who have become Americans have sought ways to develop and reproduce their heritage cultures as members of this diverse polity, and that, moreover, this alternative tradition can and should serve as a model for the country's future development.

Cultural pluralism did not find its first real philosopher until Horace Kallen (1924 [1970]) began to publish essays on the subject early in the twentieth century. Nevertheless, practices of cultural pluralism were prevalent in American society from the very beginning of its existence. In seeking to reproduce their cultural practices, moreover, ethnolinguistic communities have employed a wide variety of organizational forms, especially religious institutions, schools, ethnic organizations, and the mass media.

From the vantage point of our own more secularized milieu, it is important to recall that religion was far more central to the civic lives of most Americans in the eighteenth and nineteenth centuries than it is today. Further, during those centuries religious beliefs and practices were closely intertwined with ethnocultural sentiments and traditions. Thus, many non-Anglo groups in the early days of American history saw ethnolinguistic cultural freedom as an integral part of their claims to religious freedom. Simply put, having the right to worship in one's own way meant having the right to worship in one's own tongue and according to one's cultural traditions as well. Many non–Anglo Americans continued to draw a close connection between perpetuating their religious faiths and maintaining their non-English languages well into the twentieth century (see, e.g., Archdeacon, 1983; Deloria, 1969 [1988]: chap. 5; Harding, 1983; Karenga, 1982; Takaki, 1989; Acuña 1988: chap. 11).

In addition, virtually all cultural communities seek to reproduce themselves in the young. Accordingly, private and parochial schools, often closely connected to efforts to maintain religiously based ethnic diversity, have also been important institutions through which various ethnic communities have sought to reproduce their languages and cultures in the young. The largest non-English-speaking U.S. ethnic community in the nineteenth century, for example, was German American, and the Roman Catholic adherents among this group supported a German-language parochial school population of 165,000 in 1886

(Kloss, 1977: 67). But this was only the largest example of a very widespread phenomenon, involving virtually all ethnic and ethnoreligious groups throughout both rural and urban areas of nineteenth- and early twentieth-century America (see, e.g., Kloss, 1966, 1977; Howe, 1976; Bennett, 1962 [1987]; San Miguel, 1987; Lissak, 1989; Takaki, 1989; Baron, 1990; Crawford, 1992).

In this context, the U.S. Supreme Court decision in *Meyer v. Nebraska* (1923), overturning an assimilationist Nebraska law prohibiting the teaching of "foreign" languages in public or private schools, is seen by pluralists as a major historical landmark for their alternative tradition (see, e.g., Crawford, 1992: chap. 7). Indeed, Heinz Kloss (1977) described the decision as nothing less than "a Magna Charta for the private nationality school" (p. 73).

The media of mass culture has been a third quasiprivate domain in which non-Anglo cultures and languages have flourished in the United States. An immense variety of non-Anglo books, magazines, and newspapers have been published throughout our history for readers of languages other than English. Many passed from view within a few short years, but others have remained and prospered for many decades. Ethnic communities have also supported English and/or bilingual versions of magazines and newspapers, seeking to maintain ethnic cohesion and to foster intergroup communication. Similarly, most ethnic communities have employed theater and other forms of mass entertainment to express and enjoy their own vision of the "human comedy," often in languages other than English (see, e.g., Howe, 1976: pt. 3).

In the twentieth century, non-English movie houses, radio, and television have provided abundant and expanding electronic media for cultural expression and maintenance. Through each of these forms of communication, ethnolinguistic communities have found a way to express their distinctive visions, engage in internal dialogue and debate, and maintain a degree of group cohesion within the larger national community.

Finally, another important source of private institutional support for cultural pluralism has been the rich diversity of ethnic organizations. Early in our history, Alexis de Tocqueville (1835 [1964]: chap. 30) remarked on the unusual degree to which Americans created "civil associations" for an immense variety of purposes, and we have been described as "a nation of joiners" on many occasions since. Accordingly, mutual aid societies and fraternal organizations among immigrant and subordinated ethnic groups have been commonplace at virtually all times and places in U.S. history. While the names change, the organizations have nearly always performed the same functions: to help ethnic group members find solace and joy through the renewal of their relationships with each other, and to negotiate collectively the difficult and often daunting process of coming to terms with life in the United States.

Similarly, political parties in the diverse cities and countrysides of the United States in the late nineteenth and early twentieth centuries were typically organized along ethnic lines, piecing together ethnic subgroups into an electoral and (they hoped) governing coalition (see, e.g., Hofstadter, 1955; Buenker, 1973). Ethnic geographic enclaves have also provided an environment in which a wide range of ethnically based economic institutions have flourished in U.S. history, giving members of these communities structural support for economic development and advancement that is also compatible with culturally pluralistic goals (see, e.g., Light, 1972; Portes and Bach, 1985). Organizations of wage laborers, too, have often found a more effective foundation in ethnic loyalties than in the more abstract concept of "class" (see, e.g., Mink, 1986; Olzak and Nagel, 1986: pt. I; Portes and Bach, 1985: chap. 1).

In addition to these private efforts on behalf of ethnocultural maintenance, pluralists stress as well the tradition of public, governmental support for cultural pluralism. In his now classic study *The American Bilingual Tradition*, German-born linguist Heinz Kloss (1977) documented a wide range of governmental policies in U.S. history that were "promotion-oriented" toward non-English languages. In terms of the policy categories outlined in Chapter 1, Kloss (and more recent scholars) have detailed numerous examples of state-supported non-English-language schools and linguistic access measures, as well as official language policies supportive of non-English languages.

Several scholars (see, e.g., Kloss, 1977; Lissak, 1989; Crawford, 1989, 1992; Perlmann, 1990), for example, have pointed to the prevalence of non-English-language public school programs in the nineteenth and early twentieth centuries. Once again, as the largest non-English-speaking group in that period, German Americans were most successful in getting public schools to support instruction in their language, either monolingually or bilingually with English. Other language groups, however, achieved successes on a more limited scale.

With respect to linguistic access, Kloss documented a large number of instances in which federal, state, and local governments have systematically employed non-English-languages to communicate with their citizens and residents. These examples, too numerous to describe here, range from the promulgation of laws and other official actions to the maintenance of non-English-language materials in public libraries throughout the country. Similarly, scholars (see, e.g., Kloss, 1977; Baron, 1990) have noted that several states and municipalities adopted official language policies promoting languages other than English in both the nineteenth and twentieth centuries. In addition, some pluralist advocates have argued that the 1848 Treaty of Guadalupe Hidalgo provided protection for the rights of annexed Mexicans that was understood at the time to have included the right to maintain their language and culture, although this claim is subject to dispute among historians (see, e.g., Frakes and Solberg, 1971: 36–42; Crawford, 1992: 67–68). And Native American activists, too, have argued that treaties entered into by the U.S. government provided guarantees of public support for the development and enhancement of their cultural traditions and practices, including language.

In short, supporters of bilingualism want to emphasize that cultural pluralism is not the radical innovation that its critics frequently assume. Rather, they stress, it has been part of the American tradition since the beginning of this country, and in arguing for the elaboration of culturally pluralistic policies in the form of language policy innovations, they seek to draw upon and extend these historical practices.

In summary, then, linguistic pluralists view U.S. history as constitutive of our linguistic diversity, our racialized ethnic categories, and our ethnolinguistic stratification. Diversity in languages and cultures became characteristic of the United States not only through voluntary immigration, but through conquest, annexation, and the foreign policy initiatives of a twentieth-century global giant. The manner of incorporation of new populations into U.S. society is important, moreover, because forcible incorporation constructs a different moral relationship between dominant and subordinate groups than does voluntary individual migration. The issues of identity politics can only be understood in this historical context. Thus, even contemporary immigrants (most of whom are peoples of color) and their children are being incorporated into a racially segmented society in which their (new) identities are partially defined by the history of the United States, and not solely by their own memories of history in their countries of origin (see, e.g., Rumbaut, 1994; Oboler, 1995).

Second, pluralists argue that racialized ethnic stratification in the contemporary United States is a direct result of two centuries of systematic conquest, annexation, domination, exclusion, and discrimination against peoples of color, and that language and culture have played an important role in the implementation and maintenance of our ethnic inequalities over time. Understanding the need and rationale for pluralistic language policies in our own time, then, requires knowledge of these historical forces that continue to operate in the multilingual environment of the contemporary period.

IMMIGRATION AND THE LAND OF OPPORTUNITY: THE ASSIMILATIONIST HISTORICAL NARRATIVE

The history of the United States as perceived by contemporary linguistic assimilationists is very different from that of the pluralists recounted above. For assimilationists, the key to understanding present language policy problems in the United States is encapsulated in the word *immigration*. More specifically, understanding our present linguistic plight requires a knowledge of a very important disjunction between how immigrants were greeted by American political leaders and public policies in the past, and how they are being greeted today.

The Historical Past

In the assimilationist vision, the meaning of U.S. history is to be found in our virtually unique melding of disparate peoples into one unified nation. To be a nation means to be one cultural "people," and not many "peoples." While acknowledging the historical realities of racialized exclusion and discrimination in U.S. history, assimilationists believe these unfortunate realities should be understood as departures from the true dynamic of U.S. history, and not as its essential core. The core trajectory of U.S. history, rather, lies in the remarkable integration of so many diverse peoples into one national consciousness, a process that has roots in the very beginnings of our history as an independent country and that must continue into the future if we are to remain the most successful multiethnic country in the world.

Further, a cornerstone of that historical process of successful integration has been, and remains, the willingness of immigrants to assimilate to the English language.

Many contemporary assimilationists point to the writings of J. Hector St. John de Crèvecoeur as foundational for the American model of national integration. A French American immigrant, Crèvecoeur settled in rural New York in 1759, married an American woman, and published his classic *Letters from an American Farmer* during the Revolutionary War. Historian Arthur M. Schlesinger, Jr. (1992), picks up the story from there in the Foreword to his critique of contemporary multiculturalism:

> This eighteenth-century French American marveled at the astonishing diversity of the other settlers—"a mixture of English, Scotch, Irish, French, Dutch, Germans, and Swedes," a "strange mixture of blood" that you could find in no other country.
>
> He recalled one family whose grandfather was English, whose wife was Dutch, whose son married a Frenchwoman, and whose present four sons had married women of different nationalities. "From this promiscuous breed," he wrote, "that race now called Americans have arisen." . . . . What, Crèvecoeur mused, were the characteristics of this suddenly emergent American race? *Letters from an American Farmer* propounded a famous question: "What then is the American, this new man?" (Twentieth-century readers must overlook eighteenth-century male obliviousness to the existence of women.)
>
> Crèvecoeur gave his own question its classic answer: "*He* is an American, who leaving behind him all his ancient prejudices and manners, receives new ones from the new mode of life he has embraced, the new government he obeys, and the new rank he holds. The American is a new man, who acts upon new principles. . . . *Here individuals of all nations are melted into a new race of men*." (p. 12 [emphasis in original])

Schlesinger adds his own gloss to Crèvecoeur's words to summarize aptly the assimilationist understanding of our historical dynamic with respect to ethnic diversity:

> *E pluribus unum.* The United States had a brilliant solution for the inherent fragility of a multiethnic society: the creation of a brand-new national identity, carried forward by individuals who, in foresaking old loyalties and joining to make new lives, melted away ethnic differences. Those intrepid Europeans who had torn up their roots to brave the wild Atlantic *wanted* to forget a horrid past and to embrace a hopeful future. They *expected* to become Americans. Their goals were escape, deliverance,

assimilation. They saw America as a transforming nation, banishing dismal memories and developing a unique national character based on common political ideals and shared experiences. The point of America was not to preserve old cultures, but to forge a *new* American culture.

. . . . From the Revolution on, Americans have had a powerful national creed. The vigorous sense of national identity accounts for our relative success in converting Crèvecoeur's "promiscuous breed" into one people and thereby making a multiethnic society work. (p. 13, emphasis in original)

As Schlesinger sees it, this model of national integration has been the dominant (although not the only) evolutionary dynamic throughout U.S. history, and he traces its articulation by a wide range of participants in and observers of the process, including Presidents George Washington and John Adams, Alexis de Tocqueville, James Bryce, Gunnar Myrdal, Frederick Jackson Turner, Henry James, and Israel Zangwill (Schlesinger, 1992: chap. 1).

A similar historical narrative was offered by Harvard sociologist Nathan Glazer, before his rueful conversion to a kind of grudging multiculturalism in the mid-1990s (see Glazer, 1997). Although he himself is not a historian, Glazer's 1970s critique of ethnically framed egalitarian public policy initiatives took its bearings from a sweeping interpretation of the trajectory of U.S. history. In Glazer's (1975 [1978]) understanding, a national consensus was reached in the mid-1960s in support of three important decisions culminating "the development of a distinctive American orientation to ethnic difference and diversity with a history of almost 200 years" (p. 5).

Like Schlesinger, Glazer acknowledged the obstacles to assimilation raised historically by nativists and racists against both immigrants and nonimmigrant peoples of color. Having made this acknowledgment, however, Glazer (1975 [1978]) criticized the purported view of pluralists that "racism defines our history," asserting instead

that the American polity has . . . been defined by a steady expansion of the definition of those who may be included in it to the point where it now includes all humanity; that the United States has become the first great nation that defines itself not in terms of ethnic origin but in terms of adherence to common rules of citizenship; that no one is now excluded from the broadest access to what the society makes possible; and that this access is combined with a considerable concern for whatever is necessary to maintain group identity and loyalty. (pp. 6–7)

The three specific decisions that were reached by the American people and their political leaders in the 1960s were articulated by Glazer (1975 [1978]) as follows:

First, the entire world would be allowed to enter the United States. The claim that some nations or races were to be favored in entry over others was, for a while, accepted, but it was eventually rejected. And once having entered into the United States—and whether the entry was by means of forced enslavement, free immigration, or conquest—all citizens would have equal rights. No group would be considered subordinate to another.

Second, no separate ethnic group was to be allowed to establish an independent polity in the United States. This was to be a union of states and a nation of free individuals, not a nation of politically defined ethnic groups.

Third, no group, however, would be required to give up its group characteristics and distinctiveness as the price of full entry into the American society and polity. (p. 5)

Like others in the assimilationist camp, Glazer expressed considerable frustration over the seeming irony that just as the European-origin American public finally decided to cast aside its historic exclusionary prejudices against peoples of color and welcome racial minorities into the fold of its universalistic and individualistic ethic, political leaders of the previously subjugated groups began to attack the long-held goal of assimilation. The nation's "new threat," Glazer (1975 [1978]) argued, came not from white supremacist opposition to integration, but from "the pressure of those recently subordinated to inferior status." And the nature of the threat was

that the nation would . . . be permanently sectioned on the basis of group membership and identification, and that an experiment in a new way of reconciling a national polity with group distinctiveness would have to be abandoned. (p. 7)

These articulations by Schlesinger and Glazer encompass most of the assimilationist narrative of U.S. history with respect to ethnocultural diversity. Acknowledging injustices in the past against African Americans, Native Americans, and (sometimes) other peoples of color, assimilationists nevertheless see the dominant theme of the U.S. past as one of steady progress toward an inclusive integration of individuals into membership in one united nation. The victorious army in the Civil War, after all, was composed predominantly of white Euro-Americans committed to a fight *against* slavery. World War II was fought *against* the racist ideologies of Hitler and his allies. The civil rights movement, in the finest hours of its achievements, was a coalition of Americans from all races and ethnic groups, united in the belief that the United States should become a "color-blind" society.

And underlying this vision of the past is the key role of immigration in making the United States the unique country that it is. It was the massive influx of immigrants in the nineteenth and early twentieth centuries that ensured that the United States would not become a society partitioned permanently into ethnic enclaves and competing groups. As Schlesinger and other assimilationists understand the past, most immigrants looked forward to assimilating as individuals into the uniquely free and liberating culture of the United States. While obviously having to make difficult adjustments to a new land, these earlier immigrants appreciated the opportunities available to them in their new homeland and evaluated their personal sacrifices (including those of a cultural and linguistic nature) in the light of the advantages these would provide for their children and grandchildren.

It was the children, in the end, who represented hope for the future to earlier immigrants. Although immigrants typically wanted their children to respect their parental prerogatives and traditional values, they nevertheless pushed their offspring to participate in schooling, work, and other social activities that would lead to success in America. Prominently included in this process was the push by immigrant parents for their children to learn English. Parents and children alike recognized and accepted that upward social mobility in the United States required linguistic acculturation into English. This dynamic of encouragement and tension between old and new cultural values yielded a highly Americanized second generation that was prepared and eager to move into the mainstream of the national life. And institutionally, it was the public schools that provided the foundation for the transformation of immigrant children into fully Americanized adults: "Our public schools in particular have been the great instrument of assimilation and the great means of forming an American identity" (Schlesinger, 1992: 17).

Those who favor a contemporary policy of linguistic assimilation, then, tend to see the social dynamic of the past as one in which most Anglo Americans welcomed newcomers from all parts of the world into their midst, although others (e.g., nativists and racists) did fight against this inclusionary process. Immigrants, meanwhile, fought to be included in the national community, and, working together with Anglo American integrationists and the children of previous immigrant generations, they were ultimately victorious over the exclusionary efforts of the prejudiced. The incorporation of immigrant individuals into the national community, moreover, established an assimilative pattern that the country was finally ready to apply to peoples of color in the 1960s, only to have it rejected by many political leaders of these previously excluded and subordinated groups. And it was this rejection of integration that set up the unfortunate political dynamic in which language policy is currently enmeshed, the subject to which we now turn.

The Historical Present

As noted, the key to the assimilationist historical narrative is the recognition and understanding of an important disjunction between past and present in American life. The process of assimilation described above, thought to work so successfully in the past to incorporate vast numbers of diverse newcomers into the national community, is today threatened by two forces that—in combination—could very well undo our standing as the most successful and harmonious multiethnic democracy in world history. These two threats are (1) a massive influx of non-English-speaking immigrants that shows no signs of abating; and (2) the ideology and policies of cultural pluralism that encourage the new immigrants to avoid making the assimilative adaptation to U.S. nationality that previous newcomers made.

The New Immigration   In 1965, the United States made its first major change in immigration policy in over forty years (Glazer, 1985: chap. 1). Abandoning the discriminatory national-origins quota system established early in the century (which had been designed to ensure that most immigrants would continue to come from northern Europe), the new law signaled a fresh wave of immigration that has continued to expand in size and scope of diversity during the three-plus decades since.

The 1965 immigration law established more equitable immigration limits for all regions of the world, and placed family reunification and occupational skills needed in the United States at the top of the priority hierarchy. According to Glazer (1985: 7–8), virtually no one in either Congress or the Johnson administration expected the sweeping changes that were to come. Nevertheless, by the end of the 1970s the size and shape of the new immigration had become evident: The numbers of immigrants began to increase dramatically, and their origins underwent a startling shift as well.

In the first twenty years following the 1965 reform, 9.2 million immigrants were officially admitted to the United States, as contrasted with 4.8 million during the preceding twenty-year period (U.S. Immigration and Naturalization Service [INS], 1987: 1). The third decade following the 1965 reform, 1987–96, saw the pace double yet again, with more than 10 million immigrants formally admitted to the United States (INS, 1997: 30). The ranks of the undocumented, of course, would bring these figures even higher, although how much higher remains in dispute. It is known with certainty, however, that over 3 million undocumented migrants applied for legalized status under the amnesty provisions of the 1986 Immigration Reform and Control Act (Silver, 1989).

Even more striking than the large numbers has been the shift in national origins of this recent wave of immigrants. Whereas the first and second waves of immigration to the United States came mainly from Europe, the present immigrants are overwhelmingly Latin American and Asian in origin. INS figures show, for example, that during the two decades from 1901 to 1920, 85 percent of immigrants originated in Europe, 4 percent in Asia, and 4 percent in Latin America. During the decades from 1961 to 1980, in contrast, 25 percent of documented immigrants originated in Europe, 26 percent in Asia, and 40 percent in Latin America and the Caribbean (INS, 1987: 3–4).

During the most recent decade for which data were available as of this writing, 1987–96, INS figures showed that the shift was even more pronounced, with those from Latin America and the Caribbean accounting for 51.9 percent of immigrants; Asians and Pacific Islanders, 31.6 percent; and Europeans, 11.9 percent (INS, 1997: 30–33). This change is largely responsible for the burgeoning growth of the population of non-European origin in the United States, especially Latinos (whose population increased by 53% in the 1980s) and Asian/Pacific Islanders (who had a 95% increase in the same decade) (O'Hare, 1992: 12).

Along with this striking increase in immigration during the last several decades has come the equally notable rise in the number of non-English-speaking households in the United States, described in Chapter 3. Many linguistic assimilationists are alarmed not only by the sheer growth in the number of non-English-speakers in the United States, but even more by their concentration into urban ethnic enclaves where they appear to have little incentive to learn English. The increasing numbers of linguistically isolated households, also cited in Chapter 3, add fuel to these concerns.

The Impact of the New Pluralism   These vast numbers of non-English-speaking immigrants represent a serious challenge in themselves to our national capacity for integration and assimilation. In fact, many assimilationists believe that it has become too great a challenge to meet successfully, and that consequently the United States must set the control of its own borders and a reduction in the number of new immigrants as very high policy priorities. In this sense, the organizational links between the "official English" movement and the immigration restriction movement are there with reason.

In addition, however, assimilationists believe that the inherent difficulty of integrating such a vast number of immigrants has been made immeasurably more severe by the unprecedented political power of cultural pluralism in recent decades, which occurred because cultural pluralists have amassed such strength in the educational systems, in the media, and in the government that they have been able to critically alter the public environment in which immigrants come to terms with their new home.

Consider the following influences that combine to discourage immigrants from making the assimilative adjustment to their new home that characterized the social contract between previous immigrant groups and the United States: publicly supported so-called bilingual classrooms where immigrant children appear to learn that they don't really need to speak English to be Americans; non-English ballots and other voting materials that impart the same message to adults; non-English-language rights in the workplace; non-English-language rights to commercial signage, virtually excluding English from whole urban neighborhoods; seemingly ubiquitous non-English media (e.g., radio, television, movies, magazines, newspapers, and billboards); stridently pluralistic ethnic political leaders; and the geographic concentration of ethnolinguistic neighborhoods noted above.

And all this has been made possible, assimilationist leaders believe, because pluralist political activists and intellectuals have convinced government officials to misconstrue the true nature of the ethnolinguistic situation in the contemporary United States. This is particularly the case with respect to Latinos. Assimilationist leaders argue that Latinos have been misconstrued as a conquered and annexed minority group when in fact nearly all Spanish-speakers in the United States today are voluntary immigrants. Accordingly, the pluralist claim that these "conquered" people's language and culture deserve to be treated as equal to English is a spurious distortion of the real issues.

This argument has been made most directly by U.S. English spokesperson Gary Imhoff. In Imhoff's view, the political movement for bilingualism is not a long-standing issue for Latinos. Rather, this drive began only in the 1960s, with the founding of several new Latino political organizations (i.e., the Mexican American Legal Defense and Education Fund, and the National Council of La Raza) that, together with reshaped and radicalized older organizations (the League of United Latin American Citizens and the American G.I. Forum), sought to rewrite the history of Latinos to conform to a new paradigm inspired by the political successes of African Americans:

> Prior to this period, the experience of Hispanic Americans was predominantly regarded as analogous to that of other immigrant groups. Obviously, Hispanics, especially those who did not speak fluent English, were at some times and in some locations subjected to discrimination, particularly in the Southwest, but sociologists carefully distinguished the experience of Hispanics from that of black Americans. Now, however, Hispanic Americans were to be considered as a minority group, and their experience was rewritten to be analogous to that of black Americans. The shift from the immigrant to the minority paradigm changed the entire focus of Hispanic political organization. (Imhoff, 1990: 57)

For Imhoff, then, the heart of the political conflict over promotion-oriented language rights lies in the shift in perception from Hispanics as immigrants to Latinos as a minority group. He elaborates on the importance of the difference as follows:

> The problems that arise between an immigrant and his or her society are solved primarily by the efforts of the immigrant. The stereotype of the American immigrant is that he or she learns the language of the new society, its customs and folkways, and the skills that are useful in the new land. Then the immigrant works twice as hard as native-born Americans and succeeds—"achieves the American dream"—by virtue of heroic and bittersweet industriousness, devotion, and discipline. . . .

In the minority paradigm, however, this type of effort must not be expected. The problems that arise between a minority and his or her society are presumed to be caused by—to be the fault of—the society. The responsibility for solving these problems, therefore, lies with the society. . . .

Society's responsibility to the immigrant is providing opportunity; society's responsibility to the minority is providing entitlements. Bilingual education is one of the foremost entitlement programs that can be offered to Hispanics. (Imhoff, 1990: 58)

In trying to shift the paradigm back to that of Hispanics as immigrants, rather than of Latinos as minorities, assimilationists such as Imhoff seek to correct pluralism's misreading of the historical past and present in the United States.

This critique of a misconstrued and misapplied pluralism was also made by Abigail Thernstrom (1987) in her book on the Voting Rights Act (VRA) of 1965. In explaining where Congress went wrong by making the VRA a permanent fixture in American life rather than the temporary amelioritive intended when it was first adopted in 1965 at the behest of the integrationist civil rights movement, Thernstrom's analysis pointedly questions the inclusion of Latinos and other language minorities under the act's protection.

Thernstrom's overall thesis is that the original intent of the Voting Rights Act of 1965 was carefully limited to enforcing the Fifteenth Amendment to the U.S. Constitution. This was to be done by using the power of the federal government to clear away obviously racially inspired impediments to the right to vote in certain southern states and localities still under the thrall of Jim Crow and out of step with the realities of mid-twentieth-century American democracy. Early in the act's implementation, however, the civil rights establishment succeeded in getting the U.S. Justice Department and certain federal jurists to redefine the meaning of Section 5, so that its principal aim became electing more blacks to public office and not ensuring the right of African Americans to vote. Not wishing to reopen the recent racial conflicts of the 1960s, both Democratic and Republican White Houses and congressional leaders acceded to this misinterpretation, which, through further important amendments in 1975 and 1982, made the tragic racialization of U.S. politics seemingly permanent in a new form congenial to the American left.

In Thernstrom's (1987) telling, Latinos gained coverage under the

VRA in part because the Mexican American Legal Defense and Education Fund (MALDEF) saw in the "growing importance of Section 5" a chance to "demand for its constituency the same extraordinary protection accorded blacks" (49). These political advocates faced several important difficulties before they could get into the action, however. Thus at the time that MALDEF mounted its campaign for inclusion into the act during the 1975 legislative renewal and amendment processes, Thernstrom (1987) asserts, "the evidence of Mexican-American disfranchisement was certainly thin" if one used "traditional measures of restricted access to the ballot" (p. 55). A second obstacle derived from the fact that the Fifteenth Amendment (the original constitutional touchstone for the VRA) mentioned only "race or color" as illegitimate obstacles to voting rights, yet the Census Bureau—and therefore the U.S. government—had regularly (except in the 1930 Census) classified Mexican Americans as "white."

Despite these obstacles, nevertheless, MALDEF and its allies in and out of Congress managed to secure the inclusion of Mexican Americans into the Voting Rights Act. The problem of defining Mexican Americans as a minority race was circumvented by devising the category of "language minorities" and by broadening the constitutional basis for the act to include the Fourteenth Amendment's equal protection clause. And the "thin evidence" of discriminatory "tests or devices" preventing Mexican Americans from voting was overcome "by equating the provision of ballots or other voting materials in English alone with the fraudulent southern literacy test used to bar blacks from the polls" (Thernstrom, 1987: 52).

In Thernstrom's interpretation, then, the inclusion of language discrimination in the 1975 amendments to the VRA was merely a cover for the real political aims of MALDEF and its allies. These political advocates were not really concerned that devices similar to Jim Crow laws would bar Mexican Americans from voting. Instead their main concern was that black leaders had hit upon an interpretation of the VRA that would guarantee them more elective political representation, and MALDEF was insistent upon gaining access to this new politics of minority representation:

> No one actually believed that the primary problem in the Southwest was the disfranchising effect of English-language election materials. Rather, the new formula was devised as a means of combating districting plans and other aspects of the electoral environment that the Mexican-

American groups believed discriminatory. The point of the 1975 amendments—unlike the 1965 act—was not access to the polls for citizens disfranchised in clear violation of the Fifteenth Amendment, but increased protection for minority candidates through the advantageous drawing of single-member districts. (Thernstrom, 1987: 60)

Thernstrom concludes her critique of the Voting Rights Act's "Mexican-American connection" by questioning the validity of the "analogy between blacks and Hispanics." Quoting Donald Horowitz, she suggests that " 'Mexican-American patterns are not replicas of black American patterns so much as they are consistent with the general fluidity of the American ethnic system' " (Thernstrom, 1987: 62). In short, she argues, the experience of Mexican Americans in the United States is more similar to that of other immigrant ethnics than it is to that of racialized African Americans.[4]

Nevertheless, Thernstrom and other assimilationists believe, the unfortunate group consciousness spawned by the black power movement enabled Mexican American political leaders to get Congress to define their group as a minority through the use of the new legislative category of "language minorities." In this way, pluralist language policy has helped to redefine the racial and ethnic environment within which the tremendous number of new immigrants to the United States are being incorporated into the national life.

As a consequence of the recent wave of immigration and such pluralistic legislative and bureaucratic successes, the assimilationists argue, whole areas of the United States are coming to resemble foreign countries rather than the unified America of the past. In the contemporary environment it is possible for the new immigrants to live their lives in ethnolinguistic enclaves that have little if anything in common with the vast majority of American communities. Particularly galling to assimilationists is the pride that some Latino leaders seem to take in pointing out that it is possible today for their compatriots to live both their public and private lives in Spanish.

In their book *The Immigration Time Bomb* (1985), former Colorado governor Richard D. Lamm and U.S. English spokesperson Gary Imhoff disapprovingly cited the "betrayal" of a "certain pride" in the following statement by the then-mayor of Miami, Florida, Maurice Ferrer (a Puerto Rican described by the authors as "a national spokesman for the Hispanic community"):

"You can be born here in a Cuban hospital, be baptized by a Cuban priest, buy all your food from a Cuban grocer, take your insurance from a Cuban broker, and pay for it with a check from a Cuban bank. You can get all the news in Spanish—read the Spanish daily paper, watch Spanish TV, listen to Spanish radio. You can go through life without having to speak English at all" (quoted on pp. 91–92)

The net result, assimilationists contend, is that fewer and fewer of the new immigrants or their children have either the motivation or the need to become conversant with the dominant culture and language of the country.

To round out their narrative of the historical present, assimilationists point to the fact that native-born Americans are coming increasingly to feel like foreigners in their own country. To underline this point, Lamm and Imhoff (1985) quote from *Esquire* magazine editor Phillip Moffitt's introduction to a 1983 article on "The Latinization of America":

"The genesis of the article on Hispanic Americans occurred two and a half years ago, when two of our editors made the following observations. One described walking out on the terrace of his midtown New York apartment one Saturday morning and looking down at the people on the street. Most of them were anything but your stereotypical Americans. "Where am I?" he caught himself thinking. Another editor, while describing his stay at the Omni, one of Miami's best hotels, noted how much easier it was for Spanish-speaking people to get attention and service. He, too, experienced that sensation of being in a foreign country" (quoted on pp. 90–91)

In summary, then, most intellectual spokespersons for the assimilationist position believe that in the past the United States embarked upon a grand experiment in culturally unified nation-building that was increasingly inclusive until, in the 1960s, the country was ready to embrace any person of any color or culture, from any part of the world, as a potential member of equal standing. In the past, moreover, virtually all newcomers to this land were eager to embrace their new home—including its language and culture—because it promised more freedom and opportunity than did the lands from which they had fled.

While the promise remains, however, today this dynamic of inclusive nation-building is seen as being threatened by a massive infusion of new non-English-speaking immigrants and a new politics of ethnic group consciousness that has resulted directly and unfortunately from the racial conflicts of the 1960s. Under the sway of a new racialized minority politics, ethnocentric Hispanic leaders in particular (although some Asian American leaders are attempting to emulate them) have managed to gain considerable power through a political agenda that is based on the false assumption that most of their constituents are not immigrants but "conquered" peoples whose languages and cultures have been unjustly oppressed by white European American racists. The result is an explosive situation in which the heretofore unprecedented success and harmony of America's grand and inclusive experiment in democratic nation-building is seriously threatened with divisive and destructive conflict.

A recent book co-authored by U.S. English (and Federation for American Immigration Reform) founder John Tanton, however, pushes the argument further, toward a virtually conspiratorial explanation of our historical present that is congruent with more traditional nativist arguments (Lutton and Tanton, 1994). In a chapter entitled "Immigration and the Politics of Race, Language, and Culture" (Chapter 3, pp. 48–59), Wayne Lutton and Tanton aim to demonstrate apparently strategically inspired linkages between political support of the new immigration, multiculturalist policies of linguistic pluralism, and the political empowerment of peoples of color. The chapter's subheadings neatly outline the thread of their argument: "Counting Illegal Aliens for Reapportionment," "Watering Down the English-Language Requirements for Naturalization," "Mandating Bilingual Ballots," "Extending the Vote to Noncitizens," "Registering Voters Passively," "Guaranteeing Minority Legislative Seats," "Admitting Puerto Rico to the Union of States," and "Next: Reinforcing Political Gains Through Even More Immigration."

This enhanced political clout for U.S. minorities, Lutton and Tanton predict, will be used to transform the cultural identity of the United States itself by "Institutionalizing Ethnic Divisions," as indicated in the chapter subheadings that follow: "Bilingual Education," "Multicultural Education," "Puerto Rican Statehood," and "The North American Free Trade Agreement." The critical import of these changes, particularly for European-origin Americans, is summarized by Lutton and Tanton (1994) in the following paragraphs:

> Large-scale immigration has been altering the distribution of power within the United States. It is shifting the balance between various ethnic

and racial groups in our society, and it is redistributing power among the states and within each state.

It should be emphasized that the American public has never agreed to, nor was even consulted on, this massive shift. Nevertheless, it is proceeding full speed ahead, in a series of seemingly unrelated changes that reinforce one another and make each new step appear inevitable. Together, they add up to a massive alteration of our political, ethnic, and cultural landscape, one that is transorming the U.S. into a country that more and more Americans find alienating and bewildering. (p. 48)

Followers of Patrick Buchanan's campaigns for the Republican presidential nomination in 1992 and 1996 will recognize a similarity between his argument on this issue and that of Lutton and Tanton. There is at least one branch of the linguistic assimilationist movement, in short, that explicitly links the importance of maintaining English as the dominant language in the United States with Anglo anxieties about the changed ethnic and racial make-up of the U.S. population, and their own power position within U.S. society. While Nathan Glazer has not disavowed his "open-arms-to-all races" position articulated above, other assimilationists have moved assertively toward support for a U.S. immigration policy that would tilt the demographic composition of the country back toward its traditional European-origin dominance (see, e.g., Brimelow, 1995).

This chapter has described the rhetorical conflict between U.S. linguistic pluralists and assimilationists by sketching their clashing perceptions of U.S. history. These widely different understandings of the historical reality of the country undergird and infuse the more discursive arguments made by each side in the debate in relation to the questions of justice (i.e., What does justice require for non-English-speakers in U.S. society?) and the common good (i.e., What sort of language policy will be in the best interest of the whole country?). In the next two chapters, we take up each of these questions in turn, following the debate through a series of twists and turns before offering a critical analysis of the arguments in the final section of the book.

5   Language Policy and Equality

The Search for Justice

As NOTED in Chapter 1, the argument over U.S. language policy has been conducted primarily in terms of two major public values, justice and the common good. The latter issue will be taken up in the following chapter, the former in this one. The search for justice in this debate has been focused for the most part in terms of how language policy can best promote greater equality for members of language minority groups. Although highly complex, the argument over how to answer this question takes two fundamental forms, one that is made in terms of equal rights, and another that is articulated in terms of social equality. The arguments of both assimilationists and pluralists in relation to each of these forms will be described in this chapter.

SOCIAL EQUALITY AND LANGUAGE POLICY

The Pluralist Argument

Both pluralists and assimilationists believe that the social inequality of minority ethnic groups in the United States, as described in Chapter 3, is intertwined with the question of language policy in this country. Pluralists believe that this social inequality derives not only from the fact that many have not mastered English and live in linguistically isolated households, but from the unequal treatment accorded racialized minority languages and cultures as well. Their aim, accordingly, is a society in which greater social equality is achieved through increased status equality for the multiple languages and cultures that make up the ethnocultural universe of the United States. The argument for a pluralistic language policy to achieve greater social equality has proceeded in several steps.

Transitional Bilingual Education as Egalitarian   As described in Chapter 1, the contemporary debate over language policy in the United States began in the late 1960s, with the reemergence of bilingual education for non-

English-speakers. In kicking off what would become the contemporary debate over language policy, the Bilingual Education Act's principal congressional sponsor—Senator Ralph Yarborough (D-Texas)—argued that the key issue for this policy was that of social mobility leading to greater social equality. In the expansive context of the Great Society programs of the 1960s, Yarborough and his allies stressed that bilingual education was needed because it would keep non-English-speaking (mainly Latino) youngsters from falling behind their English-speaking classmates while learning the country's dominant language. The theme developed by supporters of bilingual education was that the relatively high drop-out rates and lower-than-average educational attainments of many Latino children in the United States derive from the language barrier inherent in the fact that their home language is not English but Spanish. Similar arguments were made in relation to other limited English-proficient (LEP) students with relatively low success rates in the public school systems (e.g., Native Americans and several Asian/Pacific American groups).

Bilingual classes would help to overcome this handicap by teaching youngsters in a language they understand while they are attaining English proficiency. From the outset, then, bilingual education was justified as as a means of promoting greater educational success, which, in turn, would lead to greater social mobility and therefore greater social equality for language minority children and their communities.

This first rationale for bilingual education was entirely consistent with a temporary, transitional, and assimilative understanding of the program's goals. In this view, the aim of the program was to overcome an obstacle to equal opportunity for LEP students, which is identified as their inability to be schooled efficiently in an English-only classroom. Once that obstacle is removed, through the acquisition of English competency, the rationale for bilingual education is ended. It was this understanding of the social mobility aims of bilingual education that most legislators seemed to support, which made the critical evaluation studies of bilingual classrooms especially powerful in their ability to challenge the validity of (transitional) bilingual education.

An Egalitarian Rationale for Maintenance Bilingual Education   As also noted in Chapter 1, however, from the outset, there was a second social equality argument for bilingual education that entailed a more pluralistic maintenance version of the program. This position stressed that the social inequality of language minority communities was not just a function of their inability to speak English, but had a more politically charged basis in prejudice against non-English languages (and language-group members) in U.S. society. A 1975 report of the U.S. Commission on Civil Rights urging support for bilingual education, for example, cited the following testimony by a Mexican American student in San Antonio to illustrate the linkage between linguistic status in the schools and the inculcation of status consciousness in students' self-perceptions:

> "If they caught you talking Spanish, they would send you to the office and give you a warning. They would give you a long lecture about, if you wanted to be an American, you have got to speak English. And you were not a very good American. I mean, they are telling you that your language is bad. Your mother and father speak a bad language." (quoted on p. 34)

As the commission added:

> It is not necessary for language minority children to be taught explicitly that their group is less valued. The same idea is often conveyed when instruction does not include reference to things or experiences familiar to them or to their cultural group. Furthermore, many school textbooks carry historical inaccuracies which discredit minority groups. . . . By demanding behavior that contradicts what was learned at home, schools may foster negative self concept.
>
> [In contrast] bilingual bicultural education can overcome the implicit ethnocentricity of the school curriculum, since the values, traditions, history, and literature of the language minority children's culture as well as of the composite American culture are an integral part of the curriculum and, thus, it strengthens instead of weakens the sense of pride for the language minority group. (U.S. Commission on Civil Rights, 1975: 36–38)

In short, by creating a bilingual and bicultural schooling experience in which it is implicitly and explicitly recognized and affirmed that multiple cultures and languages are truly and equally American, students will be helped to combat the ethnolinguistic hierarchy that pervades the psychological and social milieu of the United States. This alternative educational experience, pluralists argue, will generate a more positive self-concept among language minority children, which, in turn, will lead to greater success in the educational system and greater equality in society in general.

Over the years, bilingual education scholars have refined the argument that a maintenance version of bilingual education will result in greater social equality in the United States. Two the most influential of these are Kenji Hakuta and James Cummins. Rather than plunging into the seemingly endless debate over evaluation studies of existing programs in the United States, both scholars have relied on basic research to develop pluralistic theoretical foundations for bilingual education as an egalitarian pedagogy.

Hakuta, a psychologist at Stanford University, published a widely noted book in 1986 that challenged several assumptions of the assimilationist view. He exposed as scientifically unfounded the belief, rooted in now-discredited IQ research by psychologists in the early twentieth century, that learning in two languages causes a retardation of the student's cognitive development. Instead, Hakuta sought to demonstrate that students who are educated in a genuinely bilingual manner (i.e., aiming for mastery of both languages) display consistently higher levels of performance on certain cognitive functions than do monolingually educated students. Further, bilingual students show no loss of proficiency in either their native or second languages. In short, the two languages of a bilingual student reinforce and complement each other, so that it is the children who are monolingual—in, for example, either English or Spanish—who are relatively culturally deprived, not those who are bilingual (Hakuta, 1986).

Canadian linguist Cummins (1981, 1984, 1986, 1989, 1996), in turn, has developed a more elaborate, although complementary, scholarly basis for believing that a pluralist educational policy will lead to more egalitarian results. In his early work, Cummins developed two language education principles that have been incorporated into the arguments of many linguistic pluralists in this country. The first is the "additive bilingualism enrichment principle," which reinforces the point made by Hakuta. Summarized by Cummins in a 1996 monograph, the principle states that

> the development of additive bilingual and biliteracy skills entails no negative consequences for children's linguistic, or intellectual development. On the contrary, although not conclusive, the evidence points in the direction of subtle metalinguistic, academic and intellectual benefits for bilingual children who continue to develop both their languages. (p. 109)

In short, *adding* English to proficiency in the student's native language (rather than *substituting* English for that language) is good for the language minority child's academic achievement.

Cummins (1996) explains his second principle, the "linguistic inter-dependence principle," as follows:

> In concrete terms, what this principle means is that in, for example, a Spanish-English bilingual program, Spanish instruction that develops Spanish reading and writing skills . . . is not just developing *Spanish* skills, it is also developing a deeper conceptual and linguistic proficiency that is strongly related to the development of literacy in the majority language (English). In other words, although the surface aspects (e.g., pronunciation, fluency, etc.) of different languages are clearly separate, there is an underlying cognitive/academic proficiency which is common across languages. This "common underlying proficiency" makes possible the transfer of cognitive/academic or literary-related skills from one language to another. Transfer is much more likely to occur from minority to majority language because of the greater exposure to literacy in the majority language outside of school and the strong social pressure to learn it. (p. 111, emphasis in original)

In combination these two principles are used by Cummins and other pluralists to challenge the "time-on-task" assimilationist argument that public school time spent learning the student's home language is time taken away from learning English, the language they really need to know to be successful in the United States. On the contrary, pluralists insist, helping minority language students to truly master their home language will enable them to transfer their cognitive skills to English in an additive fashion. The students will be enriched, enabling them to achieve higher levels of academic proficiency, and this investment in bilingual human capital development will lead to greater social equality as well.

A Political Rationale for Pluralist Language Education   In the last decade, Cummins has expanded his argument to a more frankly political and structural context. Recognizing that his two earlier principles do not explain why some language minority students (e.g., upper-middle-class Asians) seem to master English quickly and graduate at the top of their class, while others (e.g., working-class Mexicans) often experience academic failure in *both* their native language and English, Cummins has looked to the social and political context of education for answers. Thus, his 1989 book *Empowering Minority Students,* as well as his later work, "emphasizes the critical role that the social context in general, and in particular, the power relations between ethnic groups, play in determining minority children's language learning and academic achievement" (p. 13).

Cummins (1984) argues that students who come from "caste-like" racially dominated ethnic groups are likely to experience a variety of structurally imposed learning blockages that result in relatively poor academic performance. Echoing the pluralist historical narrative and the argument of the U.S. Commission on Civil Rights cited above, for example, Cummins (1996) summarizes the experience of history, emphasizing the contrasting experiences of voluntary and involuntary minorities in the United States:

- Subordinated groups that tend to experience the most severe academic disadvantage have never been given the opportunity to assimilate into the societal mainstream; on the contrary, they were subjected over generations to segregated and inferior schooling, they were punished for speaking their home language in school, and their pride in their cultural identity was systematically eradicated;
- The educational experiences of subordinated group students have reflected the pattern of interactions experienced by their communities in the wider society; both children and adults have been prevented from full participation and advancement in mainstream societal institutions (e.g., schools, the job market, etc.) through segregation and discrimination;
- Although early generations of immigrant children were punished for speaking their L1 [first language] and many groups did tend to experience academic difficulties, they were not discriminated against nor segregated educationally to the same extent as involuntary minorities; thus, an ambivalent and/or oppositional identity was not internalized by the group and later generations assimilated to the mainstream society and succeeded academically;
- Among both voluntary and involuntary minorities, school failure on the part of culturally diverse students was generally attributed to some inherent deficiency, either genetic or experiential (e.g., "cultural deprivation," bilingual confusion, etc.); this focus on inherent deficiencies of the bilingual child served to deflect attention away from the educational treatment that children were receiving. (pp. 35–36).

This highly inegalitarian context has distorted the work of both public educators and their students, Cummins asserts. For example, in a political context in which certain minority languages are disparaged as belonging to long-subjugated peoples, educators are under great pressure to place the students from these language groups in mainstream classrooms as quickly as possible. Consequently, educational programs for these students are likely to be transitional bilingual education (if bilingual at all), and the students are pushed to exit into regular classrooms at the earliest moment.

The result is that students who have learned to mimic oral English skills (without having truly mastered the structure of the language or of their home language, for that matter) are "tested out" into English-only mainstream classes without the academic preparation they will need to be successful. That is, if they speak as though they know English, teachers often assume that they are ready for English-only classrooms. When they subsequently fail (which occurs more often than not), these supposedly English-speaking students are typically referred to special education courses on the assumption that they suffer from motivational or cognitive problems unrelated to language. The students, then, are unfairly stigmatized several times in several ways, which negatively affects their performance as well as that of their teachers. In addition, teachers often expect students from long-subjugated language minority groups to fail, and this becomes a self-fulfilling prophecy in that the students are treated by the teachers (often unconsciously) in ways that virtually ensure that they will perform poorly on academic assignments.

Although all of these processes are important to Cummins's argument, his central point is that education occurs in an inevitably political context. Written primarily for teachers, his 1989 and 1996 books seek to convince them that their work with politically dominated minority students cannot be apolitical, for it will either empower or disable the students. In seeking to empower minority language students, Cummins argues that language education is inherently a mechanism of power.

If educators teach language minority students from an assimilationist frame of reference, a clear political message is delivered to the students and to their ethnic communities: "to survive in this society your identity must be eradicated and your community must not threaten the power and privilege of the dominant group" (Cummins, 1989: 58). Cummins describes this message as nothing short of psychological violence directed at students and their communities. As he comments, "with respect to the internalization of shame by parents and children, the results of this psychological violence may be even more devastating since the violence is covert and the institutionalized racism is hidden behind the genuine efforts of well-intentioned educators" (Cummins, 1989: 58–59).

As an alternative to the assimilationist, compensatory education model for language minority students, Cummins (1996: chap. 6) proposes a multipart framework for educational change that he believes will lead to greater empowerment and educational success. His framework emphasizes an awareness of the embededness of schooling in a structural context of institutional and social power relations ("macro-interactions"), within which individual educators should work to change their specific roles in relation to subordinated language minority students. In particular, teachers should work to change their "micro-interactions" with students and parents from coercive to collaborative relations of power, thereby becoming agents of empowerment rather than of social control. In moving in this direction, teachers and other educators need to work toward the following:

1. Promoting "cultural/linguistic incorporation" of subordinated groups by validating and developing their languages and cultures in the schools;
2. Encouraging community participation to empower parents and other significant members of students' lives through collaborative, rather than coercive, social relations;
3. Practicing a "transformative pedagogy" in which students are empowered by means of a learning process that is constructed through an "interactive critical inquiry" of student experiences and social realities, with "explicit attention to power relations" affecting social outcomes; and
4. Implementing assessment practices in which the function of formal testing becomes one of "advocacy" for student interests in a context of structured subordination, thus reversing the traditional "legitimating" role of assessment in which the origin of educational failure is located within the students and their families.

Cummins, in short, calls for supplementing a linguistically pluralist curriculum (item 1) with a directly political orientation on the part of educators: Teachers must work to directly empower both students (item 3) and their parents (item 2), and they must themselves become politicized advocates for their students by challenging the structural impediments to their students' educational success and by refusing to blame the victims for their difficulties in school (item 4).

Public education based on this model, Cummins believes, would involve shifting educators from their present political function of keeping subordinated minorities in their place to empowering them toward achieving greater equality in a more democratic society. In describing several success stories of parental involvement programs in which this more egalitarian approach was implemented, Cummins quotes from reports that document the enthusiasm of minority parents for their new-found personal power:

> Another mother said: "Ever since I know I have no need to feel ashamed of speaking Spanish I have become strong. Now I feel I can speak with the teachers about my children's education and I can tell them I want my children to know Spanish. I have gained courage. . . ."
> One of the fathers said: "I have discovered that my children can write. And I bring another story [written by his child]. But I have also discovered something personal. I have discovered that by reading books one can find out many things. Since my children want me to read them the stories over and over again, I took them to the public library to look for more books. There I discovered books about our own culture. I borrowed them and I am reading, and now I am finding out things I never knew about our roots and what has happened to them and I have discovered that I can read in Spanish about the history of this country [the United States] and of other countries." (Ada, 1988: 235–36; quoted in Cummins, 1996: 7)

Cummins (1996) concludes, "It is clear that these parents are gaining the internal resources, confidence and motivation to exert greater control over the forces that affect their lives" (p. 7).

To summarize, pluralists argue that assimilationist language policies in the schools reinforce inequality in two essential ways: (1) by impeding the development of transferable language skills (through early abandonment of the students' native language), the growth of these students' broader cognitive skills is blocked; and (2) by implicitly and sometimes explicitly disparaging their home languages and cultures, students are taught that their personal and family identities are deficient, a lesson that also undermines the development of their intellectual and political potential. In contrast, pluralistic language policies will help students master English and other academic subjects more successfully, as well as empower them for full participation as equals in American society.

In terms of the theoretical constructs outlined in Chapter 2, the pluralist position on education links the symbolic recognition functions of language policy with the generation of material outcomes in the forms of educational achievement leading to specific occupational categories and the distribution of wealth, prestige, and social standing. In short, pluralists argue that both directly, through instrumental mastery of language and literacy skills; and indirectly, through a flattening of symbolic identity hierarchies, genuinely bilingual education will lead toward greater social equality for language minority students.

Linguistic Access and Social Equality   Much more has been written by linguistic pluralists about language education and social equality than about issues of linguistic access. Nevertheless, the case for pluralist linguistic access policies rests on very similar arguments. That is, pluralists stress that English-only rules operate to keep language minority adults in a subordinate position in the political economy. U.S. citizens literate in languages other than English have been disempowered by the degree to which they are prevented from voting because they cannot read the ballot or other election materials. Their votes will not have been registered, and insofar as voting contributes to political power, they will have been cut off from a key foundation of political equality.

Similarly, the economic foundations of a more egalitarian society will have been undermined by the degree to which minority language persons are blocked from well-paying and prestigious jobs simply because an employer or other employees do not wish to hear non-English languages in the workplace. Finally, language rules that exclude language minority persons from access to social and other public services will be helping to perpetuate an inegalitarian society by the degree to which those services contribute to greater social equality in the United States. Pluralistic language access policies, on the other hand, help to move language minorities in the direction of full and more fruitful participation in the political economy, thus contributing to a more egalitarian society.

The Assimilationist Response

In their response to pluralists on the relationship between language policy and social equality, assimilationists begin from the assumption that there is no question that English is the language of power in all realms of U.S. society: in commerce, in communications, in education, in civil society, in political life. That being so, assisting language minorities toward greater equality through social mobility can only be attained through emphasis on efficient mastery of English. From a purely pragmatic and instrumental point of view, if one wishes to advance one's position in this society, the linguistic path is very plain: Learn English well, and speak English fluently on all public occasions. The greater one's mastery of the dominant language, the greater will be one's acceptance as "one of us" by the dominant ethnolinguistic society. Numerous assimilationists have argued that most non-English speakers already know this and accept it without objection. Abigail Thernstrom (1990), for example, quotes a recent immigrant as saying, "'without English we cannot work, and without work, we are nowhere.'" "But of course," Thernstrom adds, "it is time for educational 'experts' to catch on to what most newcomers have always known" (p. 48).

Those who strive to maintain their linguistic and cultural distinctiveness, on the other hand, risk the danger of permanent marginalization in U.S. society. As Stephen Steinberg (1982) has observed, "Throughout American history ethnicity has been preserved most authentically by those groups who, for one reason or another, have remained economically marginal" (p. 53).

Given this English-dominant context, assimilationists view policies of public support for non-English languages as at best a foolish experiment doomed to failure, and at worst a cruel and dangerously divisive hoax perpetrated on the relatively weakest and poorest members of ethnic communities by some of their nationalistic leaders. These policies are foolish because they detract the attention of non-English-speakers from their more immediate and important task of learning the nation's language and its cultural ways.

Bilingual Education as Segregative   Along with the pluralists, assimilationists to date have expended most of the energy—and ink—they devote to the social equality issue focusing on its relation to bilingual education programs. Bilingual education, they believe, is a wrong-headed policy that keeps language minority children segregated from the mainstream, thereby reinforcing their already existing feelings of not really belonging in U.S. society. As Rosalie Pedalino Porter (1990) has put it, children "truly want to 'belong'":

When strict bilingual education advocates speak of the great benefits of separating limited-English students from their classmates temporarily so that they can develop pride in their own language and culture and a sense of identity, they downplay the negative side of such an approach, namely, that this segregation reinforces the feeling of being different, of being a perpetual outsider. An integrative approach to bilingual education is difficult to achieve because the program itself is essentially segregative. (p. 35)

In his poignant autobiography, Richard Rodriguez (1982), who began his life in Sacramento, California, in a monolingual Spanish-speaking family, eloquently described his pain and shame at realizing that he and his family did not "own" the public language of the United States. But he later recognized that a great loss had occurred in his family when he (and his siblings) subsequently became monolingual in English:

> The special feeling of closeness at home was diminished by then. Gone was the desperate, urgent, intense feeling of being at home; rare was the experience of feeling myself individualized by family intimates. We remained a loving family, but one greatly changed. No longer so close; no longer bound tight by the pleasing and troubling knowledge of our public separateness. . . .
>
> The family's quiet was partly due to the fact that, as we children learned more and more English, we shared fewer and fewer words with our parents. Sentences needed to be spoken slowly when a child addressed his mother or father. (Often the parent wouldn't understand.) The child would need to repeat himself. (Still the parent misunderstood.) The young voice, frustrated, would end up saying, "Never mind"—the subject was closed. Dinners would be noisy with the clinking of knives and forks against dishes. My mother would smile softly between her remarks; my father at the other end of the table would chew and chew at his food, while he stared over the heads of his children. (Rodriguez, 1982: 22–23)

Nevertheless, Rodriguez believed that the sacrifice was a necessary and valuable transition for an immigrant family, because only by truly "owning" the public language of the United States (a transformation that could not occur unless he gave up the private language of his family) could he feel that he truly *belonged* as an American in the United States:

> Only when I was able to think of myself as an American, no longer an alien in *gringo* society, could I seek the rights and opportunities necessary for full public individuality. The social and political advantages I enjoy as a man result from the day that I came to believe that my name, indeed, is

Rich-heard [not "Ricardo"]. . . . I celebrate the day I acquired my new name. Those middle-class ethnics who scorn assimilation seem to me filled with decadent self-pity, obsessed by the burden of public life. Dangerously, they romanticize public separateness and they trivialize the dilemma of the socially disadvantaged. (Rodriguez, 1982: 19, 27, emphasis in original)

In short, assimilationists argue that language minority children cannot become truly equal in their own hearts and minds while they bear the linguistic and cultural marks of difference in the English-dominant society of the United States. Only by claiming an English-language cultural identity of their own—which cannot happen so long as they cling to the private cultures of their families—will these children be placed on the path toward genuine social equality.

In terms of the theoretical constructs outlined in Chapter 2, this argument is centrally based on a conception of identity politics. Only when one internalizes an American identity—in which the adoption of English as one's true language plays a central part—will genuine equality of membership take place in one's own heart and mind. In this sense, the linguistic adoption of an American identity is instrumental to the attainment of social equality.

Interestingly, one of the leading advocates of linguistic pluralism, Eduardo Hernandez-Chavez, also has written about the profound difficulty of being truly bicultural, of being truly at home in two cultural communities in the United States. Writing of "the ambivalence felt in many Chicano communities toward other Chicanos who have attained middle-class status," Hernandez-Chavez (1978) notes that the latter

> are perceived as assimilated *agringados* who, having rejected the values of the ethnic community, accept Anglo-American ways.
>
> At the same time, parents exhibit a very natural aspiration for their children to achieve educational and economic mobility and regard the learning of English as the means to do so. No contradiction is seen because there is little recognition of the extent of deculturation that is required by the educational and economic systems in order to achieve a substantial amount of mobility. The belief exists that assimilation is a personal choice, unrelated to upward mobility and the characteristics that must be acquired to attain it. (p. 547)

Bilingual Education as Preventing Mastery of English   In addition to attacking the inegalitarian effects of its segregative and marginalizing methods, and the associated identity politics, critics of bilingual education argue that this pedagogy—in practice—has *not* resulted in greater mastery of English by LEP students. While they acknowledge the necessity of special education programs for LEP students, as required by the *Lau v. Nichols* decision of 1974, assimilationists believe that both federal and state bilingual programs have become hostage to pluralistic and ethnic nationalist ideologues who refuse to allow genuine experimentation to occur with respect to the most effective methods of teaching English proficiency to these students (see, e.g., Porter, 1990; Imhoff, 1990; Chavez, 1991).

In her critique, for example, Porter (1990) recounts her own frustration with these programs as she developed greater experience as a bilingual education teacher:

> As I visited other schools and talked with teachers at professional meetings about their experiences, I began to believe, along with many of my colleagues, that the underlying rationale of native-language-based programs was wrong-headed. How else could I account for the fact that so many of my fifth- and sixth-grade students—who had never been out of the mainland United States, and had, indeed, grown up right in Springfield—had not yet learned enough English to be taught their subjects in English? (p. 24)

Ultimately, Porter (1990) came to believe that the first and most important "impediment to English-language learning" was bilingual education's devotion to "the preservation, through language, of the child's native 'culture' " (p. 25). As a consequence of this devotion, "the transition from native-language instruction to English is so gradual, and the increase in use of English and in opportunities for these students to be integrated with their English-speaking peers is so minimal, that the process is like a meandering, slow-motion dance" (p. 25).

After criticizing the theorists of bilingual education (e.g., Cummins) for an alleged lack of empirical evidence to support their theories, Porter (1990) presented her own experience-based conclusions on the most effective approaches to English-language teaching:

> 1. Providing as much time as possible for limited-English students to use and practice the English language in thoughtfully planned, real-life situations, both social and academic, produces the greatest success in English-language learning.
> 2. Providing appropriate English subject matter for classroom work, both comprehensible and challenging at the students' age level,

enhances both language learning and academic achievement in all subject areas. . . .

3. Promoting rapid language learning and early integration of limited-English students with their English-speaking classmates creates the best conditions for school achievement.

4. Enhancing the ability of limited-English students to "think" in English can be accomplished by reducing the amount of native-language use in bilingual programs and discarding the practice of "instruction by translation," which generally is confusing and ineffective.

5. Making the students feel both challenged *and* self-confident, as all good teachers know, works for all students. (p. 83, emphasis in original)

In an analysis described by some as the "time-on-task" hypothesis, then, Porter and many other assimilationist critics of bilingual education believe that an adequate foundation for educational success by LEP students requires the *maximum* use of English and the *minimum* use of the native language. And, along with most pluralists, assimilationists believe that a successful educational experience is an important precondition for greater social, economic, and political equality for these language minority children.

Linguistic Access and Social Equality If their conclusions about the harmful effects of segregative bilingual education programs are correct, assimilationists have grounds for reasoning further that the same conclusions hold for linguistic access measures promoted by linguistic pluralists. That is, any measures that encourage ethnolinguistic groups to keep themselves apart from the mainstream—through maintenance of the ethnic boundaries of language and cultural distinctiveness—can only serve to keep these groups in a marginal, and hence less than equal, place in the U.S. political economy. Such measures as non-English ballots and workplace rules, in short, will not help the members of these groups to attain higher status, power, and wealth; rather, they virtually guarantee their continued subordination.

In summary, then, pluralists and assimilationists are in profound disagreement on the causal relationships between language policy and greater social equality for language minority persons. Pluralists believe that greater social equality requires public policy support for the maintenance and status enhancement of minority languages, while assimilationists believe that such policies prevent their mastery of English and maintain language minority persons in marginalized and subordinated positions in the political economy.

LANGUAGE POLICY AND EQUALITY AS EQUAL LANGUAGE RIGHTS

While the first debate about the relationship between equality and language policy focuses on disputed causal relationships between public policy and social equality for language minority persons, a second debate has taken place in the liberal discourse of rights. In outlining this debate, it will be helpful to distinguish between two forms of language rights at issue which largely correspond with a distinction made by Heinz Kloss (1977) between "tolerance-oriented" and "promotion-oriented" language rights. This distinction, in turn, is roughly coterminus with Isaiah Berlin's (1960) famous contrast between "negative" and "positive" freedoms. The debate over toleration-oriented language rights, in other words, is focused primarily on freedom *from* discrimination in relation to the use of language in private and public sectors, as well as in civil society. In contrast, the debate over promotion-oriented language rights concerns putative responsibilities of the state to create and maintain linguistic domains in minority languages so that language minority groups can enjoy the freedom to participate equally in the life of the polity.

Freedom from Language Discrimination: The Pluralist Argument

This particular debate over equality issues centers on the liberal democratic rights to freedom of expression in the language of one's choice and to equal protection against discrimination because of one's language minority status. As noted in Chapter 1, a number of these issues have arisen in the debate over language policy. Among these are the right to nondiscrimination in education, employment, free expression (e.g., speech and public signs), and access to voting materials, a fair trial, and public services. Underlying this issue are some very basic philosophic precepts of liberal democratic thought.

The pluralist position on language discrimination begins with the liberal democrats' emphasis on the rights of the individual. In the liberal democratic system, individual personhood is the most important public value. Frequently employing a social contract theory of the state, liberal democrats hold that certain individual rights exist onto-logically prior to the authority of the state. In the language of the U.S. Declaration of Independence, the only reason that governments are "instituted" by human beings is to protect their natural or God-given rights to "life, liberty, and the pursuit of happiness."

Contemporary liberal philosophers, moreover, argue that these rights for which governments are created must be held equally by every individual (since each person is assumed to be of equal moral worth in the sight of God or in nature), and are conceived in terms of the right of each person to define and pursue his or her own individual good. Thus the good is viewed as what is best for each of us—as judged by our-selves alone, in the final analysis—and our rights are seen as the politi-cally constructed and/or protected guarantees to the essentially private definition and pursuit of these individual goods (for an overview of these concepts and beliefs, see Kymlicka, 1989: chaps. 1–2).

What linguistic pluralists want to emphasize, in this context, is that one's language and, more generally, one's cultural beliefs and practices are inherent parts of one's personhood. That is, my identity as a person is partially constructed by the language of my birth, and I cannot be compelled to lose my "mother's tongue" without losing my right to be myself—a violation of liberalism's ontological individualism. While lib-eral pluralists believe that individuals should be free to define their own relationship to the ethnolinguistic community of their birth (including forsaking it to assimilate into another), *requiring* them to leave behind the social bases of their personal identity is destructive of their funda-mental human and political rights. Or, as the authors of *Black Power* put it, "No person can be healthy, complete and mature if he must deny a part of himself" (Carmichael and Hamilton, 1967: 55). In this sense, plu-ralists see policies of both domination/exclusion and coercive assimila-tion as violations of fundamental human and civil rights.

In developing their case for a pluralistic language policy, bilingual advocates cite both international and U.S. legal precedents. Following World War II, for example, both the United Nations Charter (1945) and the Universal Declaration of Human Rights (1948) declared that lan-guage (along with race, sex, and religion) is an impermissible criterion for invidious discrimination by states, and thus is presumably a funda-mental human characteristic deserving protection and freedom of choice (McDougal, et al., 1976, quoted in Macias, 1979: 40). Several other, more recent international agreements—such as the 1966 International Covenant on Civil and Political Rights and the 1975 Helsinki Accords—articulate the right of minority groups to maintain their cultures and languages in even stronger terms (Sigler, 1983).

Within the U.S. legal system, the foundational protection for toleration-oriented language rights remains the 1923 decision in *Meyer v. Nebraska*, where the U.S. Supreme Court ruled that "the protection of the Constitution extends to all, to those who speak other languages as well as to those born with English on the tongue" (Crawford, 1992a: 237). The Court ruled that the liberty of persons to teach a language, to learn any language, or to hire a person to teach their children any language, falls under the protection of the due process clause of the Fourteenth Amendment: "No state shall . . . deprive any person of life, liberty, or property without due process of law."[1]

While there is little controversy today in the United States regarding a person's right to use and maintain a non-English language at home, the question of toleration-oriented language rights becomes contentious when the language domain is shifted to more public arenas. It is at this stage of the argument that pluralists and assimilationists often part company. Indeed, many pluralists believe that the campaign to make English the sole official language in the United States is aimed at restricting the use of non-English languages by private individuals in public arenas. The issue arises in several different ways, which will be summarized here under two headings: first, the rights of individuals to express themselves in public spaces in the language of their choice; and second, the right of individuals not to be discriminated against because of their language difference.

The Right to Free Expression   Pluralists contend that freedom of expression (as protected, for example, in the First Amendment to the U.S. Constitution) requires that individuals must be able to speak, write, and perform in any language they choose, even if they want to exercise this right in public spaces such as city streets, workplaces, and other public buildings. It is on the basis of this right that pluralist opponents of city ordinances regulating foreign-language commercial signs have based their claims (a basis affirmed by the trial court in *Asian American Business Group v. City of Pomona* [1989]). The right to free expression is also the foundation of the pluralist argument against rules requiring employees to speak only in English while on the job. And, as seen in Chapter 1, it was the principal basis for the Arizona federal trial court's decision overturning that state's restrictive 1988 "official English" initiative, as well as the Arizona Supreme Court's 1998 decision overturning the same initiative. In short, any effort to restrict public expression in non-English languages by individuals is viewed by pluralists as a violation of a fundamental human and civil right.

The Right to Nondiscrimination   In keeping with its roots in the civil rights movement, contemporary pluralists' second argument for toleration-oriented language rights in public arenas is centered on the right not to be discriminated against on the basis of one's membership in a language minority group. Here pluralists emphasize the historical record of conquest, annexation, exclusion, and domination of peoples of color, and the special place of cultural and linguistic oppression within that record.

As we saw in Chapter 4, pluralists believe that language minority groups have suffered a variety of discriminatory practices at the hands of the majority. The measure for unjust discrimination in this context is receiving unequal treatment at the hands of the state, employers, or other operators of public enterprises on the basis of language. Such discrimination is a violation of liberal democracy's criteria for equal rights. Following reasoning such as this, linguistic pluralists have won important victories in getting some federal administrative rulings, statutes and judicial decisions to recognize language as a basic characteristic of national origin, which means that it is covered under the prohibition of discrimination on the basis of race, religion, national origin, and gender in the Civil Rights Act of 1964.

From the pluralist perspective, the U.S. Supreme Court was adhering to this reasoning in finding in *Lau* that the San Francisco school district had violated Lau's civil rights by placing him in a mainstream English-only classroom (see Chapter 1). Since Lau did not understand English, putting him in that classroom placed him at an unfair disadvantage because of a central characteristic (language) of his national origin. This equal rights–based reasoning was most clearly articulated in the dissent by Judge Shirley Hufstedler[2] at the appeals court level in the *Lau* case. Her articulation of the issue seems to take its bearings from earlier judicial decisions outlawing racial segregation in the public schools:

These Chinese children are not separated from their English-speaking classmates by state-erected walls of brick and mortar, but the language barrier, which the state helps to maintain, insulates the children from their classmates as effectively as any physical bulwarks. Indeed, these children are more isolated from equal educational opportunity than were those physically segregated Blacks in *Brown;* these children cannot communicate at all with their classmates or teachers (quoted in Crawford, 1989: 36)

It was similar reasoning that led Congress to require election materials and ballots to be available in non-English languages, and to mandate states to "take appropriate action to overcome language barriers" (U.S. Congress, 1974, Section 1703(f))in their educational programs. Further, the criteria of equal rights lie behind the decisions of the U.S. Equal Employment Opportunities Commission to prohibit language discrimination by employers and of the U.S. Supreme Court to require linguistic access for persons accused of crime (see, e.g., Mirandé, 1996).

Indeed, in terms of political strategy, much of the rationale for pluralists' support of linguistic access policies—as described in Chapter 1—is articulated in these terms of wrongful discrimination against language minority group members. The application of this criterion has not yet met its outer boundaries (in that pluralist activists and attorneys continue to seek extensions of protections against linguistic discrimination), but the basic principle is clear enough: Denying members of language minority groups equal access to the legally protected rights and opportunities enjoyed by other Americans is to deny them a fundamental civil and human right. And here the key point is that providing non-English-speakers with the *same* English-language materials and/or services that English-speakers receive is *not* providing either equal access or equal treatment.

Freedom from *Language Discrimination:*
The Assimilationist Argument

As noted, most assimilationists do not challenge the liberal democratic freedom to use the language of one's choice as a private individual in one's private realm. However, they do oppose pluralist positions on the question of language discrimination at several points. One point of disagreement is on where to draw the line between private and public realms, as will be further developed below. Here it is sufficient to note that opponents of the pluralist position argue that First Amendment protections of freedom of expression do not give public employees the right to perform their duties as public servants in the language of their choice. There are justified limits on First Amendment private freedoms, critics believe, that are inherent in accepting office as a public servant who is responsible for carrying out the public good as legitimately defined by governmental authority. One of these justified limits is in the responsibility to implement an English-only requirement as public policy.

Another point of disagreement comes with respect to the rights of private employers to set the linguistic terms and conditions of employment. In particular, private employers have argued that they have the right to require their employees to speak only English while in the workplace, especially to protect the rights of monolingual English-speakers (see below) and to promote employee harmony.

More fundamentally, assimilationists are deeply at odds with the pluralist depiction of the United States as a multilingual and multicultural country. Viewing the country instead as an English-speaking nation, assimilationists take two basic tacks in opposing pluralist arguments on linguistic freedom and nondiscrimination: They argue, first, that pluralist language policies discriminate against language minorities by keeping them segregated and subordinate, and second, that these policies discriminate against monolingual English-speakers.

Language Policy and Discrimination Against Language Minorities   As a point of departure, it is important to reemphasize that assimilationists see most non-English speakers in the United States today as *immigrant* newcomers, not as members of long-standing *minority groups,* a position elaborated in Chapter 4. Here it is sufficient to reiterate that assimilationists view the social contract between immigrants and their new country as including an obligation to learn and participate in the country's language. Thus, many of the situations that appear to be "discrimination" to pluralists are seen by assimilationists as rightful "positive reinforcements" to learn English. That is, telling immigrants that they must learn English if they want to participate in this country's bountiful opportunities—such as voting, moving up the employment ladder, and receiving social services—is entirely appropriate in the social contract between newcomers and those who are receiving them.

From within this frame of reference, moreover, assimilationists view the effects of many pluralist language policies as being manifestly discriminatory against the very recipients of these supposed benefactions, since by telling non-English-speakers that they need not learn the country's dominant language will help to maintain them in segregated and marginal positions in the political economy, as argued above with respect to social equality. Former U.S. Representative Norman Shumway (R-California), a long-time sponsor of the English Language Amendment in Congress, drew the connection this way:

> In my view, existing [i.e., pluralistic] government policies are discriminatory, by keeping language minorities forever on the fringes of our society. Those who cannot communicate fluently in our common language cannot possibly avail themselves of America's many opportunities. (Shumway, 1988 [1992]: 123)

Similarly, former U.S. Senator Walter Huddleston (D-Kentucky), another sponsor of the English Language Amendment, described the effects of bilingual education programs and the non-English ballot provisions of the Voting Rights Act of 1965 as follows:

> [On bilingual education:] The unfortunate result is that thousands of immigrant and nonimmigrant children are languishing in near-confusion, suspended between two worlds, and not understanding what is expected of them. . . .
>   [On non-English ballots:] By failing to provide a positive incentive for voting citizens to learn English, we are actually denying them full participation in the political process. Instead, we are making them dependent upon a few interpreters or go-betweens for information as to how they should vote. (Huddleston, 1983 [1992]: 115–116)

In short, pluralist language policies discriminate against non-English-speakers by worsening their position in society.

Language Policy and Discrimination Against English-Speakers   Even more vexing to assimilationists than pluralism's negative impact on language minorities are its discriminatory effects on English-speakers who are not bilingual. English is this country's public language, and many assimilationists are outraged by the thought that those who are fluent in English but do not speak a "foreign" language might be disadvantaged in their own country. In the assimilationist worldview, this discrimination takes two forms, one contextual and one economic.

The contextual form of discrimination derives from the feeling of many Americans that they no longer belong in their own country, as it appears to be taking on the linguistic and cultural trappings of a foreign country. Political theorist Joanne Bretzer's (1992) insightful study of language policy conflict in Miami illustrated this sense by quoting several residents of that city; one of whom said that

> "before we had our revolution, it was laid back. You could start out in the morning and go down to Matheson Hammock [a local park], take the kids down and stop at Shorty's on the way home. Of course, people, their language—it was very easy to conduct your business, and I miss it, I miss it. I have *lost my city*." (quoted on p. 210 [emphasis added])

And less poignant but more direct is how one of Bretzer's (1992) informants described his experience of driving through Miami in the late 1980s:

> "I couldn't believe it. I mean, it was like a foreign country . . . a Spanish-speaking country. You won't see a sign that's in English. . . . It was Spanish; every word on every building—it was Spanish." (quoted on p. 213)

This contextual feeling of being unjustly deprived of one's rightful cultural landscape seems to be a central motivating force for many adherents to the assimilationist position on language policy, and it is best understood in terms of the symbolic identity politics framework outlined in Chapter 2. Although difficult to formulate in the language of equal rights, many assimilationists nevertheless articulate their dismay at the situation in terms of losing their right to feel at home in their own country. It is this articulated feeling, as well, that motivates many employers to issue English-only workplace rules in the name of employee "harmony."

A second, and more material, sense of discrimination against English-speaking monolinguals derives from the perception that an increasing number of jobs in the United States require bilingual skills, thereby depriving "Americans" of their right to equal employment opportunities in their own country. Again, one of Bretzer's (1992) respondents made the point in respect to Miami:

> "The [Cuban] culture . . . has taken over—there is no integration. . . . If you are working someplace . . . the language is mainly Spanish; if you don't know it, you don't belong here. . . . They consider this Cuba across the water." (quoted on p. 215)

Across the land, but particularly in areas with heavy concentrations of Spanish-speakers, monolingual English-speakers have complained bitterly about being discriminated against in employment and in other areas of civil society because of policies favoring those who are bilingual. Symptomatic of this argument, an organization of California teachers opposed to bilingual education (known as LEAD or Learn English Advocates Drive) grew to more than twenty thousand members in just two years in the late 1980s, in part on the strength of its opposition to "discriminatory" and "divisive" pay bonuses for bilingual teachers (Enriquez, 1989: 1).

Contrary to pluralists, then, assimilationists view policies that provide support for non-English languages in any public domain as discriminatory, although they do believe in the right of language minorities to use their languages in private forums.

Freedom to . . . : *The Pluralist Case*
for Promotion-Oriented Language Rights

Heinz Kloss's (1977) concept of promotion-oriented language policy relates to state action to promote the retention or maintenance of languages other than the dominant one. In addition to protecting minorities' right to the private use of their languages and prohibiting invidious discrimination, should public policy actively seek to help maintain non-English languages and ethnolinguistic communities in the United States? Many (but not all) linguistic pluralists answer yes, while virtually all assimilationists argue against this proposition.

In some ways the pluralist case for promotion-oriented language rights grows out of dissatisfaction with the reach of the nondiscrimination rationale for a pluralistic language policy described above. This dissatisfaction stems from the fact that the courts and most lawmakers have accepted the linguistic nondiscrimination argument only insofar as language minorities are not fluent in English. Employing this deficit model of language policy, as noted above, the Supreme Court's *Lau* decision is premised on a language barrier faced by the linguistic minority. Similarly, the language provisions of the Voting Rights Act were adopted by Congress only because educational discrimination had prevented language minorities from becoming literate in English. The assumption in both cases is that English is the only "real" public language of the United States and that speaking another language is a handicap, a barrier that must be overcome.

From a pluralist perspective, the problem with this formulation is that there is no long-term public protection for the language minority's right to cultural maintenance and reproduction. While they see nondiscrimination as an important aspect of language rights, many linguistic pluralists want public support for cultural maintenance and development as well. The core of this part of the pluralist argument derives from the belief that the United States is inherently, foundationally, a country with multiple languages and cultural groups. Given that assumption, equal treatment (equal protection under the law) by government requires that all cultural groups that are constitutive parts of the United States must be given public support for the preservation and reproduction of their cultures, including the linguistic component. As noted in Chapter 2, above, the state cannot claim to be neutral in respect to language. If the state chooses to work through only one language in a multilingual society, the speakers of that dominant language will have many advantages over the speakers of minority languages.

Ultimately, what is at stake from this perspective is the equal right to *survival* for minority language communities as ethnolinguistic groups, and their right to expect public cultural institutions (e.g., public schools) to enable and support their cultural reproduction over time. That is, as full (tax-paying) members of U.S. society, language minorities have a right to expect that institutions such as the public schools will help to maintain and further develop *their* languages and cultures, just as it does the language and culture of the dominant Anglo group.

A good example of this line of argument is the case made by Hernandez-Chavez (1984) for a maintenance version of bilingual education. Like other pluralists, he seeks to make clear the need for language minority students to learn English:

> For language minority children in the United States, strong English proficiency in all domains is essential. English proficiency is indispensable in today's world for advanced academic training. Participating adequately in business, commerce, or the occupational market without a full command of English would be extremely difficult for an individual. And the use of English for interethnic relations in most situations is natural and appropriate and thus very important. (Hernandez-Chavez, 1984: 171)

Nevertheless, he argues, it is *equally important* that education for language minority students aim for the development of their "full cognitive academic abilities in the native language" (Hernandez-Chavez, 1984: 172).

Underlying this argument for genuine bilingualism as the goal of public education is Hernandez-Chavez's (1984) conviction that there is a "deep need to revitalize ethnolinguistic communities in the United States; to give them a measure of self-determination in one of the most important areas of modern life; and, ultimately, to build the capacity of these communities for self-sufficiency" (p. 179). This is so because full and equal participation in U.S. society means not that language minorities must try to become indistinguishable from the white majority, but rather that they should "strengthen themselves from within—culturally, socially, politically, and economically" (Hernandez-Chavez, 1984: 170).

This need to revitalize the capacity of Latino communities to reproduce themselves, in turn, must be understood to include the political right to define their own educational interests as members of the U.S. polity. This right entails their freedom to maintain distinctive linguistic and cultural ties through public institutions such as the schools: "Education for language minority children . . . must serve the true interests of minority groups rather than the interests of the majority group—interests as defined by the minority communities themselves, not as they are perceived by majority group educators or scholars" (Hernandez-Chavez, 1984: 178). If this democratic right were fully realized, Hernandez-Chavez (1984) is convinced that "the goals of education would surely change from an emphasis on mainstreaming and assimilation to cultural pluralism and ethnolinguistic solidarity" (p. 178).

Although not many U.S. pluralists have pursued this line of thinking, its logic has implications beyond the institutional confines of public education. If equal treatment requires the state to devote its resources to the maintenance and reproduction of ethnocultural minority communities, then why not legislate the full range of pluralist policies adopted by the Canadian federal government several decades ago (e.g., bilingual public and commercial signs and documents, government officials, public proceedings, etc.)? The underlying logic of this position was made quite clear in 1973 by Canada's Royal Commission on Bilingualism and Biculturalism in arguing that the country's language policy should aim toward an egalitarian polity in which

everybody has the same access to the various benefits of a society without being hindered by his cultural identity. Thus, it is not enough for members of a minority group to have access to the same activities, institutions, and benefits as the members of the majority group; that simply requires an absence of discrimination against individuals as such. The equality to which we refer requires that a person who engages in some activity or associates with some institution need not renounce his own culture, but can offer his services, act, show his presence, develop, and be accepted with all his cultural traits. (p. 5)

Few U.S. political activists for linguistic minorities have argued the case to this extent, but it is important to stress that U.S. pluralists have attempted to make the case that the concept of equal rights requires state support of efforts to maintain and develop minority cultures and cultural groups. From this perspective, a state policy of assimilation not only works against genuine equality between cultural groups, but actively seeks the annihilation of important parts of the cultures of these groups, and is therefore guilty of cultural genocide.

The Assimilationist Case Against Promotion-Oriented Language Policy

It will not be surprising that U.S. assimilationists argue vociferously against state policies promoting the retention of minority languages and ethnolinguistic communities. Indeed, in some respects, this is the essence of the assimilationist position. Much of the assimilationist's rationale for this opposition rests upon their beliefs about the destructive effects of ethnocultural pluralism on national unity in the political community, and will be articulated fully in the next chapter. In addition, however, assimilationists have used two quite different lines of argument to counter the pluralist argument that is rooted in the language of equal rights.

The first basis for the assimilationist position on this issue is the necessity to maintain a strict distinction between public and private spheres in American political life. While personal freedom requires recognition of the right to use a non-English language in the privacy of one's home and family, the public reality of U.S. society—as emphasized above—is overwhelmingly and rightfully English in language. Assimilationists view this reality as long-standing and virtually coterminus with American nationhood. Accordingly, the right to maintain a non-English language and to pass it along to one's children is a strictly private right, and has been so throughout the historical development of the United States. In an early critical review of bilingual education programs, for example, journalist Noel Epstein (1977) wrote that the financing and promotion of "student attachments to their ethnic languages and cultures" have been "jobs long left to families, religious groups, ethnic organizations, private schools, ethnic publications and others" (p. 7), and he expressed considerable skepticism that these tasks are appropriate for public schools. Linda Chavez (1991) is more direct on this point:

> If Hispanic parents want their children to be able to speak Spanish and know about their distinctive culture, they must take the responsibility to teach their children these things. Government simply cannot—and should not—be charged with this responsibility. The best way for Hispanics to learn about their native culture is in their own communities. Chinese, Jewish, Greek, and other ethnic communities have long established after-school and weekend programs to teach language and culture to children from these groups. Nothing stops Hispanic organizations from doing the same. (p. 164)

One of the principal reasons for insisting on this line between public and private promotion of minority languages and cultures is the belief that state intervention in the promotion of private goods for individuals leads almost inevitably to corruption and tyranny. Chavez (1991) connects this tenet of classical liberalism with the argument against promotion-oriented language policies in her assertion that "government bureaucracies given the authority to create bicultural teaching materials homogenize the myths, customs, and history of the Hispanic peoples of this hemisphere, who, after all, are not a single group but many groups" (p. 164). In other words, state institutions (public schools in this case) should not be allowed to authorize or *de*authorize any particular version of the multiple understandings of the cultures of the highly diverse members of ethnic communities in the United States.

Any such interference by the state in the pursuit of happiness by individuals and families undermines their freedom to define the good for themselves. Latino parents should not be forced to accept the pronouncements of civil servants—whether Latino or not—about the nature and meaning of their own unique cultures. Thus, while all Americans have the right to their own definition of the pursuit of happiness—including the right to preserve the language and culture of the "old country"—this is a private matter that must be left undefined by institutions of the state. Equal protection, then, means that individuals in each cultural group must have the equal right to devote their own resources to the preservation of the family language, but by no means does it mean the state is obligated to promote equally the multiple languages that people bring with them to this land of immigrants.

Not only would the state's promotion of multiple languages be an unwarranted extension of the meaning of equal treatment, assimilationists argue, but it would lead to an absurdly expansive growth of political jockeying and public expense. Imagine attempting to require the public schools of Los Angeles to promote equally all of the one hundred or more languages brought to them by its polyglot immigrant students! And if that is not the intention of pluralists, then where do they propose to draw the line for equality between those language groups that deserve state promotion and those that do not? No, assimilationists argue, equality in this context means simply that every individual should have an equal opportunity to realize her or his dreams in the United States to the best of her or his ability and resources; it cannot require the state to enable her or him to realize those dreams in the language of her or his ancestors.

The second assimilationist equal-protection argument against promotion-oriented policies of linguistic pluralism takes its bearings from the logic of the early civil rights movement of the 1950s and 1960s. That movement's thrust was initially toward the individual integration of American blacks into the mainstream of U.S. society. Attorneys for African Americans fighting the infamous Jim Crow laws supporting southern segregation argued that policies of racial separation, such as those maintaining separate schools for black and white children, were inherently discriminatory and perpetuated racial inequality in U.S. society. Because of the preexisting inequality between races in the United States, separate schools for black children were badges of inferiority and were inherently unequal, thus violating the equal protection clause of the Constitution's Fourteenth Amendment (*Brown v. Board of Education of Topeka, Kansas* [1954]).

For the same reasons, assimilationists have argued, using state support to maintain separate ethnolinguistic groups in U.S. society will inevitably keep them in marginal and subordinate positions. Indeed, the famous *Méndez v. Westminister School District* (1947) desegregation case—a precursor to the 1954 *Brown* case—involved schools maintained in Southern California to segregate (and subordinate) Mexican American youngsters on grounds that they were Spanish-speaking. In precisely the same way, pluralistic language maintenance policies will isolate and segregate Latino and other language minority youngsters, thereby perpetuating their marginalization and subordination in respect to the issue of social equality, as argued above. The net result will be a state denial of their right to equal protection of the laws.

In a society that is overwhelmingly English-dominant, as is the United States, the only policy approach that will not deny language minorities full access to equality is one that enables them to integrate fully into the mainstream of society, in keeping with the original (and rightful) goals of the civil rights movement. Claiming the label of equality for policies promoting linguistic pluralism is tantamount to arguing that policies of apartheid are egalitarian policies. "Separate but equal" was a cruel fiction in the Jim Crow South, and it is equally a cruel fiction in respect to language policies.

SUMMARY AND CONCLUSION

This chapter has sketched the clash of arguments between linguistic pluralists and assimilationists on two debates regarding the relationship between U.S. language policy and the public value of equality. Given the emotional heat generated by the debates, it is important to notice that there are certain areas of agreement between these two sides that the protagonists themselves often tend to overlook. For example, both sides claim to respect the diverse ethnic origins of the American people, and both sides acknowledge the right of all people in the United States to learn and to use languages other than English. This in itself is a major accomplishment in a world where the direct repression of minority languages and cultures is a relatively frequent occurrance.

Further, both sides are in agreement that English is the primary language of the United States and that all U.S. residents are well advised to master this language. Indeed, English-Plus advocates (see Chapter 1) and other linguistic pluralists have been among the staunchest supporters of expanding English-language classes for both children and adults.

Nevertheless, there are important areas of disagreement between U.S. assimilationists and pluralists on the relationship between language policy and the achievement of equality for members of language minority groups. First, while both sides agree that everyone has the right to learn and to use a non-English language, they are deeply at odds as to the appropriate terrain for the exercise of this right, and about whether equality requires public recognition of and support for languages other than English in U.S. society. Pluralists believe that the principle of nondiscrimination requires public awareness and acknowledgment that language minorities in the United States are unfairly disadvantaged by the English-only practices of public authorities and others in public and civil domains. Removing these discriminatory barriers requires public acceptance and recognition of minority languages in a wide range of public spaces, including public schools, voting booths, public agencies, and workplaces.

Further, many pluralists believe that equal democratic rights for language minorities requires the promotion of minority languages through public policies that employ the power of the state to help maintain and develop minority languages and cultures. Assimilationists, on the other hand, would restrict both the terrain of and support for any language rights of non-English-speakers to the private sector. Governments, in their view, have no legitimate reasons for recognizing or promoting non-English languages in U.S. society.

Second, there is clear disagreement between assimilationists and pluralists over the causal relationship between language policy and the social mobility of language minorities. Both sides agree that social mobility should be an important consideration in the formulation of language policy, but they disagree as to the type of policy that will most effectively promote that goal. Assimilationists believe, as we have seen, that newcomers can hope to become successful individuals in the English-dominant and competitive social milieu that is the United States only if they fully adopt—heart and soul—the "American" language and culture as their own. Pluralists, in contrast, argue that their heritage of conquest and racial domination—in conjunction with continuing racial and ethnolinguistic discrimination—operates to inhibit social mobility for nonwhite language minority persons. Only when all the American cultures are recognized as equally worthy of respect and public support will the structural conditions exist for genuine social equality in the United States.

It is important to note that this latter disagreement between pluralists and assimilationists over the relationship between social equality and language policy has both a factual, instrumental aspect and a more discursive, symbolic dimension. The factual, instrumental face of that debate has been conducted largely through claims for and charges against social scientific research aiming to judge the efficacy of bilingual education in the nation's classrooms. The written materials in this war of words would easily fill a large bookshelf.[3]

While the debate over the efficacy of bilingual education raises important questions of research method and interpretation, this book will not attempt to resolve it for two important reasons. First, the debate over social scientific evaluations of bilingual education programs has been so distorted by immediate political tactics that it can contribute little to answering the fundamental questions in the language policy conflict in the United States. This underlying conflict, as has been documented in great detail above, is between pluralists and assimilationists in respect to the appropriate role of languages other than English in U.S. society. Nearly all of the hotly contested evaluation research on bilingual education, however, has focused on programs that are designed to facilitate linguistic assimilation into mainstream English-only classrooms; that is, the research debate has concentrated nearly exclusively on the efficacy of transitional bilingual education, judged in terms of the goal of exiting successfully into English-only classrooms. Thus, dual-language maintenance programs have been almost absent from the studies, even though they are a primary goal of U.S. linguistic pluralists. As a result, the evaluations of U.S. bilingual education programs offer little factual information to use in resolving this important question.[4]

The second, and perhaps more important, reason for not considering the conflict over the evaluations of bilingual education programs is that this debate misses a crucial point that is made clear by asking the following question: Just how strong would the statistical evidence need to be to convince a U.S. English activist that maintenance bilingual education programs are highly successful and should be implemented in every school district in the country? Highly committed assimilationists are not likely to be convinced by *any* statistical analysis that showed that language minority youngsters benefited from being encouraged to retain a language other than English. Nor will a mountain of statistically impeccable studies that "prove" the failure of poorly funded transitional bilingual education programs convince committed pluralists that linguistic assimilation through English immersion is a superior approach for achieving equality for language minority youths. In short, no matter how careful or judicious the social scientific study, the fundamental dispute at issue in the U.S. language policy conflict cannot be resolved politically by factual, instrumental analysis.

This is so because at the heart of the dispute over justice and equality for language minorities in the United States is a fundamental conflict over a more symbolic and discursive issue: the appropriate role of non-English languages and cultures in U.S. society. That is, each of the factual arguments between protagonists reiterated above is premised on contextual assumptions about the fundamental nature of U.S. society that are not examined or defended in the arguments themselves. The assimilationist position on each of the debates over equality outlined in this chapter, for example, is premised on the assumption that the United States is appropriately understood as a monolingual, English-speaking country, in which non-English languages and cultures are family-centered and private realities that are best seen as the temporary consequences of immigration.

In contrast, the pluralist position in each of the debates described above begins from the supposition that the United States has never been a monolingual society, and that it has continuously contained a variety of ethnolinguistic minority communities, most of which have been kept in subordinated positions by the dominant cultural community. For these groups, the image of U.S. linguistic diversity as deriving from individualistic patterns of voluntary immigration is an inappropriate and inherently inegalitarian misconception of reality. The assumption that the United States has always been, and appropriately remains, a multicultural and multilingual society, then, undergirds each of the pluralist arguments that equality for language minority groups requires pluralistic language policy goals.

In short, the question of equality in relation to U.S. language policy is deeply intertwined with the questions of identity politics, and the political divide that separates Americans in this debate cannot be resolved without coming to terms with the nature of our national identity in relation to language and ethnic diversity. As will be seen in Chapter 6, the same conclusion must be reached regarding the disputed relationship between national unity and language policy.

6 Language Policy and National Unity
The Search for the Common Good

THE SECOND question of primary values in the language policy debate is that of the common good, centering in this instance on the relationships among language, cultural identity, and national unity. And, while the debate over equality and language policy has most exercised the emotions of linguistic pluralists, it is the question of national unity that seems to most stimulate the adrenalin of assimilationists. This chapter, therefore, will begin with a description of the assimilationist argument in relation to language policy and national unity, followed by an exposition of the pluralist response, with each position tied to a conception of the common good. Following these descriptions, the chapter turns to an analysis of the deeper meanings of this debate, particularly in relation to the connections between the common good and identity politics. At the heart of this analysis is the complex web of relationships among understandings of the common good, ethnolinguistic justice, and the national interest. This analysis sets the stage for the book's final chapters, which will criticize the arguments of both pluralists and assimilationists and outline a proposed resolution of the U.S. language policy debate in terms of both justice and the common good.

ASSIMILATIONISTS ON NATIONAL UNITY AND THE COMMON GOOD

At the heart of assimilationist opposition to pluralist language policies is the belief that these policies encourage a group-based political pluralism that cannot help but divide the country into warring ethnic camps seeking to advance their own interests at the expense of others. On the question of language policy for the United States, it is nothing less than national unity that is at stake—a subject that involves everyone in the country and thus goes to the heart of the common good.

Writing on bilingual education, U.S. English spokesperson Gary

Imhoff (1990) provides an excellent overview of the assimilationist position:

> Behind bilingual education is a social theory that, in the name of pluralism and tolerance, sometimes rejects and sometimes condemns the unifying, dynamic, cosmopolitan culture of America in favor of the separatist, atavistic, changeless, exclusive cultures of ethnic groups. (p. 54)

In more hyperbolic language a similar point was made by conservative writer Tom Bethell, who wrote in a 1979 *Harper's* article that "bilingual education is an idea that appeals . . . to those who never did think that another idea, the United States of America, was a particularly good one to begin with, and that the sooner it is restored to its component 'ethnic' parts the better off we shall all be" (p. 30). Suggesting that American political leaders supportive of bilingual education are afflicted with a "death wish," Bethell (1979) questioned their patriotism by attributing to them a new national motto: "America the Bad . . . One Nation, Full of Victims . . . Divisible" (p. 31).

Similarly, though more generally, Nathan Glazer's 1983 collection of essays on *Ethnic Dilemmas* concluded with a plaintive hope that our contemporary ethnocultural diversity might somehow—even now, against all odds—follow the same assimilative path as did the last great wave of immigration, citing assimilation's role in overcoming ethnic conflict as its most important contribution:

> Leave aside the realism of expecting people to give up ethnic attributes, attachments, and loyalties within any brief period of time. This still is an ideal that is worth holding in mind. Difference, alas, is always liable to become a source of conflict. Assimilation has already proceeded so far with some groups, specifically the European ethnic groups, that it is not an unreasonable hope. If this original hope offered the best chance of a society in which ethnic and racial rivalries and conflicts could be laid to rest, there is no reason why it cannot still be held up as an ideal. Instead, it has been driven from the field of discussion of ethnic issues. The "melting pot" is now attacked not only on the empirical ground that it really didn't melt that much or that fast, but on the normative ground that it should not have been allowed to do so. And on the basis of this attack, Americanization has become a dirty word, and bilingualism and biculturalism receive government support.
>
> I doubt that this is wise. Without endorsing the rigors of the Americanization programs of World War I and the succeeding decades, I can still see the virtue of forging a single society out of many stocks, and can still see that this process deserves some public guidance (p. 336)

Glazer's wistful articulation thus explicitly links the process of assimilation with language policy. And at the heart of the assimilationist argument is the conviction that language is one of the most important mediums through which our unity as a people is forged and maintained. As the new millenium approached, American nationalism was held together by the thinnest of ties, and surely an indispensable strand in that tie is a common language. In making his case for designating English the sole official language of the United States, former U.S. senator S. I. Hayakawa (1985) articulated the point as follows:

> What is it that has made a society out of the hodge-podge of nationalities, races and colors represented in the immigrant hordes that people our nation? It is language, of course, that has made communication among all these elements possible. It is with a common language that we have dissolved distrust and fear. It is with language that we have drawn up the understandings and agreements and social contracts that make a society possible. (p. 6)

Similarly, the 1986 ballot initiative in favor of California's Proposition 63, making English the sole official language of the state, read in part:

> The State of California stands at a crossroads. It can move toward fears and tensions of language rivalries and ethnic distrust. Or it can reverse that trend and strengthen our common bond, the English language.
>
> Our American heritage is now threatened by language conflicts and ethnic separatism. Today, there is a serious erosion of English as our common bond. This amendment reaffirms California's oneness as a state, and as one of fifty states united by a common tongue. (California Secretary of State, 1986: 46)

Finally, William Bennett (1988), secretary of education during the Reagan administration and a leading cultural conservative among Republicans in the years following, provided this articulation of the thesis, explicitly linking American nationalism, political unity and a common language:

> We are, after all, one people, fellow citizens. The Civil Rights Act of 1964 was an affirmation of fellow citizenship based on our moral equality, as well as a means to individual opportunity. As fellow citizens, we need a common language, and that language is English. Our common history is written in English. Our common forefathers speak to us, through the ages, in English. . . .
>
> We are one people not by virtue of common blood, or race, or origin. We are one people, above all, because we hold these truths to be self-

evident: that all men are created equal, that they are endowed by their Creator with certain inalienable rights, and that therefore just government is by consent of the governed. And government by consent means government by discourse, by debate, by argument. Such a common enterprise requires a common language. We should not be bashful about proclaiming fluency in this language as our educational goal; and we should not be timid in reforming our policies so as to secure it. (pp. 188–89)

In short, assimilationists are convinced that a common language plays an indispensable role in creating the "one people" of the United States, in building a true nation. Pluralistic language policies, on the other hand, work against the creation of one united people by undermining the processes of linguistic assimilation into our common language. And this is not just a matter of language, per se. It is importantly a matter of political conflict as well.

This is so because the pluralist cause of bilingualism in the United States fosters and promotes the belief among language minorities that they have narrow interests not shared by the nation's people as a whole. Using government to support these special interests introduces a conflictual, zero-sum dynamic of political competition over scarce material and symbolic resources. With language policy issues on the political agenda, would-be minority political leaders have a personal stake in sharpening and maintaining their constituents' awareness of incidents and issues that divide them from other Americans, and in increasing the size of their followings.

There is, then, a built-in political dynamic providing incentives to potential ethnic leaders to "rub raw the sores of discontent" (in Saul Alinsky's famous phrase) in order to increase the size and militancy of their constituencies. These incentives lead, on the one hand, to efforts to socialize immigrants into thinking of themselves as discriminated-against minorities; and, on the other hand, to campaigns of ethnic vilification against, rather than common piety toward, long-standing symbols of national unity.

Assimilationist critics of linguistic pluralism have charged that ethnic political leaders have already gone some distance toward corrupting the political process of the country in precisely this way. Latino political elites in particular, many assimilationists believe, have used promotion-oriented language policies to pyramid their own power at the expense of the Latino-origin masses of the United States. Linda Chavez (1991), for example, wrote that for the past two decades, Hispanic leaders have convinced politicians and policy makers that Hispanics want and deserve special treatment—everything from bilingual education for Spanish-speaking children to protected status at the polls for Latino adults—and that they require protection from an alien, Anglo society in which they cannot compete. In doing so, these leaders have enhanced their own power, but their methods jeopardize the further integration of Hispanics into this society. (p. 61)

The crux of her argument is that the special treatment demanded by Latino elites—which justifies their existence *as* political elites—fosters a policy of separatism that precludes genuine inclusion and equality for Latinos in U.S. society.

A similar argument was made by former Colorado Governor Richard D. Lamm and Gary Imhoff (1995) in reference to the Voting Rights Act's requirements for non-English ballots and election materials:

[A]n immigrant who is unable to understand the labeling of voting levers as Democrat or Republican is unlikely to understand many of the issues that separate candidates or underlie referenda, as Gerda Bikales [former executive director of U.S. English] pointed out. Proponents of bilingual voting say that many people who do not speak English can follow issues in their foreign-language press or on foreign-language television stations or through their community leaders. They are able to be informed voters, they claim, without knowing English. But are they able to be *independent* voters? Gerda Bikales has said that "the ethnic leader fights for his leadership by fighting assimilation." He also preserves his power base by assuring that he is the primary, or even the sole, source of political information. (p. 116; [emphasis added])

Bilingual education too, it has been argued at length, has led to political corruption and divisiveness. In her critique of bilingual education, for example, Rosalie Pedalino Porter (1990) accuses a "bilingual education establishment"—dominated by privileged, middle-class, but nationalistic Latinos—of ignoring the needs of low-income and disadvantaged LEP children in favor of their own political agenda and power. In the interests of ethnic nationalism and their own privileged positions as ethnic leaders, this establishment has engaged in "corrupt, discriminatory practices," including the admission into undergraduate and graduate programs of "unqualified Latino students, who then received credit for courses they never attended after the first day of class"; the exclusion of "gringos" from graduate fellowships; and the employment of Puerto Rican teachers who "knew little or no English and, therefore, could hardly be called 'bilingual' " (Porter, 1990: 40, 26).

Meanwhile, the students are not learning what they need to know to succeed and are falling farther behind their English-speaking classmates. Porter (1990: chap. 2) claims as well that when she naively and idealistically sought to open a public dialogue on the lack of effectiveness of the bilingual education pedagogy, the program's bureaucratic establishment relentlessly and vindictively persecuted her in various ways. In short, she argues, pluralistic language policies support an elite of ethnic nationalists who have material and symbolic incentives to continually bring attention to and to reinforce the differences between people, which can only serve to foment divisive conflict between the various ethnic communities of the United States.

The social dynamic underlying this process has been spelled out in greater detail by Harvard sociologist Orlando Patterson (1977). His reasoning begins from the premise that because the resources of any society are finite, there will inevitably be political conflict over their allocation. But when these cleavages are cast along ethnic lines, they generate dangerously high levels of emotional intensity. In the context of the struggle over scarce resources, ethnic divisions have two reciprocally reinforcing consequences that result in destructive social conflict. The first consequence is that in the heat of competition, ethnic groups are under great pressure to close ranks and thus throw up exclusive boundaries, because group cohesion facilitates success in the struggle for society's resources (Patterson, 1977: 179).

This solidification of boundaries, Patterson (1977) argues, not only constitutes a kind of tyranny over the members of ethnic groups (i.e., under strong pressure from others in the group, they no longer feel free to develop their personalities in nonethnic ways), but it also reinforces the second consequence of ethnic competition, which is diminished communication across group boundaries:

> By emphasizing ethnicity, by encouraging its development, pluralist thinkers are emphasizing the very set of developments which will prevent communication between individual members of different groups. In the end—and sadly, we seem already to have reached this point with respect to some groups—the only kind of communication possible will be a formalized interaction of ethnic spokemen who meet like ambassadors from warring camps during a truce to work out the best ways of living beside each other with the least amount of conflict. Such a state of communal truce is indeed the very most that a society organized along pluralist lines can even hope for. There can be no such thing as a positive

consensus, a search for meaning and purpose that transcends the petty interests of each separate group. (p. 174)

Patterson judges this to be an "incredibly low, one might say base, standard" for a vision of the good society, especially for one that aspires to "moral leadership" in the world. Moreover, he argues that any society based upon this pluralistic vision cannot last, since "no society can survive for long without a common set of values whereby other members can be judged and consensus can be achieved" (Patterson, 1977: 172).

With the rise of bitter and sometimes violent ethnic conflicts in Europe following the breakup of the Soviet empire, the 1990s witnessed even more apocalyptic visions of the consequences of ethnocentric and culturally pluralistic politics. Thus, Ralph Prendas wrote in 1991:

I think ethnic conflicts can engender a level of solidarity that over-saturates the need for belongingness. It brings into play, after a certain threshold of solidarity intensity is attained, a new set of adverse effects which negate the initial value of group cohesion . . . *"the collective threshold."* When group consciousness attains a certain critical mass, it thereafter destroys the carriers themselves. (quoted in Young, 1993: 4 [emphasis in original])

Tying this destructive dynamic to language policy and the U.S. Latino political leadership once again, Hayakawa (1985) foresaw a potential for conflict between nationalistic Hispanics and Anglo Americans even more seriously divisive than that between white and black Americans:

The ethnic chauvinism of the present Hispanic leadership is an unhealthy trend in present-day America. It threatens a division perhaps more ominous in the long run than the division between blacks and whites. Blacks and whites have problems enough with each other, to be sure, but they quarrel with each other in the same language. Even Malcolm X, in his fiery denunciations of the racial situation in America, wrote excellent and eloquent English.

But the present politically ambitious "Hispanic Caucus" looks forward to a destiny for Spanish-speaking Americans separate from that of Anglo-, Italian-, Polish-, Greek-, Lebanese-, Chinese-, Afro-Americans and all the rest of us who rejoice in our ethnic diversity, which gives us our richness as a culture, and the English language, which keeps us in communication with each other to create a unique and vibrant culture. (pp. 11–12)

Summarizing, the assimilationist position on national unity is that in the kind of society promoted by cultural pluralists, which inevitably comes to be characterized by rigid and impermeable ethnic boundaries, national unity and the common good are undermined by the political encouragement of competition, separation, and (frequently) animosity between cultural groups. Attention toward national unity and the ties that bind us together as one people is deflected by cultural pluralism toward heightened ethnocentrism and mutual antagonism between the members of ethnic groups. This cannot be to the good of the national community as a whole, or to the genuine good of members of any of its constituent ethnic groups.

In contrast, an assimilative language policy would reduce the political significance of ethnic attachments, thereby reducing invidious comparisons and discrimination between groups as well. Individuals would be encouraged to think of themselves as simply "Americans" and as sharing this most important membership category with others from all walks of life and whose ancestors hailed from all parts of the globe. Moreover, the fact that an assimilative language policy would enable ethnolinguistic minority group members to more quickly move up the socioeconomic ladder would also result in greater social harmony and national unity.

This is so because an assimilative adjustment by newcomers enables them to feel that they truly belong to U.S. society (as noted by Porter [1990] and Richard Rodriguez [1982], as cited in chapter 5), thereby diminishing the grounds for conflict that result from the inevitable invidious comparisons and grievances of a segregated and divided society. Under such a solution, of course, the divisive leaders of ethnic minority political movements would have to find gainful employment, but the society as a whole would benefit: through greater productivity by formerly underemployed non-English-speakers, and through the greater political harmony resulting from a reduction of ethnocentric animosities and inequalities. In sum, then, the two assimilationist arguments intertwine: Assimilative policies will result in greater social mobility for non-English-speakers, leading, in turn, to greater productivity and social harmony that will be to the common good.

In addition, of course, the assimilationist position is in accord with the nationalist position on identity politics outlined in Chapter 2. That is, assimilationists are more in tune with the project of nation-building in the contemporary world, and they are committed to the completion of a uniquely *American* nationality, one that will be forged importantly through the bond of language. If the American nation is in fact an "imagined community," a single national language is essential for peoples' capacity to imagine themselves as one people and their country as unified. The assimilationist intent is to make *American* nationals out of *ethnic* Americans and recent immigrants, and they place a heavy weight on language policy as an instrument for realizing this intention. To assimilationists, then, the trend toward ethnolinguistic pluralism is a dangerous development, one that threatens to overwhelm the process of Americanization at a crucial moment in our national history.

The Pluralist Response on Language and National Unity

Linguistic pluralists generally have not taken the initiative in the discussion of language policy's relation to the national interest. Nevertheless, many pluralists have responded to assimilationist charges that linguistic pluralism undermines national unity by fostering divisive social and political conflicts. Perhaps the most sustained treatment of the subject by pluralist writers is an essay by sociolinguists David F. Marshall and Roseann D. Gonzalez (1990). The argument evolves in three basic steps.

The first step is to assert that assimilationists seem to begin from the assumption that monolingual societies are more unified and less internally divided than multilingual countries. However, Marshall and Gonzalez respond to this generalization by saying that it is difficult to know the truth of such a statement, since almost no monolingual countries exist in the world today. Instead, the "natural" state of most countries is one of multilingualism. Since this is so, and since most (multilingual) countries are not experiencing seriously divisive internal conflicts, it must not be the case that multilingualism results in social and political divisiveness. Thus, "one can only conclude that the proposition that a single language makes a nation stronger or more unified seems to suffer from a lack of empirical substantiation in today's world" (Marshall and Gonzalez, 1990: 31).

The second step of the argument is to try to demonstrate that where conflicted multilingual societies do exist, "very few [of the conflicts], if any, are language oriented, and . . . none are based solely on language differences" (Marshall and Gonzalez, 1990: 32). The central assertion of these pluralists is that, where deep and divisive ethnolinguistic conflicts are found in contemporary societies, the basis for such divisions is ethnic inequality and not multilingualism as such. When ethnic inequality becomes intolerable to subordinated groups, Marshall and Gonzalez argue, they often mobilize politically to seek greater equality for themselves. It is at this stage that some subordinated minority groups may organize around language as a potent symbol of their group's deprivation and/or aspirations.

> Why the deprived group turns to language as a symbol is readily apparent: as Deutsch (1975, 7) reminds us, "Language is an automatic signaling system, second only to race in identifying targets for possible privilege or discrimination." Surpassed only by the color of your skin, the sounds of your language are a means of identifying and authenticating you as a member of a specific group. (Marshall and Gonzalez, 1990: 34)

As a consequence of ethnic mobilization, pluralists argue, a stable internal peace is found only by making some accommodation to the demands of the subordinated group: "When a government accommodates a minority's needs, that minority has less reason to be disruptive" (Marshall and Gonzalez, 1990: 35). Thus,

> it is not multilingualism itself that is the possible threat to national unity, but denying the aspirations of ethnic groups; only when these aspirations are denied does the potential for sectionalism and possible disruption appear. . . .
>
> A nation's unity is threatened most when it denies what are regarded as rights by its minorities and language rights have been more and more viewed as a part of human rights in this century. It is not having more than one language that threatens national unity; on the contrary, it is denying equal opportunity. (Marshall and Gonzalez, 1990: 39)

In short, it is assimilationist policies such as "official English" that threaten national unity, not pluralistic language policies that meet the aspirations of ethnic minorities and provide avenues for equal opportunity. A similar point was made in 1986 by the Los Angeles County Board of Supervisors in rejecting a proposal to support an English-only policy:

> English as the official language resolutions will not help anyone learn English. They will not improve human relations, and they will not lead to a better community. They will create greater intergroup tension and ill will, encourage resentment and bigotry, pit neighbor against neighbor and group against group. They reflect our worst fears, not our best values.

An important aspect of the pluralist argument here is that, in the context of the struggle for equality on the part of subordinated ethnolinguistic groups, dominant-group resistance to equality is often couched in the language of "unity," and it often masks (consciously or unconsciously) a dominant-group demand for the preservation of its privileged position. That is, demands for a return to social peace and harmony, or national unity, are in fact demands for a return to a supposedly peaceful domination of one group by another (see Takaki, 1987, for a critique of Glazer's assimilationist characterizations of the trajectory of U.S. history, made along similar lines).

Following this line of analysis, Marshall and Gonzalez (1990) characterize the English-only movement as a negative reaction to increased "Hispanic economic and cultural opportunities" (p. 37). Advocates of an "official English" policy, they assert, are responding to a linguistic "threat" to unity that lacks any basis in reality. Noting that non-English-speakers make up only a minuscule portion of the U.S. population, that the language shift to English is occurring at an unprecedented rate among recent immigrant groups, and that Latinos and other non-English-speaking immigrants are flocking to English classes in hopes of greater social mobility, Marshall and Gonzalez (1990) attribute Anglo support for "official English" to a "sense of relative deprivation" that derives, in reality, from the declining hegemonic position of the United States in the international political economy, coupled with increased social mobility for Latinos and other previously subordinated groups (pp. 37–38). Seen in this light, in short, the campaign against pluralist language policies—as embodied in the drive to designate English as the sole official language of the United States—is a strategy for continued Anglo American domination, in which the discourse of national unity is merely a facade for the movement's inegalitarian goals.

The third and final part of the pluralist argument is that, far from being sources of national weakness, linguistic and cultural diversity actually *strengthens* the United States in several important ways, as Marshall and Gonzalez (1990) describe:

- *National defense:* "In time of war, multilingualism often becomes a major asset in the pursuit of victory" (p. 45).
- *Culture:* "Is not human diversity a major driving force for our curiosity and our learning, and does not multiethnicism reinforce this diver-

sity without endangering the ideals and beliefs that truly bind a nation together?" (p. 45).

- *Politics:* "As our two eyes give us depth of perception, so do two or more languages give us a 'depth of field' in the political process and its continual arguments. . . . Multilingualism is a means for citizens to become better informed, and it has long been axiomatic that the better informed the citizenry, the stronger the democracy" (p. 46).
- *Education:* Kenji Hakuta's (1986) research (see Chapter 5) demonstrates that " 'balanced bilinguals,' those who spoke two languages at roughly the same levels, evidenced a marked cognitive advantage in relation to those who were only monolingual" (p. 46).
- *National unity:* "By guaranteeing equal access, regardless of mother-tongue, a nation-state could actually utilize multilingualism as a measure of its success in unifying its varied contingents. In the United States, for example, where legislation has attacked racial and religious discrimination, further legislation attacking linguistic discrimination would serve to guarantee that language could not be used as a tool for the deprivation of opportunity" (p. 47).

Other advocates of linguistic pluralism have stressed a somewhat different formulation of the positive advantages of a multilingual U.S. population, especially in relation to the new world political economy. The days of a nationalistic "American century," when the national interest of the United States could be understood and followed without much consideration of the concerns of other peoples, are over forever. New developments in communications technology, as well as in the technologies of the production and distribution of goods, have given rise to a genuinely internationalized economy. These changes, in conjunction with the demise of the cold war, mean that we must learn new ways of interacting with increasingly more diverse and interdependent political and economic systems. Peoples that could be disparaged safely as "Hottentots" by Theodore Roosevelt now have increasing economic and political influence on the well-being of all Americans.

In this environment, linguistic pluralists argue, it is in the national interest of the United States—both economically and politically—to develop multilingual skills and multicultural understandings. These skills and understandings are crucial for enabling us to operate more effectively in competition with other nations for whom the learning of several languages is a long-standing feature of the educational system. European, Asian, Latin American, and African students routinely learn several languages before graduating from high school. It is time for Americans to awaken to the fact that our national interest lies in the development of a similar openness to other languages and cultures.

This line of argument was given high-level support two decades ago when President Jimmy Carter appointed a Commission on Foreign Languages and International Studies. In its 1979 report to the president, the commission declared:

> We are profoundly alarmed by what we have found: a serious deterioration in this country's language and research capacity, at a time when an increasingly hazardous international military, political and economic environment is making unprecedented demands on America's resources, intellectual capacity and public sensitivity. . . . Nothing less is at issue than the nation's security. . . .
>
> America's incompetence in foreign languages is nothing short of scandalous, and it is becoming worse. Historically, to be sure, America's continental position between vast oceans was a basis for linguistic as well as political isolation, but rocketry as well as communications satellites render such a moat mentality obsolete. . . . Our vital interests are impaired by the fatuous notion that our competence in other languages is irrelevant. (pp. 1–6)

A similar argument, focused more on economic security, was made by sociolinguist Joshua Fishman in 1978:

> It now increasingly behooves the former movers and shakers of monolingual efficiency and rationality to cultivate and foster their own multilingualism if they are to maintain their economic advantages in world markets. . . . The Japanese do not sell world-wide in Japanese. Can Americans insist on doing so in English? (p. 46)

In view of these global facts, pluralists insist, it is wasteful folly for U.S. educators to strip language minority students of their native languages in the elementary grades, only to try to reinstill them in other students in high school. Would it not be to the common good to establish "two-way" bilingual education programs for *all* U.S. students, so that every American high school graduate would have mastered both English and another language? The benefits of such a policy would accrue to the United States in terms of not only our national linguistic resources for political and economic interaction, but also our openness to and understanding of the cultures, values, and identities held dear by the many peoples with whom it is in our interest to interact productively.

It was this logic, at any rate, that seems to have led the President's Commission on Foreign Languages and International Studies to endorse a maintenance version of bilingual education. Viewing non-English-speaking Americans as a resource from which the nation should draw to meet its multilingual needs, the commission (1979) criticized the assumptions of assimilationists: "The melting-pot tradition that denigrates immigrants' maintenance of their skills to speak their native tongue still lingers, and this unfortunately causes linguistic minorities at home to be ignored as a potential asset" (p. 6).

Instead, the commission (1979) called for greater national support for the maintenance of our multiple linguistic resources through bilingual education programs: "We assume that Americans whose first language is not English should have every opportunity to advance their competency in that other language, without delaying their mastery of English" (p. 40). Further, the commission recommended two-way bilingual education programs in which both native English-speakers and language minority students would be encouraged to participate. The result, pluralists argue, will be a stronger, more competitive country better able to weather the increasingly diverse cross-currents of the new world order.

In summary, then, pluralists argue that policies of linguistic assimilation are not conducive to social harmony or to the common good. Rather than unifying and strengthening the country, assimilationist policies foment division and weaken the country both internally and in relation to the rest of the world. As was the case with the debate over equality and language policy, then, this discussion over language and the national interest reveals assimilationists and pluralists deeply divided.

Digging Deeper: National Identity Politics and the Language Policy Debate

At this point, it is necessary to take stock of the arguments outlined in this and the previous chapters. As seen in the conclusion to Chapter 5, it is not possible to resolve the dispute between pluralists and assimilationists over the relationship of equality to language policy without coming to terms with the appropriate ethnolinguistic character of the United States. In this chapter, too, the debate between assimilationists and pluralists over the relationship of the common good and language policy is undergirded by a deeper disagreement over the appropriate nature of the United States as a national political community. That is, each position on the relationship between language and the common good assumes that the goal (the commonweal) *embodies* its own understanding of the United States as a national community.

Assimilationists, for example, argue that governmental support for U.S. multilingualism will, by its very nature, foment destructive ethnolinguistic division and conflict. It will teach us to think of ourselves as members of distinct and primordial ethnolinguistic groups who are in competition with each other for scarce societal resources, to constantly compare our status in the competition with that of members of other groups, and to constantly demand that every governmental action achieves the ever-elusive goal of social group equality. This conception of equality, by its very nature, will lead to never-ending social and political conflict to the detriment of the public good. A policy in support of public monolingualism, in contrast, will teach us that we are all members of the same body politic, the same political community, and enable us each as individuals to achieve what we can, through our own efforts, without having to attribute our achievements—or the lack of them—to our memberships in ethnolinguistic subgroups.

Pluralists, on the other hand, begin from the assumption that multilingualism and multiethnicity are the natural, or constitutive, conditions of the United States, as they are of nearly all countries in the contemporary world. Accordingly, the common good must rest on our recognition and acceptance of this fundamental fact. Failure to do so is inherently divisive in that it requires some people to attempt to change themselves to meet the convenience, interests, and criteria of a dominant group of people. It is this demand to change, coupled with the caste-like inequality characterizing the relationships between dominant and subordinate groups, that foments social conflict and political division. The common good cannot be truly *common* if it furthers one group's interests at the expense of those of others. Both equality and the common good, in sum, require acceptance and recognition of the inherent ethnolinguistic diversity of the United States. These two public values are inextricably intertwined.

Ultimately, then, the conflict between assimilationists and pluralists in relation to U.S. language policy comes down to a fundamental disagreement over the inherent nature of the country itself and its identity as a national polity. What sort of national community are we? Are we an inherently multiethnic and multilingual political community, whose genius and national promise lie in our ability to combine cultural diversity with social equality? Or are we a transethnic, English-speaking nation, whose multilingualism is a transitional and transitory result of our generous and open-armed immigration policy?

This is the most critical chasm in the policy conflict, because the debates over the relationships between language policy, equality, and national unity cannot be resolved without coming to terms with this fundamental disagreement. The assimilationist position on U.S. ethnolinguistic equality depends on its monolingual conception of U.S. society. No amount of empirical evidence that maintenance or developmental bilingual education will result in superior academic achievement by language minority youngsters could conceivably alter the assimilationist position that continuing to speak Spanish as one's private and public language would deter a Latino NEL (non-English-language) student from achieving social equality. As Richard Rodriguez (1982) argued (see Chapter 5), it is only when English becomes *my* language, at the core of *my* identity as an American, that I can feel truly equal as a member of these United States. This is true because the United States is, at its core, an English-speaking society. By virtue of this long-standing social fact, all non-English-speaking groups are doomed to marginal and subordinate status in the society.

By the same token, the pluralist position on social equality depends on its conception of the inherently multiethnic and multilingual nature of U.S. society. And this inherently diverse national character derives not only from voluntary immigration, but from the forced inclusion of some peoples through conquest, annexation, and enslavement, and the racialized ethnocultural stratification system that derives from those experiences. The flaw in the assimilationist vision, pluralists believe, derives from its studied refusal to recognize the hidden hierarchy underlying the normalization of a hegemonic Anglo American culture. For pluralists, the call for unity through linguistic and cultural assimilation will not result in the absence of ethnic group diversity in U.S. society, nor will it usher in an era of ethnic social equality. This is manifest in the oft-retold experience of countless Latino and Asian/Pacific Americans, many of whom are third- or fourth-generation U.S. citizens, who are asked by Anglo fellow citizens, "Where did you learn to speak English so well?"

The question reveals important underlying assumptions about racial identity, language patterns, and "normal" membership in the American political community. This being so, the primary result of giving up one's linguistic and cultural heritage, many pluralists believe, is to undermine the cultural foundations of one's ethnic community, further weakening it in an inherently competitive group-based society. The point was nicely summarized by Los Angeles civil rights attorney Kathryn Imahara in the following 1993 statement to a newspaper reporter:

> I grew up in an English-only household. I was told, "You're not a Japanese. You're American." When I finally realized that it doesn't matter that I went to a top law school, that I continue to be judged by the color of my skin, the slant of my eyes, and the color of my hair . . ., without that culture I'm left with a shell. (*Orlando Sentinel Tribune*, 1993)

The linguistic pluralist emphasis on the issue of equality can best be understood in light of this understanding of the fundamental, but often obscured, ethnolinguistic *and* racial diversity of U.S. society. In a social and political context where culturally and linguistically assimilated members of minority groups are still viewed and treated as *others*, as outsiders, the arguments of assimilationists in relation to both equality and national unity seem to take on a quasi-surreal quality. This is why pluralists insist that true equality for contemporary language minorities can only be achieved when their cultures and languages have greater status equality in U.S. society.

In sum, then, pluralist support for public policies enhancing and maintaining U.S. linguistic diversity stems from the conviction that there are inevitable social consequences deriving from long-standing and apparently permanent perceptions of ethnocultural diversity. Genuine equality can only be achieved when Americans come to perceive themselves as a diverse people, a diverse nation, that encompasses multiple but equally valued ethnocultural communities. It is possible that in the end we will all speak English, but it is important to recognize and maintain the value to us all of the ethnolinguistic communities in which we dwell and that dwell among us. Until these communities are valued as equally *American,* the dream of social equality that de Tocqueville saw as the reality of American life (for European Americans) will remain permanently out of reach (as it was in de Tocqueville's day) for those from non-European backgrounds.

Assimilationists, on the other hand, cannot conceive of a truly national community that is not a nation in the singular ethnocultural sense. Those who insist on being "different" cannot be genuinely included in the national community, nor can they escape their marginality. The tragedy of our times, many assimilationists believe, is that just when the forced exclusion of racial minorities was ended through the inclusive actions of the civil rights movement, a countermovement of self-separation took hold that continues to be pursued today by adherents of linguistic pluralism. What should have been a long-overdue celebration of our new-found consensus in racial and ethnic equality, in which Martin Luther King, Jr.'s (1991) dream of transforming "the jangling discords of our nation into a beautiful symphony of brotherhood" (p. 219) would be realized, was turned instead into a new era of tribal conflict in the United States.

Is there any way to bridge these divergent understandings? If the analysis of this book is correct, there can be no consensus on U.S. language policy unless and until this national identity chasm between pluralists and assimilationists is bridged. What would it take to do so? What kinds of evidence or arguments could persuade an assimilationist that U.S. society ought to be conceived as inherently diverse along racial, ethnic, and linguistic lines, and that we should strive to realize our social equality and achieve our national unity within such a conception? Conversely, what kinds of evidence or arguments could convince a pluralist that giving up one's language and culture to join the "American" culture is the true path to social justice, equality, and national strength and unity?

The concluding section of this book will attempt to address these fundamental questions—not directly, but by recasting the debate, retaking our bearings on what is at stake in this conflict, and pointing toward a policy direction that will both promote justice for language minority group members and facilitate the common good.

III. CRITIQUE AND REFORM

7 Flaws at Every Turn

A Critique of Assimilationist, Pluralist, and Confederationist Alternatives

WE ARE now at the point of resolution for this book. We have surveyed the principal policy issues that divide many Americans over our politics of language. Further, after placing the U.S. conflict over language in theoretical, comparative, social, and historical contexts, we have also reviewed the principal arguments made by assimilationist and pluralist partisans in the contemporary battle over U.S. language policy. These arguments have been articulated in relation to the two most fundamental value issues in this conflict: how to ensure justice (equality) for language minority group members in contemporary U.S. society, and how to ensure that U.S. language policy enhances the common good by contributing toward national unity.

In the end, as we have seen, the intractability of the language policy debate seems to rest on a gaping chasm between two visions of our national self-understanding. The assimilationist vision yearns for and insists upon a national community that is monolingual and monocultural, in which linguistic diversity does not threaten to engulf us in a babel of discordant sounds signifying a shredded social fabric. The pluralist vision, in contrast, understands the United States as an ethnically diverse and multilingual society with a tragic past of racialized ethnocultural domination, but standing now at a point of historic opportunity to realize—through a policy of multicultural and linguistic pluralism—the promise of its ongoing project of democratic equality.

If this is so, then it should be clear that ultimately the language policy debate in the United States is not about language as such but about what kind of political community we are and wish to be. It is, in short, centered in identity politics. How, then, should we proceed to a fuller understanding of what is required for a U.S. language policy that would be both just and in the common interest of all members of this political community? This is the question that will preoccupy these last two chapters. This chapter will compare and critically examine the three available policy alternatives.[1] I will begin with a critical articulation of the most important weaknesses in the positions of both linguistic assimilationists and pluralists, the major partisans in the contemporary U.S. debate. Given these flaws in both arguments, I will turn next to a consideration—and critique—of the remaining alternative policy approach, linguistic confederation. Taking into account the problems with each of the available policy alternatives, I will outline my own position on the best possible approach to language policy for this country in Chapter 8.

WEAKNESSES IN THE ASSIMILATIONIST ARGUMENT

The argument for an assimilationist U.S. language policy has two fatal flaws that interlock to destroy its moral and long-term political viability. In brief, these intellectual weaknesses are as follows:

1. The assimilationist vision of U.S. history is highly romanticized and morally undermined by its seemingly willful determination to ignore the continuing significance of our national legacy of racialized ethnic injustice.
2. The assimilationist attempt to confine ethnolinguistic difference to the private sector misconstrues the nature of the relationships between individual identity, culture, the state, and equality of opportunity.

The combination of these flaws, moreover, enables the assimilationist argument to function as a defense of continued and unwarranted privilege for (especially white, European-origin) native English-speakers. Like all nations, the United States envisioned by assimilationists is an "imagined community." Given the historical and social realities of our society, this conception results in a continuation of unjustified privilege for members of the dominant ethnocultural group. I will take up each flaw in turn, and then summarize the effect of their combination to make my last point.

The First Flaw: The False History of the Assimilationist Vision

As outlined in Chapter 4, a key element of the assimilationist argument in contemporary language policy has to do with a perceived break between the social integration of immigrants in former times as compared to newcomers today. An important corollary to this position, moreover, is that the human subjects of today's U.S. language policy are best understood as immigrants similar in all important respects to those earlier-era immigrants. In the assimilationist view, then, contemporary language policy is about immigrants (not oppressed minorities) who are being manipulated by ethnic activists and misled by bad policy into avoiding the necessary efforts for cultural and linguistic assimilation. And, while many assimilationists acknowledge the presence of racial domination in the U.S. past, they see contemporary language policy as fundamentally unconnected to that history. It is on the basis of these assumptions that assimilationists can perceive the United States as an essentially monocultural and monolingual country. However, these understandings of the American past and of its fundamental cultural character are false in several important respects.

The Experience of Earlier Immigrants   First, the assimilationist understanding misconstrues and romanticizes the experiences of earlier immigrants to the United States. There is abundant historical evidence that both the first and second waves of U.S. immigrants (primarily European in origin) in the nineteenth and early twentieth centuries were in fact much more complex compared to the perception of assimilationists today. It is true that many immigrants in those earlier eras were eager to become "American" as quickly as possible through linguistic and cultural integration. But the same is true of contemporary immigrants; indeed, most evidence shows that today's immigrants learn English earlier and more efficiently than earlier immigrant generations did (see, e.g., Portes and Schauffler, 1994; Veltman, 1998).

At the same time, and as pluralist advocates have been accurately reporting, many of the earlier immigrants were no more eager to give up their languages and cultures than are contemporary immigrants. Indeed, some one-third returned home rather than staying in North America (Dinnerstein and Reimers, 1988: 46). Those who did remain, moreover, tended to live in ethnic enclaves, and to establish and support local religious and community-based organizations and media that sought to maintain the old country's language and culture as long as possible. And, of course, many ethnic activists of those eras wanted to have their children taught in their home languages, as well as in

English, by both public and private schools. Further, despite many assimilationists' romanticization of the Americanizing efforts of the public schools, the historical evidence is very strong that those earlier generations of immigrant children were less successful educationally than their contemporary counterparts (Rothstein, 1998).

While there is no doubt that all immigrants must and do make a cultural adaptation to their surroundings, few if any—either historically or in the present—have simply "melted" into the dominant cultural community without a trace. Historian John Higham (1984) has expressed this point well in stating that all U.S. ethnic groups have been created here (i.e., they are not simply unchanged transplants from another country); however, once created, *no* U.S. ethnic group has ever disappeared completely from our society (p. 178).

In short, virtually all of the assimilationist critics' complaints about present-day immigrants' "willful insistence" on maintaining their cultural and linguistic difference were also made by earlier nativist opponents of immigration and by earlier assimilationists during the first two waves of immigration to this country. The notion that there is a historical break in attitudes toward the culture of the United States between the earlier immigrants and those of today is simply false, as any close examination of the evidence will make clear.

"Immigrants" Versus "Minorities" A second flaw in the assimilationist reading of the historical context is its misconception and oversimplification of the relationship between contemporary immigrants and racialized minority status in U.S. society. That is, as was seen in Chapters 4 and 5, assimilationists typically dismiss the language-rights claims of pluralists with the argument that most contemporary non-English-speakers are voluntary immigrants, not oppressed minorities. Rather than responding directly to this position, in turn, many pluralists remain focused on their assertion that most U.S. language minorities were incorporated into U.S. society through force and not through free choice.

The social reality, while more complex than either of these positions, is more in accord with the pluralists than with the assimilationists. It is true that pluralists often fail to give sufficient recognition to the fact that most non-English-speakers in the United States today are voluntary immigrants who have chosen to come to this country and who *expect* to have to make a cultural adjustment to their new country if they are to become successful here over the long term.[2] What the assimilationist account fails to notice, on the other hand, is the nature of the social integration process for contemporary immigrants to the United States.

The important issue is the social context into which today's immigrants integrate. And while it is true that most non-English-speakers in U.S. society today are recent immigrants, their social status upon arrival, as well as their eventual social identity upon full incorporation, is conditioned by the previous history of this country and the racially stratified society that was created and maintained through that history.

One of the great romanticized myths espoused by many contemporary assimilationists is that a country's people can just decide that its past need have no effect on its present. Higham has inquired how nineteenth-century European Americans could believe in the self-evident virtue of their universalist democratic and assimilative social practices while living side by side with peoples of color whom they dominated and excluded. They could do so, he concluded, only by excluding those "others" from their thoughts altogether while thinking about their political ideals (Higham, 1984: chap. 8). In similar fashion, many contemporary assimilationists believe that the racialized ethnic categories created through past Anglo practices of domination and exclusion can simply be dismissed from public policy as no longer relevant, and that they have no relationship to the lives of contemporary immigrants from non-European countries.

Immigrant incorporation, however, is a process that occurs through time in a structured social context. As numerous sociological and historical studies of U.S. immigrants have documented (see, e.g., Portes and Bach, 1985; Massey et al., 1987; Portes and Rumbaut, 1996), the self-identity of immigrants typically goes through several stages. Very recent migrants, for example, most often see themselves as temporary sojourners in this country, here out of political or economic necessity and not out of a desire to integrate fully into the cultural and social fabric of the United States. It is often only when their children attend U.S. schools, and then mature and begin families of their own, that immigrant parents gradually begin to see the value and necessity of participation in the civic life of U.S. society, and to entertain the possibility that they and their families will not be returning permanently to the home country. The children, then, are most frequently the prime instruments of family integration and acculturation.

Only very slowly and gradually do most immigrants and their children begin to see themselves as having some kind of real membership in U.S. society. What are the nature and context of that membership? Typically, the first step in this incorporation process is identification of the immigrant family as "ethnic" Americans. As noted in Chapter 2, ethnic identities are not created in nature; rather, like national identities they are socially constructed through the establishment of boundaries that are marked and maintained both internally and externally to the group. It is not wholly unknown for individual immigrants to assimilate so fully that neither they nor those with whom they interact are able to place them in any U.S. ethnic category other than "American," but it is surely a rarity. For the vast majority of contemporary U.S. immigrant families from Latin America and Asia, this is virtually inconceivable. This is so because Latin American and Asian immigrants are usually incorporated—having had no real say in the matter themselves—into racialized minority ethnic identities that have long histories in U.S. society. Thus, while it is true that a majority of contemporary U.S. Latinos and Asian/Pacific Americans are immigrants to this country, this does not preclude their being members of U.S. racial minorities. Indeed, the point is that most are being assimilated into these minority groups, whether they wish it or not. This is particularly true, as Alejandro Portes and Ruben G. Rumbaut (1996: chap. 7) document, in inner city schools, where the children of many recent immigrants are first socialized into American society (see also Portes, 1994). Countless daily interactions with those from other groups (e.g., Anglos, African Americans, Asian/Pacific Americans, Latinos, American Indians) lead immigrants and their children to be perceived—and to begin perceiving themselves—as "Latinos," "Asians," and so on.[3]

As new members of these groups, further, most immigrants from non-European countries are heirs to the long traditions of racially segmented and stratified social practice that flow forward from that history recounted in the pluralist version of the U.S. national memory (see Chapter 4). The social forces through which this racialization takes place are complex and deeply embedded in contemporary American society. U.S. society is thoroughly interlaced with institutional structures that racially structure our social reality on a continuous basis, as Michael Omi and Howard Winant (1994), among others, have powerfully argued. Thus, to the extent that Latinos or Asians are subject to discrimination and prejudice as a result of their "race," they will be so treated whether they are recent immigrants or sixth-generation U.S. citizens.

Moreover, in part because of the large number of non-English-speaking immigrants within these minority communities, the interconnections between race and language as ethnic group boundaries are being reinforced rather than diminished. As a result, language minority members face the prospects of hostility and discrimination in which the distinction between their racialized identities and their native languages is often lost.

Some evidence indicating that this is the case is found in the public opinion surveys on language and cultural issues cited in Chapter 3. In their analysis of the sources of opposition to bilingual education among Anglos, for example, Leonie Huddy and David O. Sears (1990) found that "racial attitudes predicted more of the overall variance than did nonracial symbolic predispositions, and symbolic racism, in particular, was the most powerful variable" (p. 130).

Similarly, in their study of California survey data on (mostly) Anglo opinion regarding the state's 1986 "official English" initiative, Jack Citrin, Beth Reingold, Evelyn Walters, and Donald P. Green (1990) found that "negative sentiments about cultural minorities [i.e., Asian Americans and Latinos] are associated consistently with opposition to bilingualism and approval of the hegemony of English" (p. 553). Indeed, they concluded that "feelings about American nationality and affect toward minority groups were the primary attitudes engaged by language policy and each exerted a strong independent influence on mass preferences" (p. 556).

In a related public opinion study, Citrin, Reingold, and Green (1990) looked at (mostly) Anglo concerns about the impact of non-European-origin immigration on American national identity. Finding symbolic identity politics at the core of disquiet about the country's changing demographic composition, they stated that "a major source of opposition to cultural minorities among the majority ethnic group in America is the perception that they fail to conform to cherished notions of Americanism" (p. 1142). Further, they concluded that this perceived failure to conform is most profoundly related to the issue of language: "In the present study, we found that beliefs about American identity exerted their strongest influence on issues involving the status of English, where the problem of cultural identity is transcendent" (p. 1148).

A different kind of evidence pointing in the same direction is found in Bonnie Urciuoli's (1996) microsocial analysis tracing the linkages between racialized class identities and Spanish-language use among Puerto Ricans living in New York. She argues that in New York (and, by implication, elsewhere in the United States), the use of Spanish by Puerto Ricans is an integral part of a "race/class conflation" in which

> *black* or *Hispanic* or *Puerto Rican* become metonyms for (naturally connected to) the idea of an *underclass*. In this metonym, class/race difference becomes morally marked. Activities seen as typical of bad citizens (dropping out of school, becoming teenage mothers, taking drugs, committing crimes, going on welfare) are habitually associated with, for example, *Puerto Ricans,* and become "explanations" for their "failure." Terms that do not fit the moral picture disappear from the discourse.
>
> Language figures into this race/class conflation in several ways. Hegemonically, Spanish itself is regarded as a barrier to class mobility because it displaces English. Accents, "broken" English, and "mixing" become signs of illiteracy and laziness, which people are morally obligated to control. . . . Bilingual neighborhoods are equated with slums, an equation familiar to people who live in them. (Urciuoli, 1996: 26 [emphasis in original])

As a result of this language/race/class conflation, Urciouli (1996) concludes, "being 'low class' and Puerto Rican or black are unmarked with respect to each other, habitually and typically associated. Like a default setting, this conflation is the normal point of reference unless it is specifically (never permanently) reset" (p. 27).

In summary, the reality for many immigrants is far more complex than the argument of assimilationists that "after all, immigrants *chose* to come here *voluntarily,* and therefore they have the obligation to assimilate into *our* language and culture." To be blunt: The argument made by assimilationists like Gary Imhoff[4] is historically false in several respects. It is, first, misleading to assume that "our" language and culture are unambiguously English and Anglo-origin. Spanish, as well as numerous Native American languages, are at least as "native" to the United States as is English. Further, languages other than English have been in continuous usage in the territory of the United States since before this country existed. It is true that in most places, other language groups often were quickly outnumbered and overpowered through superior force by speakers of English. However, this set of historical facts introduces a quite different moral equation[5] than the one on which most assimilationists wish to base their position. The point is that language and culture have been contested terrain throughout U.S. history (see Limerick, 1987: 27). There was no "golden age" when all Americans belonged to one cultural community, or when English was the undisputed sole language of the United States.

Second, it is equally distorting to characterize all in-migration as voluntary in the sense that people have chosen to come here in an unambiguouly free and opportunistic personal decision to improve their circumstances as individuals. Many of us are the descendants of immigrants who made that free and voluntary decision, but many are not. Here the pluralists have a much more complete understanding of U.S. history: Many American ethnic communities—including American Indians, several Latino groups, and several Asian/Pacific Islander groups—derive their original memberships in our national community from acts of force and violence in which the boundaries of the United States were extended to "incorporate" their forebears. Once part of the American population, moreover, most who were coerced into membership were assigned racialized minority identities in which their languages have been key components of the racialization process.

And third, even among those who have freely chosen to immigrate to the United States, there are many who are being incorporated into racialized ethnic minority communities in a social process of identity reconstruction over which they have little control, and in which language perceptions and status judgments play an important role. For each of these reasons, and especially in light of their combination, the assimilationist understanding of U.S. history is misleading and distorting, and cannot be used to justify a policy of linguistic assimilation.

The Second Flaw: The Public/Private Dichotomy and Personal Identity

One of the great attractions of the assimilationist argument about language policy is that it seems to fit well with the dominant U.S. political culture, especially in respect to the relationship between cultural difference and the line between public and private social spheres. Liberal individualist assimilationists (as opposed to communitarian nativist assimilationists)[6] argue that under an "official English" policy, individuals still have the freedom to maintain the language and culture of their choice in their homes, religious institutions, and private lives; and that it would be unjust for government to impose its version of minority cultures on members of those groups. Therefore, as Linda Chavez (1991) has argued (see Chapter 5), if Latino parents want their children to learn Spanish and to maintain their cultural traditions, no one is going to stop them from sending their children to privately financed language and cultural classes, just as other immigrant parents have done throughout U.S. history.

This is an attractive understanding of the issue in that it seems to promise maximum personal freedom and minimum governmental interference in our lives. It has, however, several shortcomings that are common to most liberal individualist understandings of social reality. First, it is based on a misconception of the relationship between government and culture; and second, its attempt to contain cultural freedom within the private sphere is necessarily incompatible with a belief in *equal* liberty for *all*. In the end, the argument for separating culture from the public realm that Chavez and other liberal individualists want to make is incoherent.

The position I will articulate here follows in the main the thinking of Canadian liberal political philosopher Will Kymlicka (1989, 1995), which shows very clearly why the argument for an assimilationist language policy is not morally sustainable in a political culture, such as that of the United States, committed to the equal protection of individual well-being and freedom.

As a liberal, Kymlicka begins from the premise that the individual self is the proper moral foundation for any just political community. The well-being of individuals, each of whose life has the same moral worth or value (the equality criterion), is the key to political justice. However, this well-being ("the good") must be defined by the individual her- or himself ("from the inside"), which requires that she or he be free to define for her- or himself what is meaningful and worthwhile in her or his own life. Since learning is always possible, moreover, she or he must be free to change her or his mind about that which is most meaningful and worthwhile. Thus far, Kymlicka's argument is quite conventional in the liberal tradition (i.e., it is completely compatible with the thought of Locke, Kant, Mill, Rawls, and even Hayek).

At this point, however, Kymlicka inquires into the sources of the self, and here he begins to diverge from many other liberal thinkers. Where does the individual self get the information and criteria with which to determine for her- or himself those things that will make her or his life meaningful and purposeful? The answer is inescapable: from a cultural community. Each person becomes a *self,* as we know that term, only within the context of a cultural community. If you removed me from any human cultural community as an infant and then (assuming I had survived) observed me as an adult, I would exhibit few of the characteristics we associate with being human (e.g., speech, reasoning processes, eating and sleeping patterns, sociability, empathic capacities, etc.; see Malson, 1972). "In deciding how to lead our lives," Kymlicka (1989) says, "we do not start *de novo*" (p. 164). Rather,

> from childhood on, we become aware, both that we are already participants in certain forms of life (familial, religious, sexual, educational, etc.), and that there are other ways of life which offer alternative models and roles that we may, in time, come to endorse. We decide how to lead our lives by situating ourselves in these cultural narratives, by adopting roles that have struck us as worthwhile ones, as ones worth living (which may, of course, include the roles we were brought up to occupy).
>
> The processes by which options and choices become significant for us are linguistic and historical processes. Whether or not a course of action has any significance for us depends on whether, or how, our language renders vivid to us the point of that activity. And the way in which language renders vivid these activities is a matter of our cultural heritage. (Kymlicka: 1989: 165)

Summarizing these processes, Kymlicka describes our cultural environment as providing for us the context of choice, the necessary and inevitable social ground on which we make our personal decisions about what leading a good life entails for us. If he is correct in this reasoning, then each individual self has a deep stake in the well-being of the cultural community that makes this "self" possible: I literally need my cultural community in order to become myself.

The second step in Kymlicka's argument is to establish the equal moral standing of a society's particular cultural communities. Without this moral equality, assimilationists could still claim that members of cultural minorities should simply be asked (or even paid) to adopt the majority cultural community as their own without sacrificing anything essential to their well-being. In a line of reasoning reminiscent of the primordialist understanding of language's role in identity formation as outlined in Chapter 2, Kymlicka (1989) stresses the degree to which an individual's personal identity is shaped by membership in a *particular* cultural community:

People *are* bound, in an important way, to their own cultural community. We can't just transplant people from one culture to another, even if we provide the opportunity to learn the other language and culture. Someone's upbringing isn't something that can just be erased; it is, and will remain, a constitutive part of who that person is. Cultural membership affects our very sense of personal identity and capacity. (p. 175 [emphasis in original])

Kymlicka (1989) elaborates this last point by adding that "cultural structure is crucial not just to the pursuit of our chosen ends, but also to the very sense that we are capable of pursuing them efficiently" (p. 176).

In other words, without the structural reality of our cultural community, we would not have the choice to pursue those ends that we have chosen (from among the options available in that context) for making our lives meaningful and purposeful. Not only is membership in a cultural community central to individual well-being, then, but so is the possibility of membership in a *particular* cultural community. As discussed in Chapter 2, Iris Marion Young (1990) made a similar point by noting that membership in a "social group" (e.g., in a racial, ethnic, or gender group) has a certain "thrownness" in that "one *finds oneself* as a member of such a group, which one experiences as always already having been" (p. 46, [emphasis in original]).

So far, nothing in this discussion contradicts the argument of a Linda Chavez that, while the maintenance of one's cultural community might be important to one's well-being, doing so is a *private,* and not a public, responsibility. (It does, however, undermine the nativist communitarian version of assimilationism that objects to cultural diversity in the private sector as well.) The third step in the argument moves us into the heart of the public/private distinction for cultural communities. Here Kymlicka attacks the supposition that it is possible to separate the public authority of the state from particular cultural communities and their means of expression.

Nearly all recent political theorists, Kymlicka asserts, have been wrong in one of their central assumptions: that political communities are typically composed of single cultural communities. This mistaken assumption is as characteristic of most liberal theorists as it is of most critics of liberalism. Kymlicka aligns himself, further, with those who argue that the state, in ordering and representing the political community, cannot be neutral in the matter of culture, because it must use cultural artifacts and media to constitute and express itself, and to carry out its tasks. The state must, for example, use language in order to exist and in order to perform. If the state does not use *my* language, as we saw in Chapter 2, then I am at a disadvantage compared to those whose language(s) it does use.

This inescapable reality creates the foundation for injustice toward members of cultural minority communities in multicultural states that support only one culture, because maintaining the structure of a cultural community requires resources (e.g., time, energy, money, and authority). And if the state's own operations—which are presumed to represent fairly all the members of the political community—buttress the structural foundations for one particular cultural community but not others, then the members of the dominant cultural community are getting their culture "for free" (or, at least, at heavily discounted rates), while the members of minority cultural communities must expend their own private resources to just maintain themselves. It is for this reason, Kymlicka asserts, that justice requires that Canada's aboriginal peoples receive special rights to offset the unearned advantage held by the dominant English- and French-speaking Canadians.

The moral foundation for Kymlicka's argument is that any adequate theory of justice must take into account the fact that the choices made by individuals in the pursuit of their ends are made in contexts and circumstances not of their own making. And, while individuals should be held responsible for the *consequences* of their choices,[7] they ought *not* be held responsible for the *circumstances* of their choices. Elemental fairness requires that individual choices be made from the circumstances of an "egalitarian plateau" (Kymlicka, 1989: 182). Kymlicka (1989) summarizes the moral heart of his argument as follows:

> Differences that are due to people's choices are their own responsibility (assuming they are freely chosen, with adequate information about the costs and consequences of those choices, etc.).
> But differences which arise from people's circumstances—their social environment or natural endowments—are clearly not their own responsibility. No one chooses which class or race they are born into, or which natural talents they are born with, and no one deserves to be disadvantaged by those facts. (p. 186)

Thus, elemental fairness requires that the state underwrite the cultural structures of minority groups as it does those of the dominant group(s).

Summarizing, then, to argue for solely private maintenance of minority languages and cultures is to make a fundamentally unfair argument. The state cannot be neutral in respect to language or culture. Those who belong to the dominant cultural community enjoy a plethora of unearned advantages in comparison with those who belong to minority cultural communities, and many of those advantages are maintained and supported by governments—national, state, and local—that should treat all their members with equal respect and equal opportunity. In relation to minority cultural communities, this requires public support for those communities' cultural structures. Accordingly, justice requires that the state ensure that members of minority cultural communities have public support for the maintenance of their languages (through, e.g., language education programs and other promotion-oriented policies), and that their members are not disadvantaged in public life by virtue of their membership in a minority cultural community. This assumes, of course, that the minority cultural community speaks a language different from that of the dominant group and desires to maintain its own language. In light of this analysis, support for a pluralistic approach to language policy, one much more extensive than thus far adopted in most parts of the United States, seems required by elemental justice understood as equal respect for all individuals in the political community.

Now, of course, as assimilationists would be quick to point out, this line of reasoning does not necessarily apply to immigrants who individually and voluntarily choose to become part of the United States. Assuming that they have "freely chosen, with adequate information about the costs and consequences of those choices" (Kymlicka, 1989: 186), to become part of the U.S. political community, we can morally expect immigrant newcomers to make a cultural adaptation to their new country.

However, as we saw in the pluralist argument of Chapter 5, and in my criticisms of the assimilationist understanding of U.S. history above, this does not mean that all immigrant newcomers should be expected to assimilate as a matter of course into the dominant English-speaking, Anglo cultural community of the country. The circumstances of their choices are not that simple or clear-cut. For into which "native" U.S. cultural community will they be assimilated? To what extent do they have a free choice in determining the answer to this question? On what moral grounds would we want the state to channel newcomers from Asia or Latin America to assimilate linguistically into Anglo communities rather than into long-standing Asian American or Latino U.S. cultural communities?

The moral answer seems clear: Individuals should have a choice as to which cultural community offers the greatest degree of personal fulfillment and meaning. But if the state provides enormous resources to maintain and enhance *one* of the country's cultural communities and not its others, then the choices available to those individuals are not being provided in accordance with the presupposition that every self is of equal moral worth in the eyes of the state. This line of reasoning, of course, requires that one perceives the United States as a country with at least several constituent and constitutive cultural communities.[8] But that was the point of my analysis above, in relation to the first flaw in the assimilationist argument.

Putting these lines of criticism together renders the core of the assimilationist argument on language policy and justice untenable. More importantly, it enables us to recognize that the assimilationist position functions as a defense of unwarranted privilege for Anglophones that is blind to the circumstances of its own inegalitarianism. That is, misrepresenting our historical context allows assimilationists to present contemporary Anglos as victims, as members of a (nonethnic "national") group that is being besieged by ungrateful and culturally arrogant immigrants who ought to behave as guests should behave. Second, misconstruing the social, cultural, and governmental foundations for *all* individual identities, attainments, and freedoms enables assimilationists to remain blind to the unearned privileges and social advantages enjoyed by native English-speakers in contrast with members of minority cultural communities.

Failing to recognize their own priviliged position, further, enables assimilationists to imagine that pluralist programs are unprecedented forms of privilege that victimize English-speaking monolinguals, rendering the English-Plus program as an agenda for minority domination. The combination of these fallacies in the assimilationist argument is so powerful because it creates a relatively seamless web of misrepresentation that demonizes non-English-speakers and their pluralist allies as aggressive and destructive foreigners, wreckers of American harmony, with Anglos cast in the role of weak and threatened victims. This can occur only because of the hegemonic[9] cultural position of Anglophone Americans.

Insisting that members of racialized minority groups assimilate linguistically "for their own good," moreover, is doubly cruel because not only does it finesse the unearned privilege of Anglophones, but it also ignores the risk taken by language minority group members who shift to English monolingualism in hopes of greater social mobility.

OBSTACLES TO THE PLURALIST ALTERNATIVE

In view of the analysis above, there are strong reasons for favoring a policy of linguistic pluralism for the United States. This country *is* composed of multiple ethnolinguistic cultural communities, and many have long historical roots here. These distinct communities, moreover, have been sustained through boundary maintenance efforts by those both inside and outside the groups. Any just language policy must come to terms with the fact that we *are* a multicultural and mutilingual country and have been so throughout our history. Such a policy must also come to terms with the fact that we are a country in which multiple ethnolinguistic minority groups have been dominated and excluded by the dominant cultural majority through processes of racialization. And in re-envisioning ourselves as a complex nation that is composed of multiple cultural communities, a just language policy must likewise come to terms with the reality that government cannot be neutral in relation to language and culture, and that those who are in the dominant cultural community are unjustly privileged by that fact through no virtue of their own. These realities point toward a language policy that aims to diminish the manifest disadvantages facing members of long-standing U.S. ethnolinguistic minority communities. A pluralistic, English-Plus language policy would more successfully come to terms with these facts by embracing them as legitimate foundations for our conception of ourselves as Americans.

In the face of assimilation's weaknesses, moreover, a pluralist language policy is attractive on several other grounds. By definition, a pluralist policy would aim to support the maintenance and vitality[10] of non-English-language cultural communities that have deep roots in the United States. This would provide a more equitable foundation upon which the members of these communities could make choices for themselves, as individuals, on matters such as the degree to which they wish to help maintain the cultural communities that have shaped their own identities. At the same time *bi*lingual and *bi*cultural, the policy also promotes national unity and social integration by bringing us together while affirming the mutual value of our cultural diversity. Under such a policy we might learn to practice and embrace each other's languages and cultural traditions, thus enabling us to value each other as unique and distinct individuals. Whereas assimilation puts those who are different at a disadvantage by reinforcing inequalities, pluralism might bring us together without disparaging our differences.

Further, by supporting the maintenance of our multiple cultural communities, pluralism enables us to avoid the stultifying sameness of monocultural communalism. We would enrich ourselves through the stimulating variety of a diversity of cultural hues, rather than the dull grayness of uniformity. As Iris Young (1990: chap. 8) has proposed, the varied richness of cosmopolitan "city life" is an appropriate aesthetic model for a pluralistic society, containing many advantages over the conformist vision of Jean-Jacques Rousseau and some of his contemporary communitarian followers. Others have argued that just as biodiversity leads to greater vitality and strength in any ecosystem, so too does cultural diversity enhance any human system.

Despite its attractiveness in the face of assimilationism's weaknesses, however, the argument for a pluralist language policy must confront several important obstacles that have not yet been fully addressed by its advocates. The following paragraphs will articulate two interrelated criticisms that seriously weaken the prospects for a successful policy of linguistic pluralism in the United States. Both critiques stress that the dominant U.S. value of liberal individualism reinforces ethnolinguistic inequality to a degree that could easily prevent realization of the goals of a policy of linguistic pluralism. Unless this obstacle can be addressed successfully, the efficacy of linguistic pluralism as the appropriate response to U.S. ethnolinguisitc diversity is cast into serious doubt.

These criticisms assert that the kind of social integration of different language groups envisioned by pluralism—an integration that is individualist and voluntarist—will, on the one hand, perpetuate the very social inequality between ethnolinguistic groups that it seeks to overcome, and, on the other hand, will yield a very unstable foundation for the maintenance of the country's ethnolinguistic diversity over the long run. Thus, if my critique faults the assimilationist argument on ethno-linguistic justice for failing to come to terms with the fact that the United States is a multicultural and multilinguistic country, my analysis below questions whether the policy of linguistic pluralism is sufficient for achieving justice for language minority communities.

The First Flaw: The Limits of Individual Choice
in an English-Dominant Country

One of the great attractions of the pluralist position is its promise that members of language minority communities can have it all: They can be ethnoculturally different while still enjoying the fruits of full integration into the public and quasipublic spaces of the country, and they can do so in a way that is equal, without paying a penalty for their difference or for their maintenance of membership in a minority cultural commu-nity. This first line of criticism of pluralist language policy questions the likelihood of realizing this attractive aim in an individualistic social context and envisions important inegalitarian consequences resulting from the implementation of an incomplete pluralist policy.

I want to suggest that even the full adoption of the pluralists' stated policy aims will not be sufficient to eliminate the barriers to ethnolin-guistic equality for members of U.S. language minority groups, and might even reinforce them. Thus, even if all language minority students in the United States were educated in effective bilingual classrooms with qualified bilingual teachers, and even if all non-English-literate U.S. citizens had full access to election materials, public services, and the like in their own languages, it might well be that the inherent dynamics of ethnic group identity in an integrated society would ensure that one group would be dominant, and that the members of other groups would remain marginalized, and in some important ways, sub-ordinated. All boundaries of identity, William E. Connolly (1991) has reminded us, create difference. Difference, in turn, has consequences in the lives of those on both sides of the boundaries. Without conse-quences, the boundaries are meaningless and soon disappear.

The problem here is that pluralism makes the assumption that indi-viduals can display and assert important (ethnic) group differences while still being accepted and functioning as equal individuals in a larger context (i.e., the national or larger community public sphere). This may be an unrealistic expectation about the dynamics of most human interactions as we know them. Indeed, such is the thrust of one of the assimilationist criticisms of pluralism that we encountered in Chapter 5. Here we revisit this critique, elaborating it in a broader context.

Put simply, the argument is that encouraging minority language individuals to maintain and use their native languages only dooms them to continued marginality in the hegemonic English-dominant public world of the United States. This marginality, in turn, means that they can never be truly equal—as experienced by themselves and by others—in relation to those for whom membership in the dominant cultural community is a given. If social equality is a primary goal, this is an important argument that must be considered in greater depth.

The argument is made most compellingly by Richard Rodriguez. Not a lawyer or social theorist, Rodriguez does not take seriously American pretensions to rights-centered individualism. He *does*, however, perceive the dominant Anglo culture as being highly individualistic in its orientation, but he also assumes that that very individualism is a culture—one that is learned and practiced from within a cultural community, as is true of all cultures. Thus his major point is that, if we want Mexican American (and, by extension, other language minority) children to experience full social mobility in the United States, they must first see themselves as full-fledged individual members of this dominant cultural community. This cannot happen, he believes, so long as they maintain membership in their own, "immigrant," cultural communities.

The foundation of Rodriguez's (1994) argument against bilingual education, and against linguistic pluralism more generally, is his belief that genuine *bi*culturalism and *bi*lingualism are impossible. Even when individuals can understand and speak more than one language, they are not necessarily genuinely bilingual or bicultural. Always, he argues, a person has only one *real* language; the other is in a subordinate position in the mind and heart. Encouraging Latino children to retain and use their private family language in public spaces, then, helps them to continue thinking of English as the language of those "others," the *Norteamericanos* or even *Americanos,* and not as "ours" or "mine." The necessary consequence is that the Latino youngster becomes an adult who always feels a stranger, a foreigner, in his or her own land. Only by fully embracing the English language and the public world that it constitutes can the immigrant child, the language minority child, become a truly equal member of the body politic of the United States.

By implication, Rodriguez is also claiming that no society can be truly bilingual and bicultural, and that one language and culture will always be the dominant, or public, one. In the United States, the dominant, hegemonic language is without question English. Their failure to recognize this reality of life underlies his contemptuous dismissal of "romantic" middle-class ethnics who push poor immigrant children to maintain their family languages. The inevitable result, he argues, is that they will be doomed to perpetual marginal status, since they will always see themselves and be seen by others as outsiders for having not incorporated the English language and the public culture as their own.

Interestingly, Quebecois nationalists in Canada make an analogous argument that goes to the heart of the identity politics debate at issue here. From the perspective of U.S. pluralists, Canada's federal government policy of linguistic pluralism appears both far-reaching and eminently worthy of emulation. As summarized briefly in Chapter 2, Canada's federal government has been committed since 1969 to a policy under which every parent has the right to choose the official language (English or French) in which her or his children will be educated. Moreover, in most circumstances Canadian citizens have the right to interact (both orally and in writing) with their federal government in the official language of their choice. And a rigorously defined employment policy is in effect in those regions where both language groups reside in significant numbers to ensure that neither English-speakers nor French-speakers will be discriminated against because of their native language. Virtually every goal imagined by U.S. linguistic pluralists has been the official policy of Canada since 1969 (see Schmidt, 1998, for an elaboration of Canada's federal language policy).

And yet, Quebec's Francophones overwhelmingly deem this policy inadequate for their own province, viewing it as grossly insufficient to assure a just future for their own linguistic community in North America. Rather than embracing this federal policy designed to bring Quebeckers into the fold of the Canadian "family" on an equal footing, in 1977 Quebec adopted the Charter of the French Language (Bill 101), aimed at ensuring that French is the dominant language in the province (see Chapter 2). This law, which continues to enjoy virtually unassailable support from both of the province's major political parties, denied immigrant parents in Quebec the choice of which official language would be the primary one for the education of their children, required employers to make French alone the official language of business (and employment) in Quebec, and mandated that businesses present a French-only public *visage* to the world in their commercial signs. It also sought to deny access to English-language schools to the children of English-speaking parents moving into the province from other parts of Canada, although this provision was dropped after being ruled unconstitutional by the country's highest court. Quebec's Charter of the French Language, in short, is an attempt to move Canada toward a policy of *linguistic confederation, as opposed to linguistic pluralism.*

Why would Francophone Quebec, which had suffered linguistic discrimination and domination at the hands of Anglophones for so long, turn around and implement its own "illiberal" policy of French linguistic dominance in its own province? One major aspect of the answer follows the argument made by Rodriguez, for as the Quebecois see it, languages are naturally in competition, and one or the other will inevitably dominate in any given territory (Laponce, 1992). Further, they stress, the short-term fate of any minority language community under such circumstances is that of the exotic "other," akin to a sideshow entertaining bored members of the dominant cultural community.

While the Quebecois are quick to defend their commitment to multilingualism as a goal for individuals and for the educational system, they believe that ethnolinguistic pluralism necessarily exists within a context of dominance by one ethnolinguistic community. In Quebec, they agree, that dominant community must be Francophone, or it will inevitably be the minority Anglophones, thus relegating the majority once again to the subordinate position it occupied in the province prior to the "Quiet Revolution" of the 1960s, even though it constituted over 80 percent of Quebec's population. With manifest exasperation, Quebecois intellectual Daniel Latouche attempted to make this point clear in his reply to an Anglophone polemic by writer Philip Resnick:

> But when will you English Canadians get it through your thick collective skull that we want to live in a French society, inside and outside, at work and at play, in church and in school. Is this so difficult to understand? Do you get some kind of secret satisfaction from forcing us to repeat this simple fact time after time? . . .

For you a French society is one where French-speaking Canadians can find work in French, buy their groceries in French, and watch television or go to school in French. When you think of a French society you think of a Chinatown-like situation. This is precisely how Americans see it. This is how they see Canada and especially English Canada. Their vision of society is purely individualistic, based on the sharing of material goods and infused with patriotic symbols. (quoted in Resnick, 1990: 89–90)

Like Rodriguez, then, many Quebecois nationalists see no alternative to having one dominant cultural community in any society. And if theirs is not the dominant community, inevitably they will be relegated to the position of the exotic minority by the sheer overwhelming power of the Anglophone majority of North America. For this reason, they push to have Canada redefine its language policy as one of confederation rather than pluralism, and many now strive beyond that for independent nationhood for Quebec.[11] Using the same logic, but not perceiving confederation as a realistic or desirable egalitarian option for the United States, Rodriguez argues for a policy of assimilation.

The Second Flaw: The Long-Term Instability of Societal Bilingualism

My second criticism of the linguistic pluralist agenda for the United States looks at the same obstacle described above from a slightly different angle—the long-term viability of a policy of linguistic pluralism in a culturally hegemonic society that stresses individual free choice. The best way to approach this criticism, I think, is to recall the argument made by Will Kymlicka, summarized in my critique of the assimilationist position above: that a just language policy in a multicultural country must give each individual an equal choice between cultural communities, but that a structurally grounded egalitarian plateau is needed for that choice to be genuinely equal. Without that equal starting point, the context of choice for individuals is constrained by numerous unequal circumstances for which they should not bear responsibility.

Following this logic, let us reexamine the context of choice for individuals under the specific policies espoused by U.S. linguistic pluralists. As we saw in Chapter 4, pluralists (as well as liberal assimilationists) support a toleration-oriented government policy that allows freedom of linguistic choice in the private civil society sectors: that is, in households, by radio and TV broadcasters, in newspapers, magazines, and books, as well as by voluntary associations such as churches, private schools, clubs, and community organizations. This, pluralists believe, should be supplemented by promotion-oriented public policies of maintenance bilingual education for language minority children, and by the extension of non-English linguistic access measures to election materials, public services and institutions, and employment rights. In general, moreover, public institutions and agents should work to instill the idea in the minds and hearts of the whole public that there are multiple languages and ethnolinguistic communities that are equally and fully American and that deserve our equal respect and common support.

Will the full implementation of these measures yield a sufficiently equal plateau so that members of U.S. language minority groups have a genuine choice in choosing and pursuing their own life goals in this multicultural society? If not, what are the long-term implications for U.S. multiculturalism and multilingualism?

A negative answer to the first question was outlined in the paragraphs immediately above, where it was suggested that members of minority cultural communities might well remain marginalized and subordinated unless they can become the dominant, counterhegemonic group in territories of their own. If this is true, there are strong reasons for further doubting the long-term viability of multiculturalism and multilingualism in the United States.[12] The basic logic here is straightforward. Once again it has been elaborated extensively by Quebecois nationalists in criticizing the adequacy of the Canadian federal government's policy of linguistic pluralism. One of the Francophone majority's most important rationales for Bill 101's policy of illiberal communitarian restrictiveness is its understanding of the seriousness of the linguistic and cultural crisis faced by Francophones in overwhelmingly Anglophone North America. In its simplest terms, the argument is that without special, restrictive protections for the French language and culture in Quebec, the viability of this cultural community over the long term is in serious doubt.

The reasoning behind this pessimistic conclusion is based on the collective logic of individual choices under certain unequal circumstances. That is, if the most sought-after opportunities (employment, status, power) in a society are in the hands of one language group, individual responses to equal opportunity policies will be shaped by that very social context toward conformity with the dominant language and culture. Thus, individuals making "free" choices to improve their own life chances will decide, other things being equal, to conform with those aspects of the social context (e.g., language use and cultural identification) that will improve their own positions. If the language of power is English, individuals will choose English in the pursuit of their own advantage. Since the language of power in Quebec historically *was* English, it was not surprising that immigrants to Quebec would choose English rather than French as the preferred language for their children's education, or that Francophones admitted into the corridors of (English-dominant) corporate and commercial power would gradually assimilate into Anglophone North America.

In short, the leaders of Quebecois nationalism believed that liberal pluralism provided an inherently unstable foundation for a bilingual country. Because languages are naturally in competition, with one always dominant, the pluralist individual free choice policies of official bilingualism espoused by the federal government provided no protection against the destructive effects on the language and culture of the Francophone community following from this seemingly inexorable logic of collective behavior. The only way to alter this logic, in turn, was to make French the indisputable language of power in the province, a counterhegemonic social transformation that could not be accomplished through policies based on liberal free market principles (see Levine, 1990, for an excellent history of this transformation, centered on Montreal).

Sociolinguists use the concept of "linguistic domain" to analyze the factors conducive to either language maintenance or language shift (Fishman, 1972). As a daily social activity, languages are not typically used equally in the various domains of a given society. Bilingual individuals, therefore, tend to apportion their language use among their various social domains. Carol M. Eastman provides a common example: "Children who speak a mother tongue and use a second language in school eventually talk about school matters in the second language and domestic matters in the first language" (p. 142). This bilingualism is unstable, however, to the degree that the second language domains begin to assume greater and greater importance in the lives of these speakers: "As the school and nonhome environment begins to dominate their lives, they use the mother tongue less and less" (Eastman, 1983: 142). As a consequence, when these children grow up and establish homes of their own, *their* children are likely to grow up in an English-dominant household. French Canadian political scientist J. A. Laponce (1987), however, may have put the problem most clearly in the following formulation:

> Bilingualism is costly, in terms of memory and reaction time. Thus for an individual to become or remain bilingual, the social benefit must outweigh the mental cost; and this mental cost explains why the tendency toward unilingualism never entirely disappears . . . and merely confirms the norm: the mind works more quickly and with less effort in a unilingual semantic system; its natural inclination is toward unilingualism. (p. 15)

Does this mean that the overwhelming "English fact" of North America (to use a Quebecois formulation) will inevitably spell the doom of U.S. bilingualism under an individually voluntaristic pluralist language policy? While most sociolinguists are unwilling to make such a flat pronouncement, few have expressed surprise at the findings of recent research by Alejandro Portes and Richard Schauffler (1994) on the language preferences of second-generation immigrant schoolchildren in the Miami, Florida, area. Taking issue with U.S. English pronouncements regarding the imminent destruction of linguistic unity in the United States, they report not only that their second-generation sample is overwhelmingly competent in English (over 70% from each immigrant category reported knowing English "very well"; virtually all of them know it "well"), but that the overwhelming majority of each group also "generally prefers" to use English as its language of choice (Portes and Schauffler, 1994: 648–49). Indeed, over 93 percent of Cuban American students attending private *bilingual* schools (and living in seemingly Spanish-dominant Miami) agreed that they "generally prefer to speak" English rather than Spanish (Portes and Schauffler, 1994: 648). Not surprisingly, very similar results have been reported from a related study of second-generation immigrant students in the San Diego, California, area (Rumbaut, 1997: 939).

In sum, if achieving and maintaining stable bilingualism and biculturalism over the long term is necessary to attain the pluralists' linguistic goals, there are strong reasons to doubt that the (highly contested) policy agenda they have articulated and promoted for nearly three decades is capable—in itself—of reaching these ends. The informal social pressures toward language shift to English, coupled with the lack of incentives to expend the necessary personal resources required to maintain the active use of two languages, just seem too powerful. This point has been acknowledged and discussed by several pluralist intellectuals (see, e.g., Castro, 1976; Fishman, 1985: 337 n.99), but has never made any real impact on the pluralist linguistic policy agenda in the United States.

In a very interesting way, then, both flaws described above yield the same sort of criticism against pluralism as a public policy solution to linguistic diversity. Despite its attractions, linguistic pluralism as a societal ideal remains too ephemeral for long-term realization in the real world. Is the pluralist goal—helping language minority children attain greater social mobility by making them feel at home in the United States through a redefinition of their languages and cultural communities as equal members of a multicultural society—a quixotic dream that can only have tragic consequences for the children involved? Will the children—even under full implementation of the pluralist policy agenda—either assimilate successfully into the dominant language and culture, or remain members of marginalized and subordinate minority communities? We cannot have it both ways, both criticisms seem to conclude. The only real alternative to these options, the Quebecois would add, is to establish vital, successful, but *separate* cultural communities in which languages other than English are dominant, an approach known as confederation (a possibility explored in the next section).

In combination, then, these interrelated criticisms of the pluralist approach to language policy point to an inherent weakness in its individualistic and voluntaristic premises. Because individuals make choices in contexts, the politics of language must come to terms with the societal and structural contexts that inform language use and prestige. Gaining equality for members of U.S. language minorities cannot be achieved solely through the establishment of formal rules that seek to guarantee equal choices to individuals. This is not how societies, languages, or political communities work, and this alone cannot be the foundation for a just language policy for the United States. In the final chapter of this book, then, we must address these realities while searching for language policy criteria that will contribute to the common good and to the realization of greater equality for members of our language minority groups. This search, moreover, must come to terms with the social, moral, and political deficiencies—outlined in this chapter—that undermine both assimilationist and pluralist solutions to our language policy debate.

As we have seen, both assimilation and pluralism have important weaknesses as policy alternatives for resolving the U.S. politics of language. Assimilationists are unrealistic because their ideology posits a monocultural and monolingual country that does not exist in the real world; more importantly, the consequence of its unrealistic assumptions is the continued unjust subordination of language minority groups by the privileged Anglo, European-origin majority. Pluralists too are unrealistic in that they assume that an egalitarian society of multiple cultural communities can be achieved through a combination of individualistic rights-based free choice measures and moral exhortations to Anglos to respect linguistic and cultural diversity. The real-world consequences of these unrealistic policies could well be the continued racialized and marginalized subordination of minority language speakers and the gradual loss (through language shift to English-only) of an important part of the cultural structures of U.S. minority communities. Where, then, does a solution lie?

THE CONFEDERATION ALTERNATIVE: WOULD IT WORK FOR THE UNITED STATES?

Intellectually, an obvious answer to the above question might be linguistic confederation, in which the United States would sanction and underwrite the establishment of non-English-dominant territories that would provide structural foundations for minority cultural communities to reproduce themselves and flourish. Without a territory of its own in which to be dominant, many sociolinguists and language policy analysts agree, no language community is likely to withstand the social market pressures toward language shift to English in contemporary North America (see, e.g., Fishman, 1985; Laponce, 1987; Phillipson, 1992). Without the stability and status conferred by such a linguistic territory, further, language minority members who do not make the shift to English are likely to remain marginalized and racially stigmatized. It was for reasons such as these that confederation became the preferred solution sought by most Quebecois in Canada. Is confederation a viable option for the United States?

To begin to answer this question, it is well to recognize that a limited form of ethnolinguistic confederation already exists in the United States on the island commonwealth of Puerto Rico, and that the structural foundation for such a policy is also found on American Indian reservations on the mainland.

American Indian Reservations and Linguistic Confederation

One example of potential structural support for U.S. linguistic confederation may be found on the reservations of American Indians. As a consequence of historical U.S.–government Indian policies, several hundred American Indian tribes and nations have territories of their own for which they claim sovereignty and on which they exercise a degree of self-government. U.S.–government policies toward American Indians have gone through a variety of inconsistent convolutions over the last several centuries, but since the 1970s the policy framework for tribal governments has been known as self-determination (U.S. Commission on Civil Rights, 1981; Deloria, 1985). Under this policy framework, tribal governments have had a good deal more legal autonomy in relation to state and local governments, and increased autonomy in relation to the Bureau of Indian Affairs of the U.S. Department of Interior. To the degree that "Indian Country" provides a land-base within which native governments might chart their own courses, the structural potential exists for developing linguistic confederation policies on reservations.

Since the 1970s, some American Indian leaders and educators have sought to use their increased political autonomy to expand and strengthen tribal cultural traditions, including use of their native tongues. These efforts have been made in a context in which many sociolinguists have predicted the imminent demise of numerous Native American languages. Indeed, James Crawford (1998) has cited data estimating that 89 percent of the existing 175 U.S. indigenous languages are in a "moribund" state, without young speakers able to carry them into the next generation (p. 152). Under the self-determination policy, some American Indian tribal governments have used their increased control over Native American educational institutions to adopt and implement a maintenance version of bilingual education in the hopes of preserving and expanding the use of their original languages. No tribal government, however, has opted for making its heritage language *dominant* in its portion of Indian Country.

During the 1980s, however, many American Indian leaders became alarmed at the threat to their bilingual efforts posed by the English-only movement described in Chapter 1. Although aimed primarily at urban minority communities being inundated with new immigrants, the "official English" movement seemed as well to bring into question the bilingual goals of Native American leaders. This threat was amplified by the reduced federal funding for bilingual education wrought by the Reagan administration. At a conference held in Tempe, Arizona, in June 1988, therefore, American Indian leaders and educators drew up a proposal for a Native American Languages Act that they forwarded to Senator Daniel Inouye (D-Hawaii), who then chaired the U.S. Senate Committee on Indian Affairs. After two years of political development and negotiation, Inouye succeeded in getting the proposal enacted into law in October 1990.

In its "Findings" section, the law stipulates that "the United States has the responsibility to act together with Native Americans to ensure the survival of these unique cultures and languages" (Hinton, 1994: 184). Other key provisions in the law (in the "Declaration of Policy" section) state:

It is the policy of the United States to—
(1) preserve, protect, and promote the rights and freedom of Native Americans to use, practice, and develop Native American languages; . . . .
(5) recognize the right of Indian tribes and other Native American governing bodies to use the Native American languages as a medium of instruction in all schools funded by the Secretary of the Interior;
(6) fully recognize the inherent right of Indian tribes and other Native American governing bodies, States, territories, and possessions of the United States to take action on, and give official status to, their Native American languages for the purpose of conducting their own business.

Section 105 of the act, finally, promises a federal policy of no restrictions: "The right of Native Americans to express themselves through the use of Native American languages shall not be restricted in any public proceeding including publicly supported education programs" (Hinton, 1994: 185–86).

This 1990 act included no provisions for funding, but a 1992 follow-up law established a federal grant program authorizing a conduit through which federal monies can be used to implement its aims. If the law were fully implemented, it—in conjuction with other organizational and institutional structures on American Indian reservations—could provide a foundation for a kind of confederationist language policy for many American Indian tribes in the United States. That is, tribal leaders could implement language policies in which their native tongues would be the dominant public languages of the reservations. At present there is little interest in going beyond a bilingual policy of two languages—English *plus* the native language—but the legal and institutional foundations are in place for such a policy should some American Indian nations decide it is both desirable and necessary for the preservation of their heritage languages.

Linguistic Confederation in Puerto Rico

A more fully developed, second example of confederation-like language policy in the United States is found in the Commonwealth of Puerto Rico. As with American Indian reservations, Puerto Rico is usually not included in descriptive summaries of governments of the United States. Nevertheless, Puerto Ricans are citizens of the United States, and their island government is a part of the U.S. state structure. The population of the island is overwhelmingly Spanish-speaking. Since its acquisition by the United States in 1898 in the settlement ending the Spanish-American War, the primary political "fault lines" within Puerto Rico have revolved around the question of its appropriate political relationship to the United States. The division has been threefold: One group has wanted complete sovereign independence, a second has wanted statehood as the fifty-first state in the union, and a third has argued for retaining a semisovereign commonwealth association with the United States.

Meanwhile, U.S. policy toward Puerto Rico has gone through various permutations, but the general historical trajectory has been toward increasing self-government for the island. In 1952, its residents approved a new constitution establishing Puerto Rico as a commonwealth (the Spanish wording is *estado libro asociado,* which literally translates as "free associated state"). The constitution was subsequently amended and approved by the U.S. Congress as a "quasi-treaty" (Kloss, 1977: 220).

The exact degree of political autonomy engendered by the constitution remains a subject of controversy that need not concern us here (but see, e.g., Fernandez, 1992). Suffice it to say that Puerto Rico has a substantial degree of internal policy-making authority (similar in many ways to that of a state government), but has no vote in the U.S. Congress, despite the fact that the island is subject to the U.S. government's policies. The future of Puerto Rico's relationship to the United States continues to be highly controversial as well.

As U.S. citizen-members of the commonwealth, Puerto Ricans have free access to residence on the mainland, a fact that has significantly increased the Latino population in the eastern United States in recent decades. Our concern, however, is with the policies of the commonwealth itself that relate to the issue of ethnolinguistic diversity. And the central fact to be emphasized in this connection is the loyalty of *Puertorriqueños* to the Spanish language and their long-standing commitment to cultural self-determination. All factions of Puerto Rican politics have been united on this point. Politically, there has been virtually unanimous resistance by the Puerto Rican people to any effort by U.S. officials to impose English-language dominance on the island.

The earliest laws relating to the governance of the island under the tutelage of the United States included provisions that all executive and judicial departments and all public offices on the island would use both English and Spanish "indiscriminately." From the beginning, also, Spanish was allowed to be the exclusive language of local government on the island. Thus, related Heinz Kloss in his 1977 study of U.S. language policy, "Puerto Rico is the only territory where Congress ordered the equal status of a non-English language" (p. 229).

An unsuccessful effort at language shift to English was made by a series of American governors and commissioners of education for the island until mid-century. While the educational commissioners had retreated by 1917 to a policy of bilingualism, U.S.–appointed governors of the island continued to press for a larger role for English until 1949—a colonialist stance that contributed to the near-consensus in Puerto Rico that Spanish should be the commonwealth's dominant language (Barreto, 1997; Kloss, 1977; Navarro, 1997).[13] Indeed, Amilcár A. Barreto (1997) asserts that the hegemonic status of English in the United States, experienced locally through American efforts to impose English on the island, led directly to a counterhegemonic ideology of Spanish dominance on the part of Puerto Rican elites. Hence, although the island has been officially bilingual in Spanish and English since attaining commonweath status (except for a two-year period of an official Spanish-only policy in 1991–93), Spanish has been overwhelmingly dominant on the island. Kloss (1977) described that dominance as follows:

> Since the establishment of the Commonwealth, the session records of the legislature and the annual messages of the Governor have appeared only in Spanish. The policy of the Commonwealth has been to deemphasize English. A Spanish literacy test is required of members of the parliament, and even jurors in the criminal courts must read and write Spanish. Executive reports in English must be translated into Spanish, while the converse is not required. The Commonwealth's judiciary has ruled that English pleadings must be accompanied by a Spanish translation. (p. 231)

And, although Puerto Rican schools have long had mandatory English classes, a 1997 educational ministry policy to expand the teaching of English toward a truly bilingual educational experience was hotly contested by Puerto Rican teachers (Navarro, 1997). In contrast to the English-dominant policies and realities of U.S. state governments, then, Puerto Rico may be described even more accurately than American Indian reservations as an example of a U.S. jurisdiction operating under a confederation-like language policy regime.[14]

Linguistic Confederation for Urban America?

Despite their cogency in these special contexts, however, neither the Native American nor the Puerto Rican example deals with the metropolitan realities of language diversity that fuel the emotional heat in our contemporary politics of language. The vast majority of non-English-speakers, however, reside in highly urbanized contexts in the mainland states. As noted in Chapter 3, well over half live in only a few states concentrated in the American Southwest or along the eastern seaboard. Is confederation a potential solution in these mainstream U.S. contexts? One writer—Mario Barrera (1988)—has suggested that at least Mexican Americans in the U.S. Southwest should give more serious thought to this alternative.

Barrera began his book by articulating the dilemma—"community" versus "equality"—faced by Mexican Americans. Under the predominant realities in the United States, he asserted, Mexican Americans can either gain equality (social, economic, political) through cultural and linguistic assimilation, or retain their ties of ethnocultural community, but only at the price of continued inequality. This is the same dilemma described above, in my discussion of the obstacles to a pluralist language policy, and one of the most prominent themes of Barrera's narrative of Mexican American community is the importance of retaining the Spanish language while striving for equality. After reviewing the conditions of and policies regarding cultural minorities in four other countries (Canada, China, Switzerland, and Nicaragua), he argues for consideration in the United States of a third alternative (to community with inequality versus equality through assimilation), which closely fits my category of confederation.

The defining characteristic of Barrera's (1988) proposal for ethnic accommodation is "regional autonomy" (p. 160), which he thinks will help "to stabilize the status of minority languages and cultures" (p. 175) in the United States. After outlining a number of specific policy proposals made by Hurst Hannum and Richard Lillich (1980) for the governance of relatively autonomous ethnic regions, Barrera (1988) uses demographic projections to argue that certain specific regions of the U.S. Southwest—Southern California, northern New Mexico, and South Texas—have the Mexican American population growth patterns necessary "to make them increasingly suitable for ethnic autonomy areas" (p. 168). Within such regions, presumably, Spanish would be the dominant language of government, education, commerce, and civil society. Acknowledging that most Chicanos do not at present support an ethnic autonomy approach, he urges Chicano intellectuals and other professionals to play a vanguard role (as these functional groups have done in other countries) in convincing the rank and file that confederation is a viable solution to the cruel dilemma of "equality versus community."

Critique   Despite the logic and coherence of Barrera's case for a type of ethnolinguistic confederation in the U.S. Southwest, however, it seems very unlikely that this will become a politically viable option for urbanized U.S. language minorities, at least in the foreseeable future. Why? Careful consideration of the requisites for a successful policy of linguistic confederation, seen again through a comparative lense focused on the Quebecois of Canada, will best develop my argument here.

Canada's Quebecois reached virtual consensus on a confederationist approach to language policy because of their conviction that unless strong steps were taken to protect a Francophone-dominant territory in Quebec, the overwhelming "English fact" of North America would wipe out their language, culture, and way of life through the sheer weight of its cultural, economic, and political power. The same reasoning has led many observers to predict that the Spanish language and Chicano cultures of the U.S. Southwest are likewise in danger of extinction unless similar steps are taken to create Spanish-dominant domains in the region. Nevertheless, important historical, sociological, and political factors that make linguistic confederation appear a realistic possibility for Quebec are not present in the United States, and their absence renders the possibility of linguistic confederation in the mainland U.S. extremely unlikely. Consider the following contrasts:

- Quebec has had an overwhelming Francophone majority (more than 80% in its last census) throughout its history. Following annexation by the United States, in contrast, Mexican Americans were quickly outnumbered by Anglo settlers in both Texas and California, retaining a majority only in northern New Mexico. Despite large-scale immigration from Mexico in recent decades, no demographer has predicted anything close to an 80 percent majority for Mexican Americans in any U.S. state in the Southwest.
- After their conquest by the British in 1763, most French Canadians in the Quebec region experienced a relatively isolated but self-sufficient existence, with an agricultural land base and a leadership of Roman Catholic clergy highly resistant to absorption by the dominant Anglophone (and Protestant) society—experiences that contributed to a relatively high degree of ethnolinguistic cohesion among the Quebecois. Following annexation by the United States in 1848, in contrast, most Mexican American elites in the Southwest experienced rapid loss of their landholdings, and most Mexican Americans were integrated in a racialized and subordinate status into the developing U.S. southwestern economy (e.g., in mines, on farms, railroads, and later factories).[15] And Mexican American cohesion in the Southwest was limited by a steady, boundary-blurring infusion of newcomers from Mexico and, in recent decades, from other Latin American countries.[16] Moreover, Mexican Americans have experienced far greater social and political, as well as economic, pressure to culturally assimilate than has been true of the Quebecois, thus further limiting their ethnolinguistic cohesion.[17]
- Because of their relative cohesion, numerical dominance, institutional support by clergy, and a countrywide political culture that has been

more group-oriented, or "corporatist" (as opposed to individualistic), than that of the United States,[18] the Quebecois have a much higher level of "institutional completeness"[19] than has been true for Mexican Americans in the United States. That is, compared with the Quebecois, Mexican Americans have had far fewer public, private, civil, and societal institutional settings (e.g., schools, government offices and agencies, firms, unions, clubs, trade groups, professional associations, service organizations, churches, political parties, and community-based organizations) within which to learn, practice, and perpetuate their own ethnolinguistic culture. The different kinds of life experiences embedded within this contrast, in turn, cannot help but affect the two groups' perceptions of the relative desirability and possibility of a linguistic confederation arrangement.

• The campaign of Canada's Quebecois to achieve a successful policy of linguistic confederation within their province was facilitated by their country's relatively more decentralized federal system and its relatively more centralized provincial governmental institutions. In the United States, in contrast, Mexican American efforts to establish a confederationist language policy would operate under much less favorable governmental institutional circumstances.

On the one hand, for example, Quebecois provincial governments have been able to chart a national language policy course at odds with that of the rest of Canada and its federal government in part because Canadian provinces generally have a higher level of autonomy in relation to the federal government than is true of American states. In 1988, for example, Quebec's premier successfully blocked a federal-level supreme court decision relating to the province's language policy; it is impossible to imagine a state governor successfully doing something analogous in the United States. Further, Canada's provinces, as well as its federal government, have parliamentary forms of government, giving their chief executives and majority political parties considerably more latitude in adopting and implementing sharp changes in policy regime. In the United States, in contrast, divided governments and a system of checks and balances are designed to frustrate a majority aiming at a decidedly nonincremental public policy approach. More concretely, the political odds seem overwhelmingly against the creation of effectively functioning, relatively autonomous, ethnically framed substate regional governments (such as those proposed by Barrera for the

Southwest) within the relatively centralized U.S. federal system, composed as it is of myriad systems of mutually blocking checks and balances at the state, regional, and local levels. These political odds seem especially overwhelming if such an effort were to be met by the determined opposition of a highly committed group of opponents with the resources and knowledge to make use of the U.S. political system's multiple veto points.

- Generally, Canada's provinces also play a larger role in their economies (through, e.g., employment of state workers, direct economic activities, and more extensive regulatory policies) than is true of American state governments. Accordingly, by changing the language policy regime of the province through Bill 101, the Quebecois were able to make strong moves toward changing the language of economic power in their province from English to French. This goal was aided not only by requiring firms operating in the province to make French their exclusive language of business therein, but also by giving Francophones strong advantages in the relatively extensive governmental labor market (see, e.g., Levine, 1990). In the unlikely event that Mexican American leaders would ever be able to overcome the institutional political odds delineated above, the resulting ethnically structured regional governments would have far less economic leverage (compared with the Quebecois) through which to make Spanish, rather than English, the dominant language of economic success in those regions. But failing to accomplish this transition would greatly weaken the political attractiveness of a confederationist language policy to Mexican American workers.
- Finally, there is a vast difference between the two countries in public opinion on the language policy issue. After several unsuccessful nineteenth-century attempts at the linguistic assimilation of Francophones into English Canada, most Canadians have long accepted the reality of French as one of their country's constitutive languages. While English Canadians have demanded linguistic assimilation in English-dominant geographic areas, few English Canadians have any expectation that the Francophone Quebecois will shift to English. Since the 1960s, accordingly, the language policy debate in Canada has been over the relative merits of linguistic pluralism versus linguistic confederation, at least in respect to the Quebecois. There is virtually no assimilationist camp in relation to the Quebecois.

In the United States, as we have seen, the debate is quite different. There is no real territorial equivalent to Quebec in this country, even in the Southwest. And the vast majority of Anglos, or European-origin Americans, seem strongly committed to an assimilative approach to language policy, as was seen in Chapter 3. As also underlined in Chapter 3, Mexican Americans (along with other Latino groups) are strongly in favor of a pluralistic, bilingual approach to language policy, but there is very little support among them for a confederationist policy that would emphasize Spanish-language maintenance at the expense of learning English.

Undergirding this difference in policy opinions between the two countries, I believe, is another important difference in public opinion that was alluded to above. That is, the political culture of the United States is fundamentally framed around liberal individualism, while Canada's different past has made its publics relatively more group-oriented, or "corporatist," in their thinking (see, again, Lipset, 1990). Successfully implementing a non-English-language confederationist policy in a territory previously dominated by English would require, at minimum, acceptance of restrictions on individual free choice in order to elevate the status of the previously subordinate language. Quebec's Charter of the French Language, for example, restricts individual choice in a number of ways in order to maintain French dominance in the province against powerful market and geopolitical forces that favor English. Similar measures contravening individual free choice would be required in the U.S. Southwest to maintain Spanish dominance against even more powerful market and geopolitical forces favoring English. Given the cultural power of liberal individualism in the United States, not only among Anglos but also among Latinos, the political odds against successful adoption of these "illiberal" confederationist policies once again appear overwhelming.

In short, while there are good reasons for favoring a policy of linguistic confederation *if* the long-term maintenance of a minority language and culture is a primary objective, the odds against the successful adoption and implementation of such a policy in the U.S. Southwest seem virtually unbeatable in the foreseeable future. In view of these odds, the fact that Mexican Americans (and other Latino groups) favor

an integrative, pluralistic language policy approach rather than linguistic confederation should occasion little surprise.

It is possible, of course, that Latino public opinion on this matter
might shift in favor of a policy of linguistic confederation, thereby stimulating a move toward the aims articulated by Barrera for Chicanos.
Ironically, however, this shift would be most likely to occur under an
aggressively assimilative U.S. language policy, and not under a pluralistic language policy regime. This is so because, as anthropologist
George M. Scott, Jr. (1990) has persuasively demonstrated, "the degree
of an ethnic group's identity will vary in direct proportion to the
amount of opposition encountered by the group; the greater the opposition, the greater the degree of identity, and conversely, the lesser the
amount of opposition, the lesser the degree of identity" (p. 163). Mounting a vigorously assimilative, anti-"foreign"-language campaign tar-
geting Spanish for elimination from the public spaces of the U.S.
Southwest, as seems to be favored by some nativist communitarian
assimilationists, far more likely would result in support for an organized campaign for Spanish-dominant confederationist language
regions than would a bilingual, pluralist language policy approach. In
any case, the political odds remain very strongly against a successful
policy of linguistic confederation for most language minority persons in
the United States.

8 Pluralistic Integration
Toward Greater Justice and a More Common Good

CHAPTER 7 argued that there are important flaws in each of the language policy alternatives for the United States. The case for an assimilationist policy is compelling only if you are willing to deny equal opportunity to language minority group members in this country. This is so because of two stubborn facts that assimilationists tend to ignore. First, assimilationists ignore the fact that our history has constituted the United States a multilingual, multicultural country not only through individual voluntary immigration, but also through violence and contested annexation. And second, most assimilationists ignore the fact that government cannot be neutral toward a country's languages and cultures. Hopefully, Chapter 7 demonstrated clearly that the combination of these two facts renders the moral argument for an assimilationist language policy untenable for the United States. The assimilationist position cannot meet the test of justice because it both violates the liberal democratic norm of equal respect for individuals *and* reinforces the hidden hierarchy of racialized ethnicity that is normalized by Anglo hegemony in the United States. Any language policy that works toward justice and a truly common good must come to terms with the reality of these facts, which necessarily moves its role beyond that of seeking only the most efficient means for inducing a language shift to English by members of language minority groups.

Chapter 7 demonstrated as well, however, that the primary alternative to assimilation—pluralism—also has several flaws that need to be addressed if this policy approach is to be worthy of adoption and implementation. In particular, pluralists must face the hard reality that, in a context of hegemonic English-language domination (which is surely the case in the United States), bilingual English-Plus programs operating through individual voluntary choice are not likely to result in either status equality or long-term maintenance for minority languages. This is because, on the one hand, if such programs are successful at providing fluent mastery of English to minority language speakers, these individuals (or certainly their children) are very likely to shift from bilingualism toward monolingual English-speaking. On the other hand, if such programs are not successful at providing fluent mastery of English to minority language speakers, those individuals who are failed thereby are effectively relegated to marginalized and subordinate positions in the American political economy. In either case, if equal justice requires individual and/or societal bilingualism, it is very unlikely that a liberal, or free choice, pluralistic language policy approach will be successful at creating or maintaining that condition.

In view of these flaws in both the assimilationist and pluralist policy approaches, Chapter 7 explored the advisability of a confederationist language policy approach for the United States, which would create domains of minority language dominance through the establishment of separate territories or regions controlled by minority language groups. It was argued that, while such an arrangement might seem to offer advantages for ensuring the long-term stability of minority languages in the United States, confederation is not a viable solution for ensuring greater equality for most language minorities in this society[1] because most members of language minority groups reside in metropolitan regions, where they are only one part of the complex multiethnic mosaic of urban America. Minority language territories carved out of such mainstream, English-dominant urban areas, further, would face overwhelming social, political, and economic odds against realizing greater equality for the groups the policy seeks to aid, resulting once more in a high probability of continued marginalization and subordination along with ethnic separation. In sum, Chapter 7's critical analysis of language policy alternatives for the United States found flaws at every turn.

CLARIFYING THE CONTEXT

Despite the evident weaknesses in every available approach to language policy in the United States, avoiding the challenge of shaping such a policy would be a serious mistake. With respect to justice and the common good, making no policy decision has as much impact on our world as does making a decision. In that spirit, the task of this final chapter is to move toward a resolution of our public policy "language wars" by articulating my own view of the best possible approach for language policy in the United States today. Before doing so, it will be helpful to clarify the context for developing such a policy. We will begin by putting into perspective once again what we now know about the social and political situation regarding language diversity in the United States. Arriving at the best possible solution to our language policy conflict rests on a clear understanding of what is really at stake.

First, it should be kept firmly in mind that there is no realistic threat to the overwhelmingly dominant, indeed hegemonic, status enjoyed by the English language in the United States. Despite the fears of many assimilationists and the possible hopes of a few ethnic nationalists, there is no real possibility that English will be displaced—or even rivaled—as the language of power in any region of the United States in the foreseeable future.[2] In terms of national identity, it is clear that most people in the United States have no question that English is the country's "national" language. And, since 1906 the United States has required immigrants to demonstrate their fluency in English before being naturalized as citizens (DeSipio and de la Garza, 1998: 70). No influential participant in the language policy debates of the last thirty years has proposed to Congress that this powerful nationalist requirement be rescinded. Further, while an influx of immigrants has brought greater language diversity to the United States in recent decades, there is no evidence of their resistance to rapid acquisition of English fluency—organized or spontaneous—among any language minority population. Nor have pluralist political activists urged anyone to retain their native language at the expense of English-language mastery. As we have seen, moreover, the vast majority in the largest non-English-language group in the country—Spanish-speakers—are eager to learn English as quickly as possible. There is every reason to believe that the same is true of other non-English-language groups (e.g., the many language groups composed mainly of immigrants from Asia). And there is not even the hint of an effective political movement for a policy of linguistic confederation in the metropolitan United States. Putting the issue into an international context makes the picture even clearer: Due to technological and economic forces, as we have seen, English is literally conquering the world linguistically. Not only are most non-English-speaking residents of the United States eagerly trying to master English, so are most upwardly mobile residents in almost every country on the globe. Viewing English as a threatened language under these circumstances seems bizarre.

However, it is *equally true* that languages other than English have been native to the United States since before its inception as an independent country. And it is a near certainty as well that languages other than English will continue to be a public presence in the United States for the foreseeable future. In many metropolitan areas and media markets throughout the country, in short, all people today can expect to continue hearing the sounds of languages other than English on the airwaves and in the malls, streets, and shops for as long they live. And this will remain true even in the face of any conceivable language policy that is also politically feasible. Without truly draconian police-state measures, the notion that the United States will—or even can—become a monolingual English-speaking nation within the next century is just as fantastic as the belief that English dominance will be challenged by another language.

In this context, the central language policy conflict is not about the continued dominance of the English language as such, but over how the country should deal with its other languages in public policy. And here, as we have seen, the primary issue is not language per se, but social identities, and their relationship to justice and the common good. In general, the languages generating the most controversy have important links to ethnic identities with deep historical roots and evoke powerful memories of racialized conquest, annexation, and domination. As we have seen, moreover, most of these ethnically significant languages (especially Spanish) are also shared by those who have been the largest groups of immigrants to the United States during the last three decades. Language, then, is an important ingredient in the political conflict, but the central issue motivating that conflict is the nature of the American people and their relationships with one another. Within this identity politics context, further, it is important to remember that language policy conflict is powerfully shaped by the racialized ethnic inequality that overlaps with linguistic and cultural diversity. Simply put, the life chances of U.S. language minority group members today are shaped not only by language difference but also by structured ethnic inequalities in which culture, language, class, and race are deeply intertwined. Economics and the processes of racialization are also implicated in the social and political context of the language policy debate. Finding a way to deal appropriately with social identities and language diversity must include coming to terms with this racialized ethnic inequality as well.

PLURALISTIC INTEGRATION: A LANGUAGE POLICY PROPOSAL

The argument that I want to make here is that, despite its flaws, an enhanced pluralist language policy offers the best possibility of promoting ethnolinguistic justice and the common good. Borrowing a concept from historian John Higham (1984: 242), I propose a language policy that aims for *pluralistic integration.* Writing to revise and strengthen Horace Kallen's (1924 [1970]) influential concept of cultural pluralism, Higham (1984) suggested that pluralistic integration be understood as having the following characteristics:

> In contrast to the integrationist [i.e., assimilationist] model, it will not eliminate ethnic boundaries. But neither will it maintain them intact. It will uphold the validity of a common culture, to which all individuals have access, while sustaining the efforts of minorities to preserve and enhance their own integrity. . . . Both integration and ethnic cohesion are recognized as worthy goals. (p. 244)

In sketching out a language policy proposal that aims at pluralistic integration, it is best to begin by clarifying the goals that are at stake. This will be followed by an outline of the major components of an appropriate language policy. In the next section of the chapter I will attempt to show that the language policy presented here would best meet the needs of the United States and its language minorities.

Clarification of Goals

As we have seen at length, the discourse over language policy in this country, as elsewhere, revolves around two sets of intertwining policy values—justice and the common good. Focusing on the issue of justice directs our attention toward how the polity's social groups are treated in relation to the benefits and burdens of the common life. Attending to the issue of the common good, in turn, directs us toward examining the impacts of a policy—its benefits and burdens—for all of us, for the country as a whole.

The goal of social justice has been defined appropriately in the language policy debate in terms of achieving greater equality between ethnolinguistic groups. But language is related to equality in several important ways. In a country in which English is the dominant language of opportunity, success, and power, first, the inability to function fluently in this language is a formidable barrier to social mobility and equality. Second, however, recognition of the United States as a multi-lingual and multicultural country requires that access to minority languages be maintained and that effective protections against discrimination and the racialization of minority languages and minority language groups be provided. A language policy aiming at greater social equality must come to terms with *both* of these dimensions.

In relation to language policy, aiming for the common good should be understood as working to ensure that the benefits and burdens, the blessings and the obligations, of our mutual memberships in the American polity are truly common. With respect to the goal of social peace and political harmony over the long term, this specifically requires trying to ensure that public policies do not function to the benefit of some groups at the expense of other groups. In the context of this country's constitutive social diversity, therefore, a conception of national unity that reflects a truly common good must be understood as entailing *both* difference and interdependence. As Aristotle (1998: 1263. 35), put it so well in his criticism of Plato's *Republic*, harmony should not be misunderstood as requiring unison.[3] True national unity will thus be based on a social peace that derives from social justice and a shared commitment to the well-being of all.

Elements of a Language Policy for Pluralistic Integration

As a beginning step, federal, state, and local governments should make clear their intent to realize a pluralistic integration of the country's language diversity by adopting a strong version of the English-Plus Resolution. As noted in Chapter 1, this resolution asks U.S. governments not only to support the widest possible access to English fluency, but in addition to (1) "conserve and develop the Nation's linguistic resources by encouraging all residents of this country to learn or maintain skills in a language other than English"; (2) to assist indigenous peoples "in their efforts to prevent the extinction of their languages and cultures"; and (3) to "continue to provide services in languages other than English as needed to facilitate access to essential functions of government, promote public health and safety, ensure due process, promote equal educational opportunity, and protect fundamental rights" (Serrano, 1997). This resolution, in turn, would provide a generalized commitment for the following specific language policy elements:

1. Dual-language, two-way bilingual education should be offered to as many language minority children as possible and to as many monolingual English-speakers as possible as well. The aim should be to develop fluency and full literacy in two languages: English *plus* another language. Typically, the other language should be the home language of language minority students, where that is feasible, and the most widely used non-English language, where that is not feasible. Ultimately, the goal should be bilingual fluency for all public school students in the United States.
2. Funding of English-language classes in areas with high concentrations of non-English-speakers should be greatly increased. No permanent resident or citizen should be denied access to fluency and literacy in the country's dominant language for lack of funding.
3. Generous funding is needed to implement the Native American Languages Act. As this largely unimplemented law recognizes, indigenous languages are precious national resources that should not be lost.
4. Continuance of the language minority provisions of the Voting Rights Act, as amended in 1992, is crucial. No person eligible to vote in the United States should be prevented from doing so because he or she is not literate in English, but is literate in another language.
5. In areas with high concentrations of minority languages, the provision of public services in those languages should be facilitated through the hiring of bilingual civil servants, as well as via written and oral communications with the public. The goal should be full access to public services in the language of the community.
6. Following examples such as those found in Canada and Australia, U.S. governments should provide public funds to nongovernmental organizations (NGOs) and community-based organizations (CBOs) operated by language minority communities, thereby enabling them to provide a mix of needed services and cultural support to their members in the languages of those communities.
7. Using the EEOC guidelines as a model, the Civil Rights Act of 1964 should be amended to indicate clearly that unlawful national origin discrimination specifically includes discrimination against the languages of minority groups (see Chapter 1).

In addition to these language-specific policy proposals, a successful language policy of pluralistic integration needs to be linked with two other vitally important public policy initiatives:

1. Recognizing that most non-English-speakers in the United States today are recent migrants to this country, a substantial and concerted immigrant settlement policy is needed. This policy initiative should have dual aims: (a) to help newcomers adapt to their adopted country through programmatic assistance in areas such as adult education, housing, health, and employment; and (b) to stimulate and encourage the immigrants' incorporation into the country's political community.
2. For reasons to be explained below, high priority must be given to complementing all of the above measures with a major public policy effort aimed at reducing the growing economic inequality in the United States.

Why Pluralistic Integration?

If the public values of justice and the common good are accepted as touchstones for resolving the U.S. dispute over language diversity, the language policy components outlined above are justified by reasoning that can be summarized as follows.

Language-Specific Policy Components

As we have seen, the dualistic reality of English-language hegemony on the one hand *and* constitutive ethnolinguistic diversity in the United States on the other seems to point in opposite directions: toward the acquisition of universal English fluency *and* toward the need to support and protect threatened minority languages. To maintain openness in both directions, a conception of linguistic justice that is not only inclusive toward all individuals in the national community but also aware and protective of the integrity of diverse individual social identities is needed. While not a perfect solution, the most appropriate general response to these dual realities is surely a policy that aims at wide societal access to fluent *bi*lingualism, supplemented by specific protections for those who have not attained English-language fluency. By working to ensure that all school-age language minority members become fluently bilingual, this policy gives them full access to the country's dominant English language while also enabling them to retain and master their heritage languages with respect and dignity. By working toward bilingual fluency for *all* U.S.

students, the policy is integrative, rather than segregative, giving members of the majority cultural community access to and greater respect for cultures other than their own. As the President's Commission on Foreign Languages and International Studies (1979) argued so powerfully, moreover, this policy would also contribute to the common good by enabling our people to operate more effectively in the globalized political economy of the twenty-first century.

In addition to aiming for bilingual fluency on the part of as many people as possible, my proposed policy also includes protections and support for those who have not attained fluency in English. These aspects of the policy are necessary for several reasons. First, it is unrealistic to expect that most of the millions of persons in our country who did not gain English fluency as children will ever become fully fluent in the national language. This is not how second-language acquisition works in most cases (see, e.g., Rumbaut, 1997: 950–51). Second, as we have seen, it is wrong to view English as the sole legitimate public language of the United States, and therefore it is unjust to base public policy on the premise that not speaking English is "un-American" or even a "handicap" to full access to civil and political rights. Third, because it is important to us all that bilingual individuals have access to U.S. language communities other than English, publicly supported efforts are needed to help nourish and maintain those communities. This is necessary because, as we have seen, powerful market and culturally hegemonic forces are at work to undermine and diminish the vitality of those communities. My proposed policy, therefore, not only protects language minority members from discrimination, but also supports language minority communities through vigorous promotional efforts. For reasons spelled out in the critical analysis of Chapter 7, however, it does not aim for full-fledged linguistic confederation.[4]

Enlisting and supporting NGOs and CBOs in efforts to provide services and cultural events in minority language communities offers a flexible and potentially rich method for increasing the number of public spaces in which languages other than English can continue to function. Within the complex fluidity of urban regions, they provide a handy way to support minority ethnic communities aiming at higher levels of institutional completeness, without adopting the formalized and segregated territories required by linguistic confederation.[5] Of course, for that very reason these avenues offer less stability and security for long-term maintenance of minority languages and cultures within the hegemonic cultural space of U.S. cities. There is no way to avoid this risky trade-off, however, except to opt for the manifest disadvantages of linguistic confederation, which, again, is not advisable in these metropolitan settings.

To better envision the idea of a language policy supportive of pluralistic integration, it is useful once again to draw upon the wisdom of John Higham (1984), who suggests that the "dual commitment" to both pluralism and integration "can be met by distinguishing between boundaries and nucleus" (p. 244). What he means is that the membership of any particular individual in an ethnolinguistic community should be voluntary; the general community should not employ the power of the state to help any ethnic group police its boundaries. While "all boundaries are understood to be permeable," he argues, "ethnic nuclei," on the other hand, should be "respected as enduring centers of social action" (Higham, 1984: 244). And as we have seen, there are good reasons for providing general public support to the "nuclei" of minority language communities, enabling them to maintain a higher level of vitality against the homogenizing forces of the market and the cultural hegemony of the dominant society. In a complex, urbanized society, moreover, some individuals will experience themselves—whether through personal choice or social circumstances—as living in or close to the nucleus of their ethnic identities. Others, however, will experience themselves as living closer to highly permeable ethnic boundaries, in which their ethnic identities are little more than memories derived from talks with their grandparents. The aim should be to make both kinds of experience a matter of personal choice rather than social imposition.

This kind of pluralistic integration, Higham (1984) further suggests, "requires a general acceptance of complexity and ambiguity" (p. 245).[6] More specifically, I think, it requires that we move beyond a persistent misunderstanding of multiculturalism in relation to social identity. A good portion of the assimilationist reflex stems from the widespread assumption that individual social identity is an "either/or" proposition, and from an inability or unwillingness to distinguish between the *integrative* function of pluralism and the *segregative* function of confederation. The assimilationist argument is based on the supposition that bilingualism and biculturalism are not really possible. Similarly, it seems to take for granted the assumption that an individual cannot have an ethnic identity and also be a committed and loyal nationalist. This means, for example, that if I assertively identify myself with pride as being "Latino," I cannot also perceive myself as being fully "American," sharing a strong sense of common membership and common destiny with other Americans who are not Latinos. In this view, my ethnic identity divides me from others in a way that threatens our commonality as Americans in some deeply disturbing way. From this monoculturalist position, if English is the language of Americans, and if I insist on speaking Spanish in public places, by this "defiant" act I am dividing myself from Americans, announcing myself as being someone who is separate, as being a Latino.

In this vision so supportive of assimilationism (or confederation, for that matter), these imagined communities—"American" and "Latino"—are separate, monad-like in their composition, akin to billiard balls bumping against each other on a felt-covered table. Further, language is a critical determinant of the boundaries between these communities—even more, in some cases, than is skin color. For some, speaking Spanish in public puts me outside the pale of "normal" American identity even more quickly and surely than does having a dark skin or Asian features. This is because language use, contrary to one's outward appearance, is perceived by many as a *voluntary* act. It may be for this reason that the language issue strikes such a deep chord in the hearts of many assimilationists. Speaking Spanish in public not only separates me from you; it is also my defiant, in-your-face *rejection* of you. Not understanding what is being said makes you feel like a rejected stranger in your own land.

In the most immediate sense, this heartfelt and pained backlash against minority language use is one of the driving forces for the linguistic assimilationist movement. But this "either/or" reading of the situation is based on a misperception of the possibilities of both personal identity and human association. It is because many of us have been trained to perceive group identities as mutually exclusive that we "see" and "feel" the division and rejection described above. In fact, however, many Americans do *not* perceive themselves as so divided: For them it is perfectly possible, even natural, to understand themselves as both ethnic and fully American. Similarly, for many Americans it is possible and even natural to think of themselves as bilingual and bicultural, at ease in both Spanish and English, in both the dominant *national* culture and in their own *ethnic* culture.

In this respect, it is very important to articulate clearly the appropriate meaning of multiculturalism in relation to social identity. Public support for a language policy of pluralistic integration depends crucially on its widespread recognition as inclusive and integrative, rather than as exclusive and segregative. Nothing has been a deeper obstacle to the political success of the English-Plus agenda than the prevailing acceptance of "bilingualism" as a code-word for "non-English monolingualism."[7] Many Americans, that is, routinely use the word "bilingual" to mean someone who speaks Spanish (or another minority language) *but not English*. In similar fashion, nothing has undercut the moral influence of multiculturalism in U.S. politics more than the fact that it is commonly misunderstood as aimed at erecting walls of difference between mutually exclusive ethnic communities.

Multiculturalism as pluralistic integration, properly understood, is a form of cosmopolitanism. It is cosmopolitan because it historically contextualizes, and supports as valuable, varied social identities while yet affirming our common humanity and interdependence. Some critics of multiculturalism, however, see it as incompatible with cosmopolitanism.[8] A cosmopolitanism that would require *you* to forgo *your* differences from me, however, is a strangely narrow and monistic—not to say presumptuous—form of cosmopolitanism. In contrast, aiming toward a mutual understanding of the historical foundations for and the values of other cultures and languages builds respect for them, allowing us to reach our fellow human beings across ethnic and national boundaries. Learning another language enables me not only to understand and respect a different world but also to contextualize my own cultural world, thus making *me* more cosmopolitan by enhancing my recognition of our common humanity as well as the rich variety of the human experience. The people of the United States are deeply blessed as potential heirs to multiple languages, each of which is a door to rich human and cultural treasures, to profound expressions of the joys and the inevitable pains of human existence. A just language policy must aim to give us access to a broader range of these inherited treasures. Further, the multiplicity of our linguistic heritage is a foundation for our continued cultural vitality as a nation. For this reason, a fully developed U.S. language policy would aim at bilingualism (or more) for *all* educated individuals in the country—majority as well as minority—as is routinely accepted in most countries in Europe and around the globe.

Ultimately, ameliorating the injustices deriving from the knots of difference requires us to return to the cognitive paradoxes of personal and social identity sketched out in Chapter 2. That is, it is vitally important to come to terms with the reality that each of our personal and social identities is inseparably linked to our difference. In order to be *me*, I need *you* to be different from me. At the same time, however, I need you to be similar enough to me that you can recognize me/us, validate me, and help me/us become myself. Since different circumstances may also make me into a different *me*, moreover, I must recognize the multipotentiality of my self. That is, I must accept that the difference that makes you *you* and *not me*, in other circumstances could have made me more like you than the *me* that I "know" as myself. At one level, this point is the same as that made by the old saying, "There but for fortune go I." While that is accurate as far as it goes, the reality is even deeper and more complex: Not only could circumstances have given me your fate, but we now need each other to be different in order to be ourselves. And while each of us needs differences among people, we each also need the confidence to know that at some level others are enough like ourselves that they can help us realize our selves.

If I am deeply fearful of my own potential to be different (that is, to be like "*them*"), however, I may feel compelled to try to suppress or eliminate the sources of that fear. This dynamic of fear of difference may be the foundation for the persistent misunderstanding that causes so many of us to see segregated, non-English-language enclaves where those same so-called separatists see themselves as highly integrated bilingual and bicultural pluralists.[9] It is possible that this fear of "otherness" has origins in the very processes of individual identity formation, as some psychoanalysts and political theorists have argued (see, e.g., Young, 1990: chap. 5). Around the globe and throughout recorded human history, certainly, many peoples have shared the belief that those who speak languages different from theirs, who have cultural traditions and practices that appear "strange," and/or who have physical characteristics marking them as outsiders, are so *essentially* different that it must be impossible for all to enjoy equal membership in the same political community. Those who share this viewpoint believe that if those "others" cannot be made like themselves in language, culture, and/or physical appearance, then "they" must be kept outside the boundaries of community membership. This attitude has been a common one, perhaps even the dominant one, throughout the history of the world. Our own past is replete with examples showing that Americans too have often been unable to overcome the temptation to demonize those whose differences seem to render them essentially "other," a consciousness that embodies the very meaning of racialization.[10]

It would be foolish to believe that these oft-indulged impulses and misunderstandings can be easily or quickly eliminated from our consciousness and behavior, particularly when that consciousness and behavior is informed and sustained by a hegemonic cultural structure. Nevertheless, whatever its origins or its ubiquitousness in the world, it is necessary to challenge and overcome the fear of "otherness" that seems to drive the movement for a monolingual and monocultural conception of the American people. The world has become far too intertwined—and inescapably incorporated into our own country—to sustain such cultural and personal fears. Finding ways to overcome them remains one of the most important challenges to our national political consciousness. Once these fears are understood and contextualized, most of us would be able to recognize that an English-only conception of our national "imagined community" is not in accord with either the highest standards of justice or the common good in the United States.

In contrast, the policy proposals outlined above meet the test of justice by providing both the public institutional support for inclusive integration of language minority group members *and* institutional support and legal protections for the speakers of U.S. languages other than English. In this sense, the policy seeks to attend to both aspects of the language minority struggle for greater equality. In addition, these proposals meet the test of promoting the common good because they improve the whole country by moving toward an inclusive and just foundation for social peace and national unity, thus bringing us together without disparaging the valuable contributions of our multiple ethnolinguistic communities, and by providing greater understanding and support for our more effective participation in a globalized political economy.

Enhanced Immigrant Settlement Policy

By themselves, however, the language-specific components of my proposed policy for pluralistic integration are insufficient for successfully resolving our national conflict over language policy. One of the legitimate concerns underlying the assimilationist critique of the pluralist agenda is the latter's seeming lack of attention to the social and political disruptions that accompany large-scale immigration, and to the social responsibilities of immigrants in their new home. It is true, after all, that most non-English-speakers in the United States today are recent immigrants. And most recent immigrants, additionally, have chosen to come to the United States voluntarily. The pluralist claim that the involuntary "minoritization" of many recent immigrants warrants their inclusion in minority protection programs does not in itself address the reciprocal obligations of immigrants to their new country. How is the country as a whole made better off by granting language rights and support to immigrants—even to those who are inducted into racialized ethnic communities with little choice in the matter—unless they too have obligations to adapt themselves to their host country?

Having an insufficient answer to this question weakens the case for a pluralistic language policy, and leaves pluralists open to hostility and ridicule by their critics. Properly understood, of course, the language-specific aspects of the pluralistic integration policy outlined above already go some distance toward resolving this issue. That is, immigrants already necessarily make numerous adjustments to their new home. As noted, for example, immigrants are already required to learn English in order to become U.S. citizens. Further, the vast majority of immigrants need little policy incentive to acquire motivation to learn English—market forces and the pervasiveness of the majority culture provide tremendously strong incentives already. To reduce their disruptive impact on the communities in which they settle, what is needed are more institutionalized opportunities for learning English and other help in integrating into their new communities. The programs outlined above would provide greater access to English-language learning for both immigrant youth and working immigrant adults. Providing more assistance in finding housing, employment, health, and educational opportunities in a new and strangely different society would also offer a more secure foundation from which immigrants can make more successful and prosperous contributions to the general economy as well as to their own well-being.

In addition, however, it would be good to provide recent arrivals to the United States with positive incentives and institutionalized opportunities for recognizing that they have important roles to play in improving and maintaining of their neighborhoods, cities, states, and new country. Understandably, many immigrants are focused on their country of origin's political and economic circumstances, and sometimes they are expecting to return home in the near future as well (see, e.g., Jones-Correa, 1998; Portas and Rumbaut, 1996). And, while many do return home—at least for a time—most do not. In this context, it will help both immigrants and the country as a whole to stimulate more recent arrivals to recognize that their neighborhood schools need their participation and support if their own children—and the children of their neighbors—are to prosper and flourish. Similarly, the time, energy, and attention—as well as tax dollars—of immigrants are needed to attend to other neighborhood, city, state, and national concerns. Cities such as Los Angeles, Miami, New York, El Paso—and hundreds of others—cannot effectively meet the challenges facing them unless large percentages of recent immigrants feel that these challenges are their own, and that they too are responsible for the evolving quality of life in their immediate surroundings.

Many immigrants, of course, have already taken up these challenges and responsibilities in highly energetic and creative ways under frequently difficult circumstances. However, a more coherent and elaborate immigrant settlement policy is needed, and one founded on principles of mutual obligation, as well as on the immediate needs of recent immigrants, would offer many advantages for both immigrants and for the entire country.[11] There is no need, however, to leap from support for the principle of mutual obligation to the conclusion that immigrants should be pressured to assimilate to English-only monolingualism or to give up their cultural practices and traditions. While they are learning English, and continuing thereafter, publicly funded, ethnically oriented community-based organizations could provide highly effective institutional means for connecting recent immigrants to their new social and political environment. These connections, in turn, could enable them to see new ways in which they can contribute to the amelioration of social problems in their new communities and enhance the well-being of their new country.[12] Citing evidence from a U.S. study of immigrant incorporation politics (Harles, 1993), political philosopher Will Kymlicka (1995) summarizes the point nicely:

> It has become clear that the overwhelming majority of immigrants want to integrate, and have in fact integrated, even during the periods of large-scale influxes. Moreover, they care deeply about the unity of their new

country. To be sure, they want the mainstream institutions in their society to be reformed, so as to accommodate their cultural differences, and to recognize the value of their cultural heritage. But the desire for such polyethnic rights is a desire for inclusion which is consistent with participation in, and commitment to, the mainstream institutions that underlie social unity. (p. 178)

The underlying rationale for this immigrant settlement program, in short, is that reaching out expansively and proactively to draw recent immigrants into community-building activities, thereby helping them to find roles through which to connect their personal well-being with the common good, will pay far greater dividends than will a mean-spirited, immigrant-bashing campaign to demand their immediate cultural and linguistic assimilation. Integrative, rather than segregative, this approach fosters greater national unity as well by addressing common problems through collaborative effort.[13]

Economic Egalitarian Measures

Equally important for enhancing the prospects of success of a policy of pluralistic integration is the need to attend to the growing economic inequality in the United States, especially as it intersects with and reinforces our racialized ethnic inequality. Without greater material equality among social groups, cultural pluralism is a formula for the continued marginalized domination of language minority groups. As an agenda for democratic respect, linguistic pluralism presumes social equality, but by itself cannot achieve this goal. In light of this reality, as we saw in Chapter 7, one fundamental weakness in the contemporary English-Plus agenda is its inability to overcome the structural barriers to social equality for language minority group members. As a consequence, minority languages are destabilized and members of minority language groups are faced with an unjust choice between a risky assimilation strategy for greater individual social mobility and an equally risky strategy of cohesive ethnolinguistic community. The former strategy is risky because the imposition of a racialized identity does not necessarily end with the acquisition of English-language fluency; the latter strategy is risky because it may well result in continued economic, social, and political marginalization and subordination.

The promise of pluralistic integration is that we can become a more democratic community of common purpose without requiring those of us who are "different" to deny and/or abandon important aspects of our identities. Most participants in the language policy debates, we have seen, seem to agree that both justice and national unity require more equality between ethnolinguistic groups. But the presence of significant material inequality makes the realization of pluralistic integration more problematic for at least two reasons. First, because of the tight knot linking certain minority languages with racialized identities and lower-class status (see Chapter 7), high levels of material or class inequality make much more difficult the reconceptualization of biculturalism and bilingualism as integrative rather than segregative, called for above in my defense of the language-specific portions of this policy.

To illustrate this point with the most prominent example, in most parts of the United States Latinos who use Spanish in public continue to be marked as racialized "others" and marginalized as outsiders[14] because most members of the general public appear not to see Spanish as a genuinely *American* language.[15] Removing the socially constructed, but barely conscious, linkage between culture, racial identity, and social class would make visible a wider range of personal and social possibilities. Remove the stigma of lower-class status and racial features, for example, and most of us see bilingualism not only as possible but as a personal enhancement. Few Americans would say that a blond-haired, blue-eyed, Anglo-surnamed U.S. citizen in a nicely tailored business suit is disadvantaged by the fact that he speaks fluent Spanish as well as English, or that he cannot "really" be bilingual or bicultural. And U.S. advertisers know that "accented" English is not necessarily a mark of low status, as indicated by their frequent use of French- and British-accented English-speakers to signify product associations with elegance and high social standing. Put differently, surely part of the fear and rejection driving the assimilationist reflex comes from difference that is based fundamentally in economics and class distinction, not language.

As we saw at length in Chapter 7, moreover, the second way in which material inequality undercuts the promise of pluralistic integration is that it creates very powerful material incentives to assimilate fully to the dominant culture and language as a means of personal advancement. Persons who are poor and culturally different often experience great personal pressure to give up their heritage language and culture in the hopes that so doing will improve their life chances of greater success in the highly competitive U.S. political economy. In this way, the pluralist attempt to keep open the personal choice for membership in a vital heritage ethnolinguistic community is deeply threatened by the destabilizing forces of market incentive and cultural hegemony.

From this angle of vision, one of the central challenges in building a successful language policy of pluralistic integration is to "de-racialize" and to "de-class" minority American languages such as Spanish. Enhancing a policy regime of linguistic pluralism with policies building the foundations for greater economic equality would constitute one important and necessary step toward unlinking lower-class status and minority language use. Greater material equality in the United States, that is, would provide a necessary environment, of positive social support for the symbolic status-enhancement mechanisms of bilingual programs in education, voting rights, employment, and social services. More personally, if my economic and social standing were to place me at roughly the same status as you (an "Anglo" American), I might feel less compelled by my circumstances to give up a treasured heritage language as the necessary price of admission to a life with some measure of public achievement, personal respect, and human dignity. And further, you would perhaps be less likely to misrecognize my bilingualism as a threatening rejection of your/our way of life and national community. In Kymlicka's philosophical language of liberal justice employed in Chapter 7, this enhancement to linguistic pluralism would add a necessary economic dimension to the culturally egalitarian "context of choice" that is required if individuals are to be treated justly in a multicultural state.

This is not the place to fully describe a set of policy proposals for greater economic equality, but it *is* the place to point out that many such proposals already exist in public discourse and on the political agenda. Further, much of this discourse is in agreement on the necessity to link the search for greater racial justice in the United States with a drive for greater economic equality.[16] What is needed is to link these intellectual and political efforts to achieve greater racial and economic justice with efforts to realize justice for ethnolinguistic minorities in the United States.

Of course, the prospects for such a policy drive for greater economic inequality are daunting under present circumstances. The large-scale growth of minority languages during the last three decades has coincided in time with a massive and globally-motivated economic restructuring in the United States. And the combination of these two factors has worked to reinforce—rather than reduce—key parts of the tangled knot of class, race, and language. The gap between rich and poor in the United States is greater now, at the end of this three-decade restructuring, than it has been at any time since World War II. Not coincidentally, the important mechanism of social mobility—the middle-class way of life that was accessible to relatively unskilled and unschooled unionized workers in large-scale and centralized industrial enterprises—which was available to several previous generations of "newcomers" to the U.S. political economy, has atrophied in this restructuring.

In light of these trends, it is important to emphasize that the consequent "downsizing" in opportunity and well-being for large segments of the American populace is not due to any moral or personal shortcomings of those so affected. Low-income persons have not become less inclined to work hard on behalf of themselves or their families in the last several decades, just as those thrown out of work during the Great Depression of the 1930s were not rendered poor by their sudden loss of a work ethic. As well, there is bountiful evidence that most immigrant newcomers are working longer hours, at more jobs, than previous immigrants and than more established groups in an effort to counteract the effects of economic restructuring.

My central point is that these changes wrought by our economic restructuring have worked against the achievement of both justice and the common good for a United States conceived as an integrated democratic political community. Political theorist John H. Schaar made this point well even before the significant growth of this "opportunity gap" over the last several decades. Democratic equality, he argued, requires

> the establishment of the material conditions necessary for a generous measure of freedom of choice for all members of the community, and the establishment of the conditions necessary for relations of mutual respect and honesty among the various economic and social groups within a society. This is not some kind of leveling demand for equality of condition. It is no more than a recognition of the obvious fact that the great material inequality that prevails in America today produces too much brutishness, impotence, and rage among the lower classes, and too much nervous vulgarity among the middle classes. (Schaar, 1981: 204)

Rather than moving us toward the requirements of justice and a more common good, however, our most powerful governmental and economic institutions have charted a course in an opposite direction. The economic restructuring of the past several decades has been accompanied by reductions in governmental and private-sector programs targeted for lower-income working families (e.g., public spending on education, health care benefits, job training and retraining programs, and other social and physical infrastructure investments), relative to the expansion of benefits and opportunities available to those in upper-middle and upper income categories. The magnification of corporate profits and stock-market winnings in this period has been wrought not only by productivity growth, but also by relatively lower payments to labor and government. For purposes of this analysis, the point to emphasize is that because most of the "winners" in this political economic restructuring have been English-speaking European Americans, and a disproportionate number of the "losers" have been both native-born and immigrant peoples of color (many of whom are non-English-speakers), these changes have reinforced, rather than reduced, the links binding together the U.S. knot of race, class, and language.

A serious reversal of these trends through a concerted set of public policy initiatives—in combination with pluralistic language policy and immigrant settlement programs—would offer the best opportunity for enhancing the social mobility of U.S. language minority members while protecting their individual rights and equal respect as culture-bearing persons. As noted, breaking the link between language and lower-class status would better enable the symbolic recognition functions of programs designed to maintain and develop non-English-language use among U.S. language minorities. This unlinking requires an egalitarian social and material context that is deeper and richer in substance than can be provided by language policy alone.

At the same time, it is equally crucial to expand the ethnocultural and linguistic parts of the pluralist agenda, particularly in relation to the necessity of deracializing minority languages and cultural communities. Reenvisioning the United States as a multicultural and multiethnic nation is central to this process, so that the structural "normalization" of Euro-"whiteness" that has typified U.S. social relations since its founding is finally brought to a close.[17] It is for the reasons outlined above, then, that both justice and the common good will be met best through a public policy regime of pluralistic integration. And that regime, in turn, requires a combination of pluralistic language-specific policies, an enhanced immigrant settlement policy, and a concerted policy effort toward greater material equality.

TOWARD A POLITICS OF PLURALISTIC INTEGRATION

Having outlined and explained the virtues of a language policy of pluralistic integration does not mean, of course, that it will be adopted by our country's political authorities. That requires political support so powerful that it can overcome the immense forces of inertia in U.S. governments, in addition to the well-organized opposition that already exists to any pluralist language policy agenda. I have no illusions that overcoming these obstacles will be an easily realized goal.

Where might such powerful political support arise? As a beginning point, the discursive analysis contained in this book will, I hope, strengthen the conviction and political persuasiveness of those already supportive of linguistic pluralism in the United States. In particular, I hope that those now engaged in the struggle for an English-Plus language policy agenda—e.g., Latino, Asian/Pacific Islander, and Native American political leaders and activists; bilingual educators; civil rights organizations; and the like—will find in this book a substantial and persuasive analysis in support of their efforts. To be successful, however, much more political backing is needed. Following are some potential political sources from which to fashion a long-term strategy for obtaining political support for a policy of pluralistic integration.

Appeal to Assimilationists

If they are truly of an open mind, first, many thoughtful assimilationists should be able to recognize that their own goals are better served by a policy of pluralistic integration than a policy of forced assimilation. This should be true particularly of those assimilationists who are genuinely committed to greater justice for language minorities in the United States. To many committed to seeing more social equality for U.S. minorities, the hegemonic, commonsense reality of English-language dominance in this society makes linguistic assimilation seem an obviously necessary path to greater social mobility for non-English-speakers. Any language policy that fails to provide access to English-language fluency is, indeed, an obstacle to social mobility and greater equality under current conditions. I hope, however, that my analysis has been persuasive in showing that a simple English-only policy of linguistic assimilation is a path to continued injustice for U.S. language minorities. And I hope I have demonstrated effectively that the policy of pluralistic integration offers a much greater hope for ethnolinguistic justice than does English-only assimilation. This is because it offers both access to English-language fluency *and* the retention and protection of minority languages, thus enriching the lives of those thereby made bilingual and of the country as a whole as well.

As outlined at some length in Chapter 6, many assimilationists are even more concerned with the socially "divisive" character of a pluralistic language policy than they are about the issue of ethnolinguistic justice. They fear that a language policy supporting the use of languages other than English will thereby encourage the development of mutually antagonistic ethnic enclaves, led by self-promoting ethnocentric leaders more concerned with their own political advantage than with the needs of language minorities or with the common good.

These assimilationists too, on deeper reflection, should be persuaded that a language policy of pluralistic integration is much more likely to lead to greater national unity and to a truly common good than is a policy that tries to force English-only on an inherently diverse populace. This is so because this policy builds bridges between individuals and between communities by encouraging all of us to learn more about, and to gain greater respect toward, each other's cultural traditions and languages. If this policy were successfully implemented, not only would we have a common language—English—but we would also have access to multiple other *American* languages and language communities. This would enable more of us to understand the rich strength that comes from a genuine harmony, rather than the false and weak sameness that comes from unison. In addition, as I have argued, the notion that we can build national unity on a false social peace that robs some of their rights and their human dignity in order to convenience or advantage others, is not a worthy foundation for a truly *common* good. An honest rethinking, then, should convince many assimilationists that a language policy of pluralistic integration is more likely to reach their own stated goal of national unity than is a divisive campaign for English-only assimilation.

Of course, there are other assimilationists—"communitarian nativists," as I have termed them in this book—who oppose a pluralistic language policy, even an integrationist one, because they cannot imagine living contentedly in a society that contains multiple ethnolinguistic communities. These people seem to find offensive the very presence of "foreign" language communities in their own country. This group of assimilationists is not motivated, in truth, by either justice for all or by a truly common good, but rather by a vision of American nationhood that is exclusive and that is willing to tolerate as "one of us" only those who appear to be close replicas of themselves. This is a vision of unity that in our history has been responsible for the policies of racialized exclusion and domination that were repudiated in the 1960s, but that still form an important strain of thinking in our national civic culture. As Rogers Smith (1997) has demonstrated so thoroughly, this is an inegalitarian civic ideal of American nationhood that has stood alongside, and competed with, the civic ideals of liberalism and republicanism throughout our country's history.

I am sure that my analysis and arguments will not persuade those who are deeply motivated by this communitarian nativist way of thinking about American social and linguistic diversity. To them I can only urge: Think again; this country does not belong only to you. But my hope is that most assimilationists really do care about equal justice for language minorities and really do believe that a truly common good is the surest path to lasting national unity.

Appeal to the Political Center

As indicated in the introduction to this book, most Americans are probably unaware that language diversity has become a "hot" political issue. As Selma K. Sontagg (1990) has suggested, the issue has low salience for most people in this country. And to the extent that it does make it onto their political radar screens, these political centrists are most likely to engage it with a reflexively assimilationist response. This is due, I think, to the commonsense hegemonic power of the English language in U.S. society. To anyone with little knowledge of U.S. history and an awareness only of our mainstream cultural, economic, and political institutions, it must seem "obvious" that English is our *only* national language. Anyone who thinks otherwise clearly must be a "nut" or a political extremist. End of discussion.

Reaching this relatively uninvolved centrist population, which often functions as a swing vote in American elections and as the opinion poll touchstone for many U.S. politicians, is probably the most daunting challenge facing any effort to build broad political support for a language policy of pluralistic integration. As indicated, this policy approach, running against the preexisting conventional wisdom fostered by our hegemonic culture, requires a large capacity for both complexity and ambiguity. For that reason, pluralistic integration is not an easy concept to sell in electoral campaigns of twenty-second sound-bites, the prototypical method of appeal to this portion of the population. Because of its complexity and ambiguity, a language policy of pluralistic integration will necessarily depend on strong backing from influential political elites. Once political and other community leaders become aware of its benefits to the common good as well as to language minorities, there is reason to believe that a pluralistic integration policy can succeed.

One recent example of such a successful campaign can be found in Miami, Florida, where a coalition of local business, educational, and political leaders developed widespread support for an inclusive bilingual, bicultural educational program for *all* public school students. In March 1998 (almost simultaneously with California voters' adoption of Proposition 227), accordingly, the school board of the Dade County School District unanimously approved a plan to implement a dual-language, two-way Spanish-English bilingual education program for the district's 340,000 students from kindergarten through grade twelve (Anderson, 1998; Wheat, 1998).

According to news reports and an edited monograph (Fradd and Lee, 1998) prepared by University of Miami educators, the key to that city's political coalition was a shared belief that the whole community would be made better off through universal bilingualism, particularly through the economic benefits. University of Miami geographer Thomas Boswell's 1998 analysis of correlations between income and language use based on the 1990 Census was prominently featured at both the conference and in news reports in the community. Finding that in Florida there is a strong correlation between bilingualism and income, his analysis indicated, for example, that the average Latino Spanish-monolingual family of four had an income of $18,240 in 1990, whereas the average Latino English-monolingual family of four had an income of $32,800. However, an average Latino family of four that was fully bilingual in English and Spanish had an income of $50,376. Boswell suggests that it is most likely that the economic benefits of bilingualism have become even more pronounced since 1990 (Wheat, 1998).

That many centrist, mainstream Americans might be willing to support other elite-led campaigns for pluralistic integration is suggested by a 1998 *Los Angeles Times* op-ed piece written by David Hayes-Bautista, a prominent UCLA sociologist who reported on a focus-group public opinion study commissioned by the Mexican American Legal Defense and Education Fund (MALDEF) with the explicit charge of finding common ground between Anglos and Latinos in California. In two respects, Hayes-Bautista's findings seem to support the kind of political bridge-building effort called for here. The first finding reported is a marked change in Anglo Californians' expectations regarding the requisites for being an "American," a change that seems to be in close accord with the preference of many Latinos for a bicultural understanding of their national identity:

> Thirty years ago, said the Anglos who participated in the survey, there was a relatively definite idea of what an "American" was. Today, 80% of them feel that there are many possible definitions of "American-ness." Nearly the same percentage (76%) of Anglos feel that Latinos do not have to give up their culture to become part of American society. "Assimilation doesn't necessarily mean losing your own culture, but coming and coexisting with the culture that exists in a neighborhood," said one participant.
>
> The Anglos' major reservation was a fear that Latinos might be reluctant to claim and share a common ground with them. "It's good to have your independence and to keep your heritage and all that, but you still have to have a common denominator," one said.
>
> Interestingly, most Latinos agree with this. Another, earlier study strongly indicated that Latinos feel that it is as important to learn Anglo American ways as it is to carry on their own. In essence, the norm for Latinos is biculturalism. Assimilation is a "both/and" situation, not a stark "either/or" choice. (Hayes-Bautista, 1998: M1)

As reported in Chapter 3, the Latino National Political Survey found results in accord with this latter observation by Hayes-Bautista.

The second finding in the study bearing on my argument directly concerns language. If the approach to language policy recommended here is to gain centrist political support, it must be seen as truly *bilingual* (with English fluency) and as inclusive rather than exclusive. Hayes-Bautista (1998) indicates that when Anglos understand this as the goal, they are quite supportive of bilingualism for both Latinos and for their own children:

In surveys, Anglos consistently have said that Latinos should learn at least some English. But they also have said that learning English does not have to come at the expense of Spanish. In the MALDEF survey, more than 90% of the Anglos felt that Latinos should speak both English and Spanish. Less than 10% felt that Latinos should speak English only.

The worry expressed by Anglos was not that Latinos might want to maintain their Spanish, but, rather, that Latinos might not want to learn English. One focus-group participant said, "If they come to the U.S. as a grown-up, it's very difficult to learn English . . . but I think they should at least make the attempt."

Latinos agree with this sentiment. More than 90% of Latino adults in the MALDEF survey agreed that learning English is important, and that everyone in California should know some English.

Both Anglo and Latino parents also are concerned about their children's language skills. Both agree that people who know two languages are better equipped for success than those who know only one. The vast majority of Anglo and Latino parents would like their children to learn Spanish as well as English. (p. M6)

This report suggests that bilingual education advocates might have been able to fend off the success of Proposition 227, if they had been able to convince Anglo voters that the program was helping LEP children to become fluent in English and that Latinos more generally wanted to be fully included in U.S. society as equally participating, bicultural Americans. Developing a successful strategy to convince centrist voters that *bi*lingualism is what pluralistic integration can and will achieve—for their own children as well as for members of language minority groups—is a major task awaiting effective political leadership. While difficult, the examples given indicate that it is not an impossible task.

Appeal to the Democratic Left

Although gaining support from thoughtful assimilationists and from relatively unmotivated political centrists would be important for building a broad base of support for a policy of pluralist integration, perhaps the most critical element in such a campaign is the democratic left, that loose coalition of political activists and leaders usually found in the progressive wing of the Democratic party, and drawn from labor, antiracist organizations, feminist organizations, community activist groups, universities, and other progressive institutions. Terming this loose coalition a "group" is risky, of course, as in truth it is a highly diverse and often contentious array of organizations and individuals committed to a wide range of political activities. Nevertheless, this sector of the political spectrum has spearheaded virtually every twentieth-century effort to address the vitally important issues of economic inequality and racial injustice in the United States.

The analysis in this book should help to convince a broader range of these political progressives that the political agenda for social justice in the United States must include *ethnolinguistic* justice. That is, this book should facilitate a needed interrogation of the concepts of "class" and "race" that feature so prominently in the discourse of progressive democrats in this country. This analysis of language policy conflict as a form of identity politics should have demonstrated to those inclined toward a class-based politics that cultural forms and failures of recognition have very real material consequences for both "winners" and "losers." Similarly, it should have shown why those engaged in the struggle for social justice should not understand the issue of race in the United States solely in terms of a black/white dichotomy.

Let there be no misunderstanding: The struggle against the racialization experienced by African Americans is a central drama in the U.S. movement for social justice that must continue forcefully if democracy is to be achieved in this country. That drama, however, is not the whole story for the effort to realize greater racial justice in the United States. This effort must include attending to racialization processes experienced by many Latinos, Asian/Pacific Islanders, and Native Americans, and in these efforts language and other cultural forms play important roles not only in the processes of racialization but also in the effort to gain greater equality for members of these communities.

In this sense, it is important to note that many of the most important books published in recent years by progressive democratic intellectuals, books that attempt to revitalize and rethink the struggles for racial and economic justice, have not engaged this larger vision of American society.[18] Although making important contributions to our rethinking of the relationships between economic and racial injustice, for example, Roberto Unger and Cornel West's *The Future of American Progressivism* (1998) does not engage the role of ethnolinguistic difference as any part of the struggle for social justice. Nor does Unger's more fully developed *Democracy Revitalized* (1998), Appiah and Gutmann's wonderfully subtle analyses in *Color Conscious* (1996), or Jennifer L. Hochschild's well-researched and deeply thoughtful *Facing up to the American Dream*

(1995). Similarly, and with few exceptions, Adolph Reed, Jr.'s edited collection of essays, *Without Justice for All* (1999), which powerfully calls for a relinking of the struggles for racial and economic equality, defines the racial struggle almost exclusively in terms of a black/white dichotomy. "Race" is understood in virtually all of these important works as an exclusively black/white issue. Where ethnicity enters the picture at all, it is typically understood in terms of Euro-American white ethnics who feel threatened by black advances.

My point, again, is not that these analyses are wrong or that they are not important. Rather, it is that a successful national political campaign for pluralistic integration is unlikely unless the principal advocates for racial and economic justice in the United States embrace a conception of that struggle that includes linguistic and cultural injustice. This will require, in addition, that they incorporate into their understanding the experiences and aspirations of racialized ethnic groups for whom these are primary issues. This may not be an easy task. Los Angeles civil rights attorney Angela Oh, appointed a member of President Bill Clinton's Initiative on Race commission, for example, generated great controversy—both on the commission and outside it—by suggesting that this national conversation incorporate a multiracial, rather than biracial, understanding of the United States. Yet how can a truly national reckoning of racial injustice in the United States *not* incorporate the racialization processes of the groups in focus in this book? As black scholar Gerald Horne (1997) concluded in an op-ed essay in the *Los Angeles Times* reviewing the controversy over Oh's suggestions, "Discussions on race have to become more complex, more sophisticated—and all-encompassing—and soar far beyond the black-white dyad." An embrace by the democratic left of a language policy of pluralistic integration, in short, is indispensable in helping language minorities to more fully realize the promise of American democracy. At the same time, it would also help U.S. progressive leaders gain a more national and comprehensive understanding of the requisites of a democratic order in the United States.

Based on this book's complex understandings of language policy conflict as a form of identity politics, this concluding chapter has argued that the best policy approach—one that is realistic as well as congruent with the public values of justice and the common good—lies in pluralistic integration. Further, the chapter has assessed the most likely

sources of expanded political support for such a policy. Given the hegemonic cultural, political, and economic odds against it, adoption of a
language policy of pluralistic integration in the United States must seem
unlikely. Still, history records that highly improbable goals can be
reached by those who understood that the odds should never be
allowed to stand in the way of achieving justice and a more common
good.

Notes

Chapter 1

1. As of this writing, a heated campaign over an Unz-sponsored anti-bilingual education initiative was shaping up in Arizona.

2. I am grateful to Luis Fraga for bringing this important case to my attention.

3. Accent discrimination has been of particular concern to attorneys and political activists working on behalf of Asian/Pacific Americans (see, e.g., Imahara, 1993: 245–46).

4. For a thoughtful description of the U.S. legal system's presumption in favor of employer independence, see Moran, 1991: 810–13.

5. Raymond Tatalovich (1995) has written a very detailed and comprehensive study of official English legislation at the state level.

6. As of this writing, however, only twenty of these policies are in force. Arizona's was declared unconstitutional by the state supreme court, as noted below; and Alaska's 1998 policy was stayed by a judge, pending appeal by opponents claiming that the law is unconstitutional.

Chapter 2

1. It is acknowledged here that the term "minority" is problematic in contemporary scholarly discourse. As used here, "minority" is not a numerical signifier, but represents the descriptive perception that dominant ethnolinguistic groups have minoritized less powerful ethnic groups and their languages in multiple ways.

2. The most prominent exceptions, of course, were the leaders of Marxist-Leninist states during their heydays following the Soviet Revolution in Russia. Most scholars, however, believe that the ideology of Marxist internationalism never successfully overcame the political imperative to pursue the national interest as the top priority, even within what was known until the revolutions of 1989 as the "communist world." See, e.g., Connor, 1984.

3. Alexis de Tocqueville (1835 [1964]: 6) articulated the theme early in the nineteenth century:

In running over the pages of our history for seven hundred years, we shall scarcely find a single great event which has not promoted equality of condition. . . . The gradual development of the principle of equality is, therefore, a Providential fact. It has all the chief characteristics of such a fact: it is universal, it is durable, it constantly eludes all human interference, and all events as well as all men contribute to its progress.

4. One of the most powerful evocations of both misrecognition and non-recognition I have read is that of Ralph Ellison in *The Invisible Man* (1952 [1995]).

5. Both Rachel F. Moran (1987) and Raymond Tatalovich (1995) describe U.S. language politics in terms of a conflict over values about ways of life.

6. Some scholars, in fact, argue that the primary function of both racial (Miles and Torres, 1996) and "ethnic" identities (Wilmsen and McAllister, 1996) is the creation and perpetuation of structures of social inequality.

7. I use this term in the sense of David D. Laitin's (1986) reformulation of Antonio Gramsci: Hegemony is "the political forging—whether through coercion or elite bargaining—and institutionalization of a pattern of group activity in a state and the concurrent idealization of that schema into a dominant symbolic framework that reigns as common sense" (p. 19).

Chapter 3

1. Dorothy Waggoner (March 1993a: 2) defines "language minority children" as those who live in homes where a non-English language is usually spoken, and "limited English proficient" students as those who scored below the twentieth percentile (the low figure cited for each date) or below the fortieth percentile (the high figure cited) in the 1982 English-Language Proficiency Study.

2. This is significant because it is impossible for researchers to assess the accuracy of self-reports on English proficiency, as used in the Census.

3. In this book the term "Anglo American" is used to designate English-speaking Americans of European ethnic heritage.

4. In this book the terms "Latinos" and "Hispanics" are used to designate Americans with roots in Latin America and the Spanish-speaking parts of the Caribbean.

5. Although U.S. language policy includes Asian Americans and American Indians as language minorities, this author has found no systematic public opinion data that would enable an analysis of these groups' views on language issues.

6. The Univision poll surveyed 755 eligible Latino voters between April 5 and 18 in eight cities: San Francisco, Los Angeles, Miami, New York, Chicago, Houston, Dallas, and San Antonio. It was conducted by Clinton pollster Mark Penn and former Reagan official Michael Deaver (Roth, 1998).

7. Proposition 227 was approved by California voters by a 61 to 39 percent margin.

8. "For the most part" because not all "white" Americans are of European origin; some Latinos designate themselves as "white" but would not necessarily describe themselves as "European Americans." Another prominent boundary question exists in relation to persons with origins in the Middle East (e.g.,

Israel, Iran, or Egypt) who do not clearly fit any of the five principal categories, depending on how they are conceptualized.

9. Since November 1997, this has given rise to an option on official U.S. government forms to check more than one of the racial/ethnic categories.

Chapter 4

1. It should be noted that there were also Mexican-origin Tejanos fighting against Santa Ana and his forces for Texas's independence, and some of them died at the Alamo. By the time of Texas statehood, however, they had been marginalized and racialized as "Mexicans" (see, e.g., Weber, 1982: 252–255).

2. Under the Platt Amendment of 1901, for example, the United States maintained a tutelary role over Cuba that ultimately helped to create the anti–U.S. posture of the Castro regime and created an obligation for U.S. receptivity for Cubans fleeing Castro's policies. U.S. interventions in Central America created similar dynamics in relation to its peoples as well.

3. See Smith, 1997, for a detailed historical description and analysis of public policies creating and maintaining racial and ethnic inequalities in relation to civic identities.

4. This argument is also made by Peter Skerry (1993) in relation to Mexican American politics generally, although not with specific reference to language policy. See Magaña, 1994, for critiques of Skerry's analysis by other political scientists.

Chapter 5

1. See Wong, 1988, for another discussion of the *Meyer* decision.

2. Hufstedler was later the first secretary of education in the Carter administration.

3. For representative samples, see August and Hakuta, 1997; Baker and de Kanter, 1981; *Bilingual Research Journal*, 1992; Ramírez et al., 1991; and Willig, 1985.

4. There is, however, plenty of evidence from programs in other countries (see, e.g., Baker, 1993: chap. 12). For the record, the evidence seems to argue very powerfully that—*when properly and fully implemented in a dual-language program that is integrative rather than segregative*—a genuinely bilingual maintenance approach is more effective at promoting both greater mastery of English and greater overall educational achievement for language minority students than a policy of rapid immersion into mainstream English-only classes.

Chapter 7

1. Since domination/exclusion is explicitly inegalitarian, I will not consider it as a policy alternative available to the United States (see Chapter 2).

2. The Latino National Political Survey, for example, found that over 90

percent of its Mexican- and Cuban-origin non–U.S.-citizen respondents (i.e., those who are very likely to be immigrants) thought that all citizens and residents of the United States should learn English. At the same time, an equally large percentage believed that public services in the United States should be provided in Spanish (de la Garza et al., 1992: 176–77).

3. One irony in this process is that among "insiders" of U.S. racialized ethnic communities, clear (and sometimes contentious) distinctions are often made between the native-born and immigrants. See, e.g., Gutierrez, 1995; Kingston, 1990.

4. See Chapter 4 for the historical argument made by Gary Imhoff (1990) and other assimilationists, who contend, for example, that "Hispanics" are not generally perceived to be a racial minority group, and did not see themselves as such until their self-proclaimed leaders redefined themselves in this way in the 1960s.

5. See, for example, the argument of Thrasymachus in Plato's *Republic* that justice is "nothing other than the advantage of the stronger" (Plato, 1968: 15).

6. I make this distinction because, as seen in Chapter 4, some of the supporters of assimilationist language policy believe there are valid grounds for excluding from U.S. membership altogether those who are "essentially" different from the dominant ethnolinguistic group (see Brimelow, 1995, as well as Lutton and Tanton, 1994). The critique that follows applies to the liberal version of assimilationism, which aims at an inclusionary approach based on universalistic individualism.

7. For example, the state is under no obligation to ensure that the future-oriented saver/investor and the profligate wastrel enjoy the same incomes.

8. To say that many Latin American– and Asian-origin immigrants freely choose to come to this country in full knowledge of its racial stratification and cultural hegemony does not alter the moral requirement that each member of a U.S. minority community (immigrant or native) should have an equal right to decide to participate in and maintain that community's cultural structure.

9. I refer once again to David D. Laitin's (1986) definition of hegemony as "the political forging—whether through coercion or elite bargaining—and institutionalization of a pattern of group activity in a state and the concurrent idealization of that schema into a dominant symbolic framework that reigns as common sense" (p. 19).

10. For an insightful depiction of vitality as a valued feature of cultural communities, see Laitin, 1998.

11. For a more elaborate comparison of language policy conflicts in Canada and in the United States, see Schmidt, 1998, and Bourhis and Marshall, 1999.

12. The philosopher Charles Taylor (1994: pp. 40–41n) has criticized Kymlicka's liberal defense of cultural pluralism along these same lines, arguing that they do not secure the survival of minority cultural communities

13. One (unsuccessful) effort was even made to "Americanize" the island by changing its name to "Porto Rico."

14. In 1998, however, several Republican members of the U.S. Congress attempted to attach an English-only requirement on legislation that would authorize another plebiscite on the possibility of statehood for Puerto Rico, and U.S. English has made the dominance of Spanish in Puerto Rico a prominent issue in its lobbying efforts (see Gugliotta, 1998; Reyes, 1998).

15. See, e.g., Almaguér, 1994; Barrera, 1979; Montejano, 1987.

16. For a discussion of the "politics of naming" in relationship to ethnic identity among Mexican Americans and Latinos, see Giménez et al., 1992.

17. See, e.g., Garcia, 1989, for a good historical overview of these pressures, and the responses of Mexican American leaders during the period 1930–60.

18. On this point, see Lipset, 1990.

19. This very helpful concept was originally developed by Raymond Bretón (1964).

Chapter 8

1. Excepting Puerto Rico, and potentially, some American Indian reservations.

2. Again, Puerto Rico excepted.

3. He also wrote that "a city-state consists not only of a number of people, but of people of *different kinds*, since a city-state does not come from people who are alike. . . . But things from which a unity must come *differ in kind*" (Aristotle, 1998: 1261.23–24, 29; [emphasis added]).

4. In principle, linguistic confederation for language minorities that are constitutive parts of the United States is justified; however, this approach should only be adopted where the language minority community is firmly committed to that goal, as is the case today in Puerto Rico. Such a community commitment arises only when most members of a language minority community are convinced that they would truly be better off in an ethnolinguistic enclave. For reasons outlined in Chapter 7, I consider such widespread support to be highly unlikely for peoples living in mainstream metropolitan regions of the United States. The most likely scenario for generating such a commitment would involve a set of highly repressive antiminority language policies aimed at forced assimilation.

5. See Schmidt, 1988, for a fuller discussion of CBOs in providing institutional support for cultural pluralism.

6. K. Anthony Appiah appears to aim for a similarly voluntaristic approach to social identity. See, e.g., Appiah, 1994, and Appiah and Guttmann, 1996: esp. pt. 2.

7. For the best of reasons, even the pluralist James Cummins has fallen into this unfortunate pattern of misrecognition. Seeking to avoid the politically charged term "minority," in his 1996 revision of his powerful book on bilingual education (first published in 1989 under a different title), he substituted the term "bilingual student" for "language minority student." In fact, these LEP/NEP

students are not, for the most part, "bilingual," although enabling them to become so should be the aim of educational policy. On that point, Cummins is absolutely correct.

8. See, e.g., Schlesinger, 1992.

9. Examples of this persistent misperception abound. A 1999 piece by *Los Angeles Times* columnist Agustin Gurza, lamenting the loss of Spanish-language fluency by many successful California Latino political leaders, for example, generated a stormy backlash of letters accusing Gurza of "fomenting cultural strife, of creating conditions for a domestic Kosovo by advocating the Balkanization of America." The fact that Gurza supported the retention of these leaders' childhood language was taken to mean that he felt that they should not have learned English, which in fact was quite the opposite of his intended meaning.

10. And since the 1960s a steadily expanding literature by historians and social scientists, too enormous to be cited here, has provided both general and specific narratives documenting this reality. See the citations in Chapter 4 for examples.

11. As Louis DeSipio and Rodolfo de la Garza (1998: chap. 4) have emphasized, helping recent immigrants to make a successful adaptation to this country through a coherent settlement policy might go a long way toward reducing the conflict so frequently experienced in high-immigration regions of the country.

12. See Schmidt, 1988, 1996, for an elaboration of these points.

13. It remains a hindrance to such a proactive settlement policy, of course, that we ask so little of our own citizens in regard to the betterment of their neighborhoods, cities, states, and the country as a whole. Beyond paying taxes and obeying the law, Americans are required to think and do little to enhance the good of all. Asking more of immigrants will remain problematic until a more proactive conception of democratic citizenship becomes the norm for *all* Americans.

14. As suggested in Chapter 7, see Urciuoli, 1996, for an insightful anthropological analysis of the linkages between race, class, and language in relation to Puerto Rican Spanish-speakers in New York City. More concisely, in a 1998 *Los Angeles Times* op-ed piece, Richard Rodriguez (1998) observed that in California, Spanish is "the language of cheap labor" (p. M6).

15. To avoid misunderstanding, I want to emphasize that I am aware that more "Americans"—that is, people of the Americas, North and South—speak Spanish than speak English. The reference is to U.S. public opinion, not to hemispheric reality.

16. Among the most significant of these are recent books by Appiah and Gutmann (1996), Stanley B. Greenberg and Theda Skocpol (1997), Jennifer L. Hochschild (1995), Adolph Reed, Jr. (1999), Roberto Unger (1998), Roberto Unger and Cornel West (1998), and William Julius Wilson (1996).

17. The complex difficulty, as well as the fundamental necessity, of this project are insightfully explored by Lawrie Balfour (1998), bell hooks (1992), and Iris Marion Young (1990).

18. See n. 16 above.

References

Acuña, Rodolfo. 1988. *Occupied America: A History of Chicanos*, 3rd ed. (New York: Harper & Row).

Ada, A. F. 1988. "The Pajaro Valley Experience: Working with Spanish-Speaking Parents to Develop Children's Reading and Writing Skills in the Home Through the Use of Children's Literature," in T. Skutnabb-Kangas and J. Cummins, eds., *Minority Education: From Shame to Struggle* (Clevedon, England: Multilingual Matters), pp. 66–91.

Akinnaso, F. Niyi. 1989. "One Nation, Four Hundred Languages: Unity and Diversity in Nigeria's Language Policy," *Language Problems and Language Planning* 13:2 (Summer), pp. 133–46.

Allardt, Erik. 1985. "Bilingualism in Finland: The Position of Swedish as a Minority Language," in William R. Beer and James E. Jacob, eds., *Language Policy and National Unity* (Totowa, NJ: Rowman & Allanheld), pp. 79–96.

Almaguér, Tomás. 1994. *Racial Fault Lines: The Historical Origins of White Supremacy in California* (Berkeley: University of California Press).

Anderson, Benedict. 1983. *Imagined Communities: Reflections on the Origin and Spread of Nationalism* (London: Verso Press).

Anderson, Nick. 1998. "A Boomtown of Bilingual Education," *Los Angeles Times* (May 25), pp. A1, A28.

Appiah, K. Anthony. 1994. "Identity, Authenticity, Survival: Multicultural Societies and Social Reproduction," in Amy Gutmann, ed., *Multiculturalism: Examining the Politics of Recognition* (Princeton: Princeton University Press), pp. 149–63.

Appiah, K. Anthony, and Amy Gutmann. 1996. *Color Conscious: The Political Morality of Race* (Princeton: Princeton University Press).

Appleton, Nicholas. 1983. *Cultural Pluralism in Education: Theoretical Foundations* (New York: Longman).

Apte, Mahadev L. 1976. "Multilingualism in India and Its Socio-Political Implications: An Overview," in William M. O'Barr and Jean F. O'Barr, eds., *Language and Politics* (The Hague: Mouten & Co.), pp. 141–64.

Archdeacon, Thomas J. 1983. *Becoming American: An Ethnic History* (New York: The Free Press).

Arendt, Hannah. 1958. *The Human Condition* (Chicago: University of Chicago Press).

Aristotle, 1998. *Politics*, translated by C. D. C. Reeve (Indianapolis: Hackett).

Arizonans for Official English v. State of Arizona 520 U.S. 1141 (1997).

Association Mixta Progresista v. HEW, Pov.L.Rep. (CCH) Par.20,335 (N.D. Cal 1974).

August, Diane, and Kenji Hakuta. 1997. *Improving Schooling for Language-Minority Children* (Washington, DC: National Academy Press).

Baker, Colin. 1993. *Foundations of Bilingual Education and Bilingualism* (Clevedon, England: Multilingual Matters).

Baker, K., and A. de Kanter. 1981. *The Effectiveness of Bilingual Education Programs: A Review of the Literature. Final Draft Report* (Washington, DC: U.S. Department of Education).

Balfour, Lawrie. 1998. "'A Most Disagreeable Mirror': Race Consciousness as Double Consciousness," *Political Theory* 26:3 (June), pp. 346–69.

Barabak, Mark Z. 1997. "The *Times* Poll: Bilingual Education Gets Little Support," *Los Angeles Times* (October 15), p. A-1.

Baron, Dennis. 1990. *The English-Only Question: An Official Language for Americans?* (New Haven: Yale University Press).

Barrera, Mario. 1979. *Race and Class in the Southwest: A Theory of Racial Inequality* (Notre Dame, IN: University of Notre Dame Press).

Barrera, Mario. 1988. *Beyond Aztlan: Ethnic Autonomy in Comparative Perspective* (New York: Praeger).

Barreto, Amilcár A. 1997. "U.S. Language Policies and the Rise of Puerto Rican Nationalism," paper presented at the Annual Meeting of the American Political Science Association, Washington, DC (August).

Beer, William R., and James E. Jacob, eds. 1985. *Language Policy and National Unity* (Totowa, NJ: Rowman & Allanheld).

Benhabib, Seyla, ed. 1996. *Democracy and Difference: Contesting the Boundaries of the Political* (Princeton: Princeton University Press).

Bennett, Lerone, Jr. 1962 [1987]. *Before the Mayflower: A History of Black America,* 6th ed. (Chicago: Johnson).

Bennett, Lerone, Jr. 1975. *The Shaping of Black America* (Chicago: Johnson).

Bennett, William J. 1988. *Our Children and Our Country: Improving America's Schools and Affirming the Common Culture* (New York: Simon and Schuster).

Berlin, Isaiah. 1960. *Four Essays on Liberty* (New York: Oxford University Press).

Bernstein, Dan. 1997. "Nearly 70% Want to End Schools' Bilingual Education," *Sacramento Bee* (December 9), p. A-1.

Bernstein, Richard. 1990. "In U.S. Schools, a War of Words," *New York Times Magazine* (October 10), pp. 34, 48, 50, 52.

Bethell, Tom. 1979. "Against Bilingual Education," *Harper's* (February), pp. 30–33.

Bilingual Research Journal (formerly *The NABE Journal*). 1992. Special issue on *Final Report: Longitudinal Study of Structured English Immersion Strategy, Early-Exit, and Late-Exit Transitional Bilingual Education Programs for Language-Minority Children* 16:1–2 (Winter–Spring), pp. 1–245.

Boswell, Thomas. 1998. "Implications of Demographic Changes in Florida's Public School Population," in Sandra H. Fradd and Okhee Lee, eds., *Creating Florida's Multilingual Global Work Force: Educational Policies and Practices for*

Students Learning English as a New Language (Tallahasee: Florida Department of Education), pp. 11–123.

Bourhis, Richard Y., and David F. Marshall. 1999. "Language and Ethnic Identity in the United States and Canada," in Joshua Fishman, ed., *Handbook of Language and Ethnic Identity* (New York: Oxford University Press), pp. 244–64.

Bretón, Raymond. 1964. "Institutional Completeness of Ethnic Communities and the Personal Relations of Immigrants," *American Journal of Sociology*, vol. 70, pp. 193–205.

Bretzer, Joanne. 1992. "Language, Power, and Identity in Multiethnic Miami," in James Crawford, ed., *Language Loyalties: A Source Book on the Official English Controversy* (Chicago: University of Chicago Press), pp. 209–16.

Brimelow, Peter. 1995. *Alien Nation: Common Sense About America's Immigration Disaster* (New York: Random House).

Buenker, John D. 1973. *Urban Liberalism and Progressive Reform* (New York: Charles Scribner's Sons).

Bureau of the Census, U.S. Department of Commerce. 1992. "Voting Rights Act Amendments of 1992, Determinations Under Section 203; Action: Notice" (September 18) (Washington, D.C.: U.S. Government Printing Office).

California Secretary of State, comp. 1986. *California Ballot Pamphlet*, General Election (November 4) (Sacramento: State of California).

California State Department of Education. 1984. *Studies on Immersion Education: A Collection for United States Educators* (Sacramento: California State Department of Education).

Camarillo, Albert. 1984. *Chicanos in California: A History of Mexican Americans in California* (San Francisco: Boyd & Fraser).

Canada, Government of. 1977. *A National Understanding: Statement of the Government of Canada on the Official Languages Policy* (Ottawa: Minister of Supply and Services Canada).

Canada, Royal Commission on Bilingualism and Biculturalism. 1973. *Bilingualism and Biculturalism; An Abridged Version of the Royal Commission Report* (Canada: McClelland and Stewart, in cooperation with the Secretary of State Department and Information Canada).

Carmichael, Stokely, and Charles V. Hamilton. 1967. *Black Power: The Politics of Liberation in America* (New York: Vintage Books).

Castro, Ray. 1976. "Shifting the Burden of Bilingualism: The Case for Monolingual Communities," *The Bilingual Review* 3:1 (January–April), pp. 3–30.

Cerrón-Palomino, Rodolfo. 1989. "Language Policy in Peru: A Historical Overview," *International Journal of the Sociology of Language*, vol. 77, pp. 11–33.

Chaudhuri, Joyotpaul. 1982. "American Indian Policy: An Overview of the Legal Complexities, Controversies, and Dilemmas," *The Social Science Journal* 19:3 (July), pp. 9–21.

Chavez, Linda. 1991. *Out of the Barrio: Toward a New Politics of Hispanic Assimilation* (New York: Basic Books).

Citrin, Jack, Beth Reingold, and Donald P. Green. 1990. "American Identity and the Politics of Ethnic Change," *Journal of Politics* 52:4 (November), pp. 1124–54.

Citrin, Jack, Beth Reingold, Evelyn Walters, and Donald P. Green. 1990. "The 'Official English' Movement and the Symbolic Politics of Language in the United States," *The Western Political Quarterly* 43:3 (September), pp. 535–60.

Citrin, Jack, Ernst B. Haas, Christopher Muste, and Beth Reingold. 1994. "Is American Nationalism Changing? Implications for Foreign Policy," *International Studies Quarterly*, vol. 38, pp. 1–31.

Connolly, William E. 1991. *Identity/Difference: Democratic Negotiations of Political Paradox* (Ithaca: Cornell University Press).

Connolly, William E. 1995. *The Ethos of Pluralization* (Minneapolis: University of Minnesota Press).

Connor, Walker. 1984. *The National Question in Marxist-Leninist Theory and Strategy* (Princeton: Princeton University Press).

Connor, Walker. 1994. *Ethnonationalism: The Quest for Understanding* (Princeton: Princeton University Press).

Crawford, James. 1989. *Bilingual Education: History, Politics, Theory, and Practice* (Trenton, NJ: Crane).

Crawford, James. 1992. *Hold Your Tongue: Bilingualism and the Politics of "English Only"* (Reading, MA: Addison-Wesley).

Crawford, James, ed. 1992a. *Language Loyalties: A Source Book on the Official English Controversy* (Chicago: University of Chicago Press).

Crawford, James. 1997. *Best Evidence: Research Foundations of the Bilingual Education Act* (Washington, DC: National Clearinghouse for Bilingual Education; on-line at http://www.ncbe.gwu.edu/ncbepubs/reports/bestevid.html, November 3, 1997).

Crawford, James. 1998. "Endangered Native American Languages:What Is to Be Done, and Why?" in Thomas Ricento and Barbara Burnaby, eds., *Language and Politics in the United States and Canada: Myths and Realities* (Mahwah, NJ: Lawrence Erlbaum), pp. 151–65.

Crawford, James. 1999. "Issues in U.S. Language Policy: Language Legislation in the U.S.A.," on-line at http://ourworld.compuserve.com/homepages/JWCRAWFORD/langleg.htm#stateleg, October 5, 1999.

Cummins, James. 1981. "The Role of Primary Language Development in Promoting Educational Success for Language Minority Students," in *Schooling and Language Minority Students: A Theoretical Framework* (Los Angeles: California State University Evaluation, Dissemination, and Assessment Center), pp. 3–49.

Cummins, James. 1984. "The Language Minority Child," in Stan Shapson and Vincent D'Oyley, eds., *Bilingual and Multicultural Education: Canadian Perspectives* (Clevedon, England: Multilingual Matters), pp. 71–92.

Cummins, James. 1986. "Empowering Minority Students: A Framework for Intervention," *Harvard Educational Review* 56:1 (February), pp. 18–36.

Cummins, James. 1989. *Empowering Minority Students* (Sacramento: California Association for Bilingual Education).

Cummins, Jim. 1996. *Negotiating Identities: Education for Empowerment in a Diverse Society* (Ontario, CA: California Association for Bilingual Education).

d'Anglejan, Alison. 1984. "Language Planning in Quebec: An Historical Overview and Future Trends," in Richard Y. Bourhis, ed., *Conflict and Language Planning in Quebec* (Clevedon, England: Multilingual Matters), pp. 29–52.

Das Gupta, Jyotirindra. 1985. "Language, National Unity, and Shared Development in South Asia," in William R. Beer and James E. Jacob, eds., *Language Policy and National Unity* (Totowa, NJ: Rowman & Allanheld), pp. 198–216.

de le Garza, Rodolfo O., Louis DeSipio, F. Chris Garcia, John Garcia, and Angelo Falcon. 1992. *Latino Voices: Mexican, Puerto Rican, and Cuban Perspectives on American Politics* (Boulder: Westview Press).

Deloria, Vine, Jr. 1969 [1988]. *Custer Died for Your Sins: An Indian Manifesto* (Norman: University of Oklahoma Press).

Deloria, Vine, Jr., ed. 1985. *American Indian Policy in the Twentieth Century* (Norman: University of Oklahoma Press).

DeSipio, Louis, and Rodolfo O. de la Garza. 1998. *Making Americans, Remaking America: Immigration and Immigrant Policy* (Boulder, CO: Westview Press).

de Tocqueville, Alexis. 1835 [1964]. *Democracy in America*, edited, abridged, and with an introduction by Andrew Hacker (New York: Washington Square Press).

Deutsch, Karl. 1975. "The Social Significance of Linguistic Conflicts," in J.-G. Savvard and R. Vigneault, eds., *Les Etats multilingues* (Quebec: Laval University Press).

Deutsch, Sarah. 1987. *No Separate Refuge: Culture, Class, and Gender on an Anglo-Hispanic Frontier in the American Southwest, 1880–1940* (New York: Oxford University Press).

Dinnerstein, Leonard, and David M. Reimers. 1988. *Ethnic Americans: A History of Immigration*, 3rd ed. (New York: Harper and Row).

Eastman, Carol M. 1983. *Language Planning: An Introduction* (San Francisco: Chandler & Sharp).

Ellison, Ralph. 1952 [1995]. *Invisible Man* (New York: Vintage Books International).

Enriquez, Sam. 1989. "Bilingual Foes Force a Vote on Bonus Pay," *Los Angeles Times* (February 29) section II, pp. 1, 4.

Epstein, Noel. 1977. *Language, Ethnicity, and the Schools: Policy Alternatives for Bilingual-Bicultural Education* (Washington, DC: Institute for Educational Leadership, George Washington University).

Fernandez, Ronald. 1992. *The Disenchanted Island: Puerto Rico and the United States in the Twentieth Century* (New York: Praeger).

Fishman, Joshua. 1972. *The Sociology of Language* (Rowley, MA: Newbury House).

Fishman, Joshua. 1978. "Positive Bilingualism: Some Overlooked Rationales and Forefathers," in James E. Alatis, ed., *GURT 1978: International Dimensions of Bilingual Education* (Washington, DC: Georgetown University Press), pp. 42–52.

Fishman, Joshua A. 1985. "The Ethnic Revival in the United States: Implications for the Mexican-American Community," in Walker Connor, ed., *Mexican Americans in Comparative Perspective* (Washington DC: The Urban Institute Press), pp. 309–54.

Fishman, Joshua. 1988. " 'English Only': Its Ghosts, Myths, and Dangers," *International Journal of the Sociology of Language*, vol. 74, pp. 125–40.

Fleischman, H. L., and P. J. Hopstock. 1993. *Descriptive Study of Services to Limited English Proficient Students*. Vol. 1, *Summary of Findings and Conclusions*. Prepared for the Office of the Undersecretary, U.S. Department of Education, by Development Associates, Inc., Arlington, VA.

Fradd, Sandra H., and Okhee Lee, eds. 1998. *Creating Florida's Multilingual Global Work Force: Educational Policies and Practices for Students Learning English as a New Language* (Tallahasee: Florida Department of Education).

Frakes, George E., and Curtis B. Solberg, eds. 1971. *Minorities in California History* (New York: Random House).

Fraser, Nancy. 1997. *Justice Interruptus: Critical Reflections on the "Postsocialist" Condition* (New York: Routlege).

Frontera v. Sindell, 522 F.2d 1215 (6th Cir. 1975)

Garcia, Mario T. 1989. *Mexican Americans: Leadership, Ideology, and Identity, 1930–1960* (New Haven: Yale University Press).

Garcia v. Gloor 618 F.2d 264 (5th Cir. 1980)

Garcia v. Spun Steak Co., 998 F.2d 1480 (9th Cir. 1993).

Griggs v. Duke Power Co., 401 U.S. 424, 433–34 (1971).

Geertz, Clifford. 1973. *The Interpretation of Cultures* (New York: Basic Books).

General Accounting Office. 1987. *Bilingual Education: A New Look at the Research Evidence* (Washington, DC: U.S. General Accounting Office).

Giménez, Martha E., Fred A. Lopez III, and Carlos Muñoz, Jr., eds. 1992. "The Politics of Ethnic Construction: Hispanic, Chicano, Latino . . . ?" *Latin American Perspectives* 19:4(Fall), pp. 3–78.

Glazer, Nathan. 1975 [1978]. *Affirmative Discrimination: Ethnic Inequality and Public Policy* (New York: Basic Books)

Glazer, Nathan. 1983. *Ethnic Dilemmas, 1964–1982* (Cambridge: Harvard University Press).

Glazer, Nathan, ed. 1985. *Clamor at the Gates: The New American Immigration* (San Francisco: Institute for Contemporary Studies Press).

Glazer, Nathan. 1997. *We Are All Multiculturalists Now* (Cambridge: Harvard University Press).

Gonzalez, Gilbert G. 1997. "Culture, Language, and the Americanization of Mexican Children," in Antonia Darder, Rodolfo D. Torres, and Henry Gutiérrez, eds., *Latinos and Education: A Critical Reader* (New York: Routledge), pp. 158–73.

Gonzalez, Mario, and Elizabeth Cook-Lynn. 1999. *The Politics of Hallowed Ground: Wounded Knee and the Struggle for Indian Sovereignty* (Urbana: University of Illinois Press).

Gray, Tracy C., H. Suzanne Convery, and Katherine M. Fox. 1981. *The Current*

Status of Bilingual Education Legislation, Bilingual Education Series 9 (Washington, DC: Center for Applied Linguistics).

Greenberg, Stanley B., and Theda Skocpol, eds. 1997. *The New Majority: Toward a Popular Progressive Politics* (New Haven: Yale University Press).

Gugliotta, Guy. 1998. "Puerto Rico Bill Could Harm GOP's Hopes to Woo Hispanics; Language Amendment Draws Opposition of Many," *Washington Post* (March 4), p. A–4.

Gurza, Agustin. 1999. "A Second Language Is a Wonderful Thing to Gain," *Los Angeles Times* (June 8), p. B-1.

Gutierrez, David G. 1995. *Walls and Mirrors: Mexican Americans, Mexican Immigrants, and the Politics of Ethnicity* (Berkeley: University of California Press).

Gutierrez v. Municipal Court., 838 F.2d 1031 (9th Cir. 1988), vacated as moot, 57 U.S.L.W. 3687 (4/18/89)

Guy, Gregory R. 1989. "International Perspectives on Linguistic Diversity and Language Rights," *Language Problems and Language Planning* 13:1 (Spring), pp. 45–53.

Hakuta, Kenji. 1986. *The Mirror of Language: The Debate on Bilingualism* (New York: Basic Books).

Hannum, Hurst, and Richard Lillich. 1980. "The Concept of Autonomy in International Law," *The American Journal of International Law* 74:4 (October), pp. 858–89.

Harding, Vincent. 1983. *There Is a River: The Black Struggle for Freedom in America* (New York: Vintage Books).

Harles, John. 1993. *Politics in the Lifeboat: Immigrants and the American Democratic Order* (Boulder, CO: Westview Press).

Hayakawa, S. I. 1985. *One Nation . . . Indivisible? The English Language Amendment* (Washington, DC: Washington Institute for Values in Public Policy).

Hayes-Bautista, David. 1998. "The Pull of the Center: Changing Anglo-Latino Perceptions Creating New Ground," *Los Angeles Times* (June 7), pp. M1, M6.

Henry, Sarah. 1990. "English Only: The Language of Discrimination," *Hispanic: The Magazine for and About Hispanics* (March), pp. 28–32.

Hernandez v. State of New York 500 U.S. 352 (1991)

Hernandez-Chavez, Eduardo. 1978. "Language Maintenance, Bilingual Education, and Philosophies of Bilingualism in the United States," in James E. Alatis, ed., *GURT 1978: International Dimensions of Bilingual Education* (Washington, DC: Georgetown University Press), pp. 527–50.

Hernandez-Chavez, Eduardo. 1984. "The Inadequacy of English Immersion Education as an Educational Approach for Language Minority Students in the United States," in California State Department of Education, *Studies on Immersion Education: A Collection for United States Educators* (Sacramento: California State Department of Education), pp. 144–83.

Higham, John. 1984. *And Send These to Me: Immigrants in Urban America,* rev. ed. (Baltimore: Johns Hopkins University Press).

Hinton, Leanne. 1994. *Flutes of Fire: Essays on California Indian Languages* (Berkeley: Heyday Books).

Hochschild, Jennifer L. 1995. *Facing up to the American Dream: Race, Class, and the Soul of the Nation* (Princeton: Princeton University Press).

Hofstadter, Richard. 1955. *The Age of Reform* (New York: Random House).

Hollinger, David A. 1995. *Postethnic America* (New York: Basic Books).

hooks, bell. 1992. *Black Looks: Race and Representation* (Boston: South End Press).

Hoover, Kenneth. 1997. *The Power of Identity: Politics in a New Key*, with James Marcia and Kristen Parris (Chatham, NJ: Chatham House).

Hornberger, Nancy H. 1988. "Language Planning Orientations and Bilingual Education in Peru," *Language Problems and Language Planning* 12:1 (Spring), pp. 14–29.

Hornberger, Nancy H. 1990. "Bilingual Education and English-Only: A Language Planning Framework," *The Annals of the American Academy of Political and Social Sciences* 508 (March), pp. 12–26.

Horne, Gerald. 1997. "America's New Racial Divide Is East-West, not North-South," *Los Angeles Times* (August 24), p. M-1.

Horowitz, Donald L. 1985. *Ethnic Groups in Conflict* (Berkeley: University of California Press).

Horsman, Reginald. 1981. *Race and Manifest Destiny: The Origins of American Racial Anglo-Saxonism* (Cambridge: Harvard University Press).

Howe, Irving. 1976. *World of Our Fathers: The Journey of the East European Jews to America and the Life They Found and Made* (New York: Simon and Schuster).

Hubler, Shawn, and Stuart Silverstein. 1993. "Schooling Doesn't Close Minority Earning Gap," *Los Angeles Times* (January 10), p. A1.

Huddleston, Walter. 1983 [1992]. "The Misdirected Policy of Bilingualism," *Congressional Record*, 98th Congress, 1st session, September 21, 1983, pp. S12640–43. Reprinted in James Crawford, ed., *Language Loyalties: A Source Book on the Official English Controversy* (Chicago: University of Chicago Press), pp. 114–18.

Huddy, Leonie, and David O. Sears. 1990. "Qualified Public Support for Bilingual Education: Some Policy Implications," *The Annals of the American Academy for Political and Social Science* 508 (March), pp. 119–34.

Huggins, Nathan Irvin. 1977. *Black Odyssey: The Afro-American Ordeal in Slavery* (New York: Pantheon Books).

Imahara, Kathryn K. 1993. "Language Rights Policy: Language Rights Issues to the Year 2020 and Beyond," in *The State of Asian Pacific America: Policy Issues to the Year 2020* (Los Angeles: LEAP Asian Pacific American Public Policy Institute and UCLA Asian American Studies Center), pp. 233–52.

Imhoff, Gary. 1990. "The Position of U.S. English on Bilingual Education," *The Annals of the American Academy of Political and Social Science* 508 (March), pp. 48–61.

Isaacs, Harold R. 1975. *Idols of the Tribe: Group Identity and Political Change* (New York: Harper & Row).

Jackson, Robert L. 1992. "Rise in Immigrants, Drop in Car-Poolers," *Los Angeles Times* (May 30), p. A2.

Jones-Correa, Michael. 1998. *Between Two Nations: The Political Predicament of Latinos in New York City* (Ithaca: Cornell University Press).

Kallen, Horace. 1924 [1970]. *Culture and Democracy in the United States: Studies in the Group Psychology of the American Peoples* (New York: Boni and Liveright: reprinted by Arno Press and the *New York Times*).

Karenga, Maulana. 1982. *Introduction to Black Studies* (Los Angeles: University of Sankore Press).

King, Martin Luther, Jr. 1991. "I Have a Dream," in James M. Washington, ed., *The Essential Writings and Speeches of Martin Luther King, Jr.* (New York: HarperCollins), pp. 217–20.

Kingston, Maxine Hong. 1990. *Tripmaster Monkey: His Fake Book* (New York: Vintage Books).

Kloss, Heinz. 1966. "German-American Language Maintenance Efforts," in Joshua A. Fishman, et al., *Language Loyalty in the United States* (The Hague: Mouton & Co.), pp. 206–52.

Kloss, Heinz. 1977. *The American Bilingual Tradition* (Rowley, MA: Newbury House).

Kloss, Heinz. 1978. *Problems of Language Policy in South Africa* (Vienna: Wilhelm Braumuller, Universitats-Verlagsbuchhandlung).

Kuri v. Edelman, 491 F.2d 684 (7th Cir. 1974)

Kymlicka, Will. 1989. *Liberalism, Community, and Culture* (New York: Oxford University Press).

Kymlicka, Will. 1995. *Multicultural Citizenship: A Liberal Theory of Minority Politics* (New York: Oxford University Press).

Laitin, David D. 1986. *Hegemony and Culture: Politics and Religious Change Among the Yorubas* (Chicago: University of Chicago Press).

Laitin, David D. 1998. "Liberal Theory and the Nation," *Political Theory* 26:2 (April), pp. 221–36.

Lamm, Richard D., and Gary Imhoff. 1985. *The Immigration Time Bomb: The Fragmenting of America* (New York: Truman Talley Books/E. P. Dutton).

Laponce, Jean A. 1987. *Languages and Their Territories*, translated by Anthony Martin-Sperry (Toronto: University of Toronto Press).

Laponce, J. A. 1992. "What Kind of Bilingualism for Canada: Personal or Territorial? The Demographic Factor," in Anthony M. Messina, Luis R. Fraga, Laurie A. Rhodebeck, and Frederick D. Wright, eds., *Ethnic and Racial Minorities in Advanced Industrial Democracies* (New York: Greenwood Press), pp. 265–78.

Lash, Scott, and Jonathan Friedman, eds. 1992. *Modernity and Identity* (Cambridge: Blackwell).

Lau v. Nichols, 414 U.S. 563 (1974)

Lee, Chae-Jin. 1986. *China's Korean Minority: The Politics of Ethnic Education* (Boulder, CO: Westview Press).

Leibowitz, Arnold H. 1982. *Federal Recognition of the Rights of Minority Language Groups* (Rosslyn, VA: National Clearinghouse for Bilingual Education).

Levine, Marc V. 1990. *The Reconquest of Montreal: Language Policy and Social Change in a Bilingual City* (Philadelphia: Temple University Press).

Light, Ivan. 1972. *Ethnic Enterprise in America* (Berkeley: University of California Press).

Limerick, Patricia Nelson. 1987. *The Legacy of Conquest: The Unbroken Past of the American West* (New York: W. W. Norton & Company).

Lipset, Seymour Martin. 1990. *Continental Divide: The Values and Institutions of the United States and Canada.* (New York: Routledge).

Lissak, Rivka Shpak. 1989. *Pluralism and Progressives: Hull Houseand the New Immigrants, 1890–1919* (Chicago: University of Chicago Press).

Locke, Steven I. 1995. "Language Discrimination and English-Only Rules in the Workplace: The Case for Legislative Amendment of Title VII," *Texas Tech Law Review*, vol. 27, pp. 33–72.

Los Angeles County Board of Supervisors. 1986. Statement quoted in March Fong Eu, comp., *California Ballot Pamphlet for November 1986 Election* (Sacramento: State of California), p. 47.

Los Angeles Times. 1998. "Profile of the Electorate," (June 4), p. A-30.

Lutton, Wayne, and John Tanton. 1994. *The Immigration Invasion* (Potesky, MI: The Social Contract Press).

Macias, Reynaldo. 1979. "Choice of Language as a Human Right—Public Policy Implications in the United States," in Raymond V. Padilla, ed., *Bilingual Education and Public Policy in the United States* (Ypsilanti: Eastern Michigan University), pp. 39–57.

Macias, Reynaldo. 1995. Preliminary research findings, presented at the Annual Conference of the American Association for Applied Linguistics, Long Beach Hilton Hotel, Long Beach, CA (March).

MacIntyre, Alasdair. 1984. *After Virtue*, 2nd ed. (Notre Dame, IN: University of Notre Dame Press).

Magaña, Lisa, ed. 1994. *Mexican Americans: Are They an Ambivalent Minority?* (Claremont: The Tomas Rivera Center).

Malson, Lucien. 1972. *Wolf Children and the Problem of Human Nature* (New York: Monthly Review Press).

Marshall, David F. 1991. "Update and Implications for English Teachers of English Only Legislation," ERIC Documentation Reproduction Service, No. ED322497.

Marshall, David F. 1996. "The Role of Language in the Mobilization of Soviet Ethnic Nationalities," in Hans R. Duz, ed., "Language Planning and Political Theory", *International Journal of the Sociology of Language* 118, pp. 7–46.

Marshall, David F., and Roseann D. Gonzalez. 1990. "Una Lingua, Una Patria? Is Monolingualism Beneficial or Harmful for a Nation's Unity?" in Karen L. Adams and David T. Brink, eds., *Perspectives on English Only* (Berlin and New York: Mouton DeGruyter), pp. 29–51.

Massey, Douglas, Rafael Alarcón, Jorge Durand, and Humberto Gonzalez. 1987. *Return to Aztlan: The Social Process of International Migration from Western Mexico* (Berkeley: University of California Press).

McClain, Paula D., and Joseph Stewart, Jr. 1998. *Can We All Get Along? Racial and Ethnic Minorities in American Politics*, 2nd ed. (Boulder, CO: Westview Press).

McDougal, M., H. Laswell, and L. Chen. 1976. "Freedom from Discrimination in Choice of Language and International Human Rights," *Southern Illinois University Law Journal*, vol. 1 pp. 151–74.

McRae, Kenneth D. 1975. "The Principle of Territoriality and the Principle of Personality in Multilingual States," *International Journal of the Sociology of Language*, vol. 4, pp. 33–54.

Meyer v. Nebraska, 262 U.S. 390 (1923)

Miles, Robert, and Rudy Torres. 1996. "Does 'Race' Matter? Transatlantic Perspectives on Racism After 'Race Relations,' " in Vered Amit-Talai and Caroline Knowles, eds., *Re-Situating Identities: The Politics of Race, Ethnicity, and Culture* (New York: Broadview Press), pp. 24–46.

Mink, Gwendolyn. 1986. *Old Labor and New Immigrants in American Political Development: Union, Party, and State, 1875–1920* (Ithaca: Cornell University Press).

Mirandé, Alfredo. 1996. "En la Tierra del Ciego, El Tuerto Es Rey (In the Land of the Blind, the One-Eyed Person Is King)," *New Mexico Law Review*, 26 (Winter), pp. 75–105.

Montejano, David. 1987. *Anglos and Mexicans in the Making of Texas, 1836–1986* (Austin: University of Texas Press).

Moran, Rachel F. 1987. "Bilingual Education as a Status Conflict," *California Law Review*, vol. 75, pp. 321–62.

Moran, Rachel F. 1991. "Irritation and Intrigue: The Intricacies of Language Rights and Language Policy," a review of *Only English? Law and Language Policy in the United States* by Bill Piatt (Albuquerque: University of New Mexico Press, 1990), *Northwestern University Law Review* 85 (Spring), pp. 790–823.

Muir, Frederick M. 1990. "Bradley Proposes Linking the City to 140-Language Service," *Los Angeles Times* (August 22), p. B4.

Muller, Thomas, and Thomas J. Espenshade. 1985. *The Fourth Wave: California's Newest Immigrants* (Washington, DC: The Urban Institute Press).

Mydans, Seth. 1990. "Pressure for English-Only Job Rules Stirring a Sharp Debate Across U.S.," *New York Times* (August 8), p. A10.

Navarro, Mireya. 1997. "Puerto Rico Teachers Fight Teaching in English," *New York Times* (May 19), on-line ed.

Norton, Anne. 1988. *Reflections on Political Identity* (Baltimore: Johns Hopkins University Press).

O'Barr, William M., and Jean F. O'Barr, eds. 1976. *Language and Politics* (The Hague: Mouton & Co.)

Obledo, Mario, and Carlos Alcala. 1980. "Discrimination Against the Spanish Language in Public Service: A Policy Alternative," in D. J. R. Bruckner, ed., *Politics and Language: Spanish and English in the United States* (Chicago: University of Chicago Center for Policy Study), pp. 155–62.

Oboler, Suzanne. 1995. *Ethnic Labels, Latino Lives: Identity and the Politics of (Re)Presentation in the United States* (Minneapolis: University of Minnesota Press).

Ogbu, John U. 1978. *Minority Education and Caste: The American System in Cross-Cultural Perspective* (New York: Academic Press).

O'Hare, William P. 1992. "America's Minorities—The Demographics of Diversity," *Population Bulletin* 47:4 (December), pp. 2–47.

Olzak, Susan, and Joane Nagel, eds. 1986. *Competitive Ethnic Relations* (Orlando: Academic Press).

Omi, Michael, and Howard Winant. 1994. *Racial Formation in the United States, from the 1960s to the 1990s*, 2nd ed. (New York: Routledge).

Ong, Paul, research director. 1993. *Beyond Asian American Poverty* (Los Angeles: LEAP Asian Pacific American Public Policy Institute and UCLA Center for Asian/Pacific American Studies).

Orlando Sentinel Tribune. 1993. "For Many Americans, English Is What You Speak Outside of Home" (April 28), p. A1.

Pabon v. Levine, 70 F.R.D. 674 (S.D.N.Y. 1976)

Parliman, Gregory C., and Rosalie J. Shoeman. 1994. "National Origin Discrimination or Employer Prerogative? An Analysis of Language Rights in the Workplace," *Employee Relations Law Journal* 9:4 (March 22), pp. 551–79.

Patterson, Orlando. 1977. *Ethnic Chauvinism, the Reactionary Impulse* (New York: Stein and Day).

Perlmann, Joel. 1990. "Historical Legacies: 1840–1920," in Courtney B. Cazden and Catherine E. Snow, eds., *English Plus: Issues in Bilingual Education. The Annals of the American Academy of Political and Social Science* 508 (May), pp. 27–37.

Phillipson, Robert. 1992. *Linguistic Imperialism* (Oxford: Oxford University Press).

Piatt, Bill. 1990. *Only English? Law and Language Policy in the United States* (Albuquerque: University of New Mexico Press).

Pitt, Leonard, ed. 1985. *California Controversies* (San Rafael, CA: ETRI).

Plato. translated by Alan Bloom 1968. *The Republic of Plato,* (Chicago: University of Chicago Press).

Pool, Jonathan. 1978. "Soviet Language Planning: Goals, Results, Options," in Jeremy R. Azrael, ed., *Soviet Nationality Policies and Practices* (New York: Praeger).

Porter, Rosalie Pedalino. 1990. *Forked Tongue: The Politics of Bilingual Education* (New York: Basic Books).

Portes, Alejandro, guest ed. 1994. Special issue on "The New Second Generation," *International Migration Review* 28:4 (Winter), pp. 632–864.

Portes, Alejandro, and Robert L. Bach. 1985. *Latin Journey: Cuban and Mexican Immigrants in the United States* (Berkeley: University of California Press).

Portes, Alejandro, and Ruben G. Rumbaut. 1996. *Immigrant America: A Portrait,* 2nd ed. (Berkeley: University of California Press).

Portes, Alejandro, and Richard Schauffler. 1994. "Language and the Second Generation: Bilingualism Yesterday and Today," *International Migration Reivew* 28:4 (Winter), pp. 640–61.

President's Commission on Foreign Languages and International Studies. 1979.

Strength Through Wisdom: A Critique of U.S. Capability (Washington, DC: U.S. Government Printing Office).

Prucha, Francis Paul. 1985. *The Indians in American Society: From the Revolutionary War to the Present* (Berkeley: University of California Press).

Ramírez, J. David, Sandra D. Yuen, Dena R. Ramey, David J. Pasta, and David K. Billings. 1991. *Final Report: Longitudinal Study of Structured English Immersion Strategy, Early-Exit, and Late-Exit Transitional Bilingual Education Programs for Language-Minority Children*. Executive Summary (San Mateo, CA: Aguirre International).

Reed, Adolph, Jr., ed. 1999. *Without Justice for All: The New Liberalism and Our Retreat from Racial Equality* (Boulder, CO: Westview Press).

Regan, Timothy. 1986. "The Role of Language Policy in South African Education," *Language Problems and Language Planning* 10:1 (Spring), pp. 1–13.

Rein, Martin. 1971. *Social Science and Public Policy* (New York: Penguin Books).

Resnick, Philip. 1990. *Letters to a Quebecois Friend, with a Reply by Daniel Latouche* (Montreal and Kingston: McGill-Queen's University Press).

Reyes, Gerardo. 1998. "Puerto Rico Language Battle: It Could Be Key to Referendum Vote in Congress," *Miami Herald* (March 4), on-line ed.

Rial, James. 1985. "Spain: Regional Languages in a Lingua Franca Dominant State," in William R. Beer and James E. Jacob, eds., *Language Policy and National Unity* (Totowa, NJ: Rowman & Allanheld), pp. 97–105.

Ricento, Thomas and Barbara Burnaby, eds. 1998. *Language and Politics in the United States and Canada: Myths and Realities* (Mahwah, NJ: Lawrence Erlbaum).

Rodriguez, Alfredo, and Roy Christman. 1988. "Spanish-Language Voters and English-Language Ballots in Santa Clara County," paper presented at the Annual Meeting of the Western Political Science Association, San Francisco (March).

Rodriguez, Richard. 1982. *Hunger of Memory: The Education of Richard Rodriguez* (Boston: David R. Godine).

Rodriguez, Richard. 1994. Discussion with faculty and students at California State University, Long Beach (October 4).

Rodriguez, Richard. 1998. "A Campaign for Another Country," *Los Angeles Times* (May 31), pp. M1, M6.

Ronen, Dov. 1979. *The Quest for Self-Determination* (New Haven: Yale University Press).

Roth, Bennett. 1998. "Many Back Bilingual Education. Poll of Hispanics Also Indicates 64% Believe Effort Has Succeeded," *Houston Chronicle* (April 23), on-line ed.

Rothstein, Richard. 1998. "Bilingual Education: The Controversy," *Phi Delta Kappan* 79:9 (May), pp. 672–78.

Rubin, Joan. 1968. *National Bilingualism in Paraguay* (The Hague: Mouton & Co.).

Rumbaut, Rubén G. 1994. "The Crucible Within: Ethnic Identity, Self-Esteem, and Segmented Assimilation Among Children of Immigrants," *International Migration Review* 28:4 (Winter), pp. 748–94.

Rumbaut, Rubén G. 1997. "Assimilation and Its Discontents: Between Rhetoric and Reality," special issue of *International Migration Review* 31 (Winter), pp. 923–60.

Salomone, Rosemary C. 1986. *Equal Education Under Law: Legal Rights and Federal Policy* (New York: St. Martin's Press).

San Miguel, Guadalupe, Jr. 1987. *"Let All of Them Take Heed": Mexican Americans and the Campaign for Educational Equality in Texas, 1910–1981* (Austin: University of Texas Press).

Sanchez v. Norton, Civil Action No. 15732 (D. Conn. June 3, 1974)

Schaar, John H. 1981. *Legitimacy in the Modern State* (New Brunswick, NJ: Transaction Books).

Schlesinger, Arthur M., Jr. 1992. *The Disuniting of America: Reflections on a Multicultural Society* (New York: W. W. Norton).

Schmidt, Ronald. 1988. "Cultural Pluralism and Public Administration: The Role of Community-Based Organizations," *American Review of Public Administration* 18:2 (June 1988), pp. 189–202.

Schmidt, Ronald, Sr. 1996. "The Political Incorporation of Immigrants in California: An Institutional Assessment," *California Politics and Policy* 2 (November), pp. 1–19.

Schmidt, Ronald, Sr. 1997. "Latinos and Language Policy: The Politics of Culture," in F. Chris Garcia, ed., *Pursuing Power: Latinos in the Political System* (Notre Dame, IN: University of Notre Dame Press, 1997), pp. 343–67.

Schmidt, Ronald, Sr. 1998. "The Politics of Language in Canada and the United States: Explaining the Differences," in Thomas Ricento and Barbara Burnaby, eds., *Language and Politics in the United States and Canada: Myths and Realities* (Mahwah, NJ: Lawrence Erlbaum Associates), pp. 37–70.

Schmidt, Ronald, Sr., and F. Chris Garcia. 1996. "Mexican American Public Opinion on U.S. Language Policy," paper presented at the Annual Conference of the Western Political Science Association, San Francisco (March).

Schneider, Susan Gilbert. 1976. *Revolution, Reaction, or Reform: The 1974 Bilingual Education Act* (New York: Las Americas).

Scott, George M., Jr. 1990. "A Resynthesis of the Primordial and Circumstantial Approaches to Ethnic Group Solidarity: Towards an Explanatory Model," *Ethnic and Racial Studies*, vol. 13:2, pp. 147–71.

Serrano, Jose. 1997. *English Plus Resolution*, introduced in the U.S. House of Representatives as H. Con. Res. 4, January 7 (Washington, DC: U.S. Government Printing Office).

Shumway, Norman. 1988 [1992]. "Preserve the Primacy of English," testimony presented before the U.S. House Committee on the Judiciary, Subcommittee on Civil and Constitutional Rights, *English Language Constitutional Amendments: Hearing on H.J. Res. 13, H.J. Res. 33, H.J. Res. 60, and H.J. Res. 83*, 100th Congress, 2nd session, May 11, 1988, pp. 36–44. Reprinted in James Crawford, ed., *Language Loyalties: A Source Book on the Official English Controversy* (Chicago: University of Chicago Press), pp. 121–24.

Sigler, Jay A. 1983. *Minority Rights: A Comparative Analysis* (Westport, CN: Greenwood Press).

Silver, Lori. 1989. "States Want Fewer Curbs on Funds for Immigrant Aid," *Los Angeles Times* (July 11), p. A20.

Skerry, Peter. 1993. *Mexican Americans: The Ambivalent Minority* (New York: The Free Press).

Smith, Anthony D. 1981. *The Ethnic Revival* (Cambridge: Cambridge Univ Press).

Smith, Anthony D. 1983. *Theories of Nationalism* (New York: Holmes & Meier).

Smith, Rogers. 1997. *Civic Ideals: Conflicting Visions of Citizenship in U.S. History* (New Haven: Yale University Press).

Sonntag, Selma K. 1990. "Political Saliency of English as Official Language," paper presented at the Annual Meeting of the Western Political Science Association, Newport Beach, CA (March 22–24).

Stampp, Kenneth M. 1956. *The Peculiar Institution: Slavery in the Ante-Bellum South* (New York: Vintage Books).

Stein, Colman Brez, Jr. 1986. *Sink or Swim: The Politics of Bilingual Education* (New York: Praeger).

Steinberg, Stephen. 1982. *The Ethnic Myth: Race, Ethnicity, and Class in America* (Boston: Beacon Press).

Sundquist, James L. 1968. *Politics and Policy: The Eisenhower, Kennedy, and Johnson Years* (Washington, DC: The Brookings Institution).

Takaki, Ronald T. 1982. *Iron Cages: Race and Culture in Nineteenth Century America* (Seattle: University of Washington Press).

Takaki, Ronald T. 1987. "Reflections on Racial Patterns in America," in Ronald Takaki, ed., *From Different Shores: Perspectives on Race and Ethnicity in America* (New York: Oxford University Press), pp. 26–37.

Takaki, Ronald T. 1989. *Strangers from a Different Shore: A History of Asian Americans* (Boston: Little, Brown).

Tatalovich, Raymond. 1995. *Nativism Reborn? The Official English Language Movement and the American States* (Lexington: The University Press of Kentucky).

Taylor, Charles. 1994. *Multiculturalism: Examining the Politics of Recognition*, edited and introduced by Amy Gutmann, with responses by K. Anthony Appiah, Jurgen Habermas, Steven C. Rockefeller, Michael Walzer, and Susan Wolf (Princeton: Princeton University Press).

Thernstrom, Abigail. 1987. *Whose Votes Count? Affirmative Action and Minority Voting Rights* (Cambridge: Harvard University Press, for the Twentieth-Century Fund).

Thernstrom, Abigail. 1990. "Bilingual Miseducation," *Commentary* (February), pp. 44–48.

Tienda, Marta, and Lisa J. Neidert. 1985. "Language Education and the Socio-economic Achievement of Hispanic-Origin Men," in Rodolfo O. de la Garza, Frank D. Bean, Charles M. Bonjean, Ricardo Romo, and Rodolfo Alvarez, eds., *The Mexican American Experience: An Interdisciplinary Anthology* (Austin: University of Texas Press), pp. 359–76.

Tseng, Pao-chien. 1985. "Language and National Unity: China," in William R. Beer and James E. Jacob, eds., *Language Policy and National Unity* (Totowa, NJ: Rowman & Allanheld), pp. 178–97.

Unger, Roberto. 1998. *Democracy Realized: The Progressive Alternative* (New York: Verso).

Unger, Roberto, and Cornel West. 1998. *The Future of American Progressivism* (Boston: Beacon Press).

U.S. Congress. 1974. Equal Educational Opportunities Act of 1974, quoted in Rosemary C. Salomone, 1986, p. 100.

U.S. Commission on Civil Rights. 1975. *A Better Chance to Learn: Bilingual-Bicultural Education* (Washington, DC: U.S. Government Printing Office).

U.S. Commission on Civil Rights. 1975a. *The Voting Rights Act: Ten Years After* (Washington, DC: U.S. Government Printing Office).

U.S. Commission on Civil Rights. 1981. *Indian Tribes: A Continuing Quest for Survival* (Washington, DC: U.S. Government Printing Office).

U.S. Commission on Civil Rights. 1981a. *The Voting Rights Act: Unfulfilled Goals* (Washington, DC: U.S. Government Printing Office).

U.S. ex rel. Negron v. New York, 434 F.2d. 386 (2d Cir. 1970)

U.S. Immigration and Naturalization Service. 1987. *Statistical Yearbook of the Immigration and Naturalization Service, 1986* (Washington, DC: U.S. Government Printing Office).

U.S. Immigration and Naturalization Service. 1997. *Statistical Yearbook of the Immigration and Naturalization Service, 1996* (Washington, DC: U.S. Government Printing Office).

Urciuoli, Bonnie. 1996. *Exposing Prejudice: Puerto Rican Experiences of Language, Race, and Class* (Boulder, CO: Westview Press).

Veltman, Calvin. 1983. *Language Shift in the United States* (Berlin: Mouton, Walter de Gruyter).

Veltman, Calvin. 1998. "Quebec, Canada, and the United States: Social Reality and Language Rights," in Thomas Ricento and Barbara Burnaby, eds., *Language and Politics in the United States and Canada: Myths and Realities* (Mahwah, NJ: Lawrence Erlbaum Associates), pp. 301–16.

Vobejda, Barbara. 1992. "Land of a Thousand Tongues: English Is Increasingly Foreign in America," *Washington Post National Weekly Edition* (April 27), p. II-37.

Waggoner, Dorothy. 1993. "Native-Born Constitute Half of U.S. Multilingual Population," *Numbers and Needs: Ethnic and Linguistic Minorities in the United States* 3:6 (November), pp. 1–2.

Waggoner, Dorothy. 1993a. "Navajo Dominant Among Native American Languages Spoken by 331,600," *Numbers and Needs: Ethnic and Linguistic Minorities in the United States* 3:5 (September), pp. 2, 4.

Waggoner, Dorothy. 1993b. "Numbers of Speakers of Asian Indian Languages Lead in Increase of Multilingualism," *Numbers and Needs: Ethnic and Linguistic Minorities in the United States* 3:4 (July), pp. 1–2.

Waggoner, Dorothy. 1993c. "Types of Census Language Information," *Numbers and Needs: Ethnic and Linguistic Minorities in the United States* 3:2 (March), p. 2.

Waggoner, Dorothy. 1994. "Most Hispanic Youth Retain Spanish as Home Language," *Numbers and Needs: Ethnic and Linguistic Minorities in the United States* 4:2 (March), pp. 1, 3.

Wardhaugh, Ronald. 1987. *Languages in Competition: Dominance, Diversity, and Decline* (Oxford: Basil Blackwell).

Washburn, Wilcomb E., ed. 1988. *History of Indian-White Relations*. Vol. 4. *Handbook of North American Indians* (Washington, DC: Smithsonian Institution).

Weber, David J. 1982. *The Mexican Frontier 1821–1846: The American Southwest Under Mexico* (Albuquerque: University of New Mexico Press).

Weinberg, Meyer. 1977. *A Chance to Learn: The History of Race and Education in the United States* (Cambridge: Cambridge University Press).

Weinstein, Brian. 1983. *The Civic Tongue: Political Consequences of Language Choice* (New York: Longman).

Wheat, Jack. 1998. "Experts: Bilingualism Vital to Economy," *Miami Herald*, pp. 1B, 6B.

Wiley, Terrence G. 1998. "The Imposition of World War I Era English-Only Policies and the Fate of German in North America," in Thomas Ricento and Barbara Burnaby, eds., *Language and Politics in the United States and Canada: Myths and Realities* (Philadelphia: Erlbaum Press), pp. 211–242.

Wilkinson, Charles F. 1987. *American Indians, Time, and the Law* (New Haven: Yale University Press).

Willig, A. 1985. "A Meta-Analysis of Selected Studies on the Effectiveness of Bilingual Education," *Review of Educational Research*, vol. 55, pp. 269–77.

Wilmsen, Edwin N., and Patrick McAllister, eds. 1996. *The Politics of Difference: Ethnic Premises in a World of Power* (Chicago: University of Chicago Press).

Wilson, William Julius. 1996. *When Work Disappears: The World of the New Urban Poor* (New York: Alfred A. Knopf).

Wolfson, Nessa, and Joan Manes, eds. 1985. *Language of Inequality* (Berlin: Mouton).

Wong, Sau-ling Cynthia. 1988. "Educational Rights of Language Minorities," in Sandra Lee McKay and Sau-ling Cynthia Wong, eds., *Language Diversity: Problem or Resource?* (Cambridge: Newbury House Publishers), pp. 367–86.

Woodward, C. Vann. 1957. *The Strange Career of Jim Crow* (New York: Vintage Books).

Wright, Guy. n.d. [c. 1983]. "U.S. English," *San Francisco Sunday Examiner and Chronicle*, p. B9.

Yarborough, Senator Ralph. 1967 [1992]. "Introducing the Bilingual Education Act," speech to U.S. Senate (January 17, 1967), excerpted in James Crawford, ed., *Language Loyalties: A Source Book on the Official English Controversy* (Chicago: University of Chicago Press), pp. 322–325.

Yniguez v. Mofford, 730 F.Supp. 309 (D.Ariz. 1990).

Young, Crawford. 1976. *The Politics of Cultural Pluralism* (Madison: University of Wisconsin Press).

Young, Crawford. 1993. "The Dialectics of Cultural Pluralism: Concept and Reality," in Crawford Young, ed., *The Rising Tide of Cultural Pluralism: The Nation-State at Bay?* (Madison: University of Wisconsin Press), pp. 3–35.

Young, Iris Marion. 1990. *Justice and the Politics of Difference* (Princeton: Princeton University Press).

Index

accent discrimination, 251n
African Americans: cultural oppression, 107–8; enslavement, 102; racialized domination/exclusion, 104; as model for cultural integration, 158
Alabama, 29
Alaska, 29
"American century," 174
American Indians. *See* Native Americans
Americanization, 1, 5
Anderson, Benedict, 43
Anglo American, definition, 252n
Anglophones (Canadian), 15
Annenberg, Walter, 31
anti-immigration argument, 128–29
Appiah, K. Anthony, 248, 255n
Arabic, 62
Arizona, 3, 29, 251n
Arizonans for Official English v. State of Arizona (1997), 35
Arkansas, 29
Asian American Business Group v. City of Pomona (1989), 147
Asian languages, U.S. speakers of, 71–72
Asian/Pacific Islander Americans: and accent discrimination, 251n; exclusionary laws re, 102; racialized domination/exclusion, 105
assimilation, linguistic, 1. *See also* language shift
assimilationists, introduced, 5; communitarian nativist, 128–29, 243–44; critique by author, 184–98;

historical misperceptions, 184–91; historical perspective of, 115–29; liberal individualist, 242–43; and pluralistic integration, 242–44; position on language discrimination, 149–53; position on national unity and language, 163–71; position on "promotion-oriented" language rights, 156–59; position on social equality and language policy, 139–45
Association Mixta Progresista v. HEW (1974), 23
Australia, 38, 227; pluralist policy, 61

Bangladesh, 59
Barrera, Mario, 214–15
Barzun, Jacques, 31
Basque country, 60
Belgium, 38, confederation policy, 64
Bellow, Saul, 31
Bennett, William C., 16, 165–66
Berlin, Isaiah, 145
Bethell, Tom, 164
Bettelheim, Bruno, 31
Bilingual Education Act (1968), 11, 131
bilingual education: as egalitarian, 130–39; evaluation research, 160–61; general, 11–19; historical precedents, 111, 113; as inegalitarian, 139–44; maintenance approach, 14, 131–39; and parents, 137–38; and political empowerment, 136; as preventing learning English, 142–44; as segregative,

275

bilingual education (cont.)
140–42; and social status, 132,
134–36; transitional approach,
13–14, 130–31
bilingualism, U.S., 72–75; economic
benefits, 245–46
Bill 101 (Quebec), 65
Boswell, Thomas, 245–46
Breton, Raymond, 255n
Bretzer, Joanne, 152
*Brown v. Board of Education of Topeka,
Kansas* (1954), 158
Buchanan, Patrick, 129
Bureau of Indian Affairs (U.S. De-
partment of Interior), 210
Bush, President George, 16, 21

California, 2–3, 14, 29, 165
Canada, pluralist policy, 61;
Canada, 38, 64, 227; B&B Commission's rationale for pluralist lan-
guage rights, 155–156; British con-
quest of French (1763), 216; federal
system, 217; government roles in
economy, 218; parliamentary sys-
tems, 217; political culture as rela-
tively "corporatist," 217, 219; pub-
lic opinion, 218
Carter, President Jimmy, 175
Catalonia, 60
Cavazos, Lauro, 16
Census, 1990, U.S., 70–73
centrists, U.S. political, 244–47
Charter of the French Language
(Quebec), 65, 202–3
Chavez, Linda, 34, 157–58, 166–67;
192
Chicanos, 215–16. *See also* Mexican
Americans
China, 38; pluralist policy, 61
Chinese Exclusion Act (1882), 101
Civil Rights Act (1964), 23, 148
Clinton, President William, 17, 30;
Initiative on Race, 249
Colorado, 29

community-based organizations
(CBOs), 227, 229
confederation, linguistic: and American Indian reservations, 210–12;
appropriateness for U.S., 210–20;
critique by author, 215–20; introduced, 63–66; and Puerto Rico,
212–14; and urban U.S., 214–20
Cooke, Alistair, 31
Court Interpreters Act (1978), 24
Cousins, Norman, 31
Crèvecoeur, Hector St. John, 116
Cronkite, Walter, 31, 34
cultural oppression, U.S., 107–10; and
education policy, 109–10
cultural pluralism, U.S.: and ethnic
enclaves, 113; and ethnic organizations, 112–13; general, 110–15; and
government support, 114; and labor unions, 113; and media, 112;
and political parties, 113; and public schools, 113; and religious institutions, 111; and schooling, 111–12
culture wars, U.S., 88–91
Cummins, James, 133–38; 255–56n;
additive bilingual enrichment principle, 133; linguistic interdependence principle, 134

Dade County, Florida, 2; School District, 245
de la Garza, Rodolfo, 256n
de Tocqueville, Alexis, 251–52n
Declaration of Independence, U.S.,
146
democratic left, 247–49; social justice
agenda, 248–49; and ethnolinguistic justice, 248–49
DeSipio, Louis, 256n
Dole, Senator Robert, 3, 30
domain, linguistic, 206–7
domination/exclusion, U.S. historical, 103–10
due process clause, 147
Duke, Angier Biddle, 31

Eastman, Carol M., 206–7
Ebonics, 36
economic inequality, U.S.: argument for policies to ameliorate, 237–42; and common good, 240; and linguistic justice, 237–40; recent policies toward, 240–41
educational attainment rates, U.S., 92
Elementary and Secondary Education Act of 1965, 11
Emerson English Language Empowerment Bill (H.R. 123), 3, 30
English dominance, U.S., 1, 69–70, 139–40, 223
English First, 31
English immersion, 15
English Literacy Grants Program, 33
English Plus Resolution (U.S. Congress), 33, 226
English Proficiency Act, 33
English: as national language, 223; as requirement for U.S. naturalization, 223
English-only. See Official English
English-Plus Information Clearinghouse (EPIC), 32–33
Equal Educational Opportunities Act (1974), 13, 29, 149
Equal Employment Opportunities Commission (EEOC), 24–27, 149, 227, 229
equal rights, and language policy, 145–59
equality, ethnolinguistic, and identity politics, 161–62
Esquivel, Rita, 16
ethnic equality and language policy, general, 45–47; and pluralistic integration, 228–42
ethnic groups, definition, 45–46
ethnic inequality, U.S., 91–95
ethnic mobilization, general, 46
ethnic revival, U.S., 100
ethnicity, U.S., 86–88

Federal Communications Commission (FCC), 36
Federation for American Immigration Reform (FAIR), 31
Ferrer, Maurice, 126–27
Finland, 38; confederation policy, 64
First Amendment (U.S. Constitution), 147
Fishman, Joshua, 176
Florida, 29
Fourteenth Amendment (U.S. Constitution), 147, 158
Fraga, Luis, 251n
France, 38, 64; assimilation policy, 59
Francophones (Canada), 65, 202
freedom of expression: and Arizona Official English law, 148; and language rights, 147
Frontera v. Sindell (1975), 27

Garcia v. Gloor (1980), 27
Garcia v. Spun Steak Co. (1993), 27
Georgia, 29
German-speakers, U.S., 70
Gilder, George, 31
Glazer, Nathan, 117–18, 164–65
Goals 2000: Educate America Act of 1994, 17
Goldwater, Barry, 31
Gonzalez, Roseann D., 171–74
Great Britain, 38, 64; assimilation policy, 59
Griggs v. Duke Power Co. (1971), 25
Guidelines on National-Origin Discrimination (EEOC), 26
Gurza, Augustin, 256n
Gutierrez v. Municipal Court (1988), 27
Gutmann, Amy, 248

Hakuta, Kenji, 133
Hausa (Nigeria), 62
Hayakawa, Senator S. I., 31, 165, 169
Hayes-Bautista, David, 246–47
hegemonic language, 54, 228
hegemony, defined, 252n

Helsinki Accords (1975), 147
Herder, Johann, 44
Hernandez v. State of New York (1991), 24
Hernandez-Chavez, Eduardo, 142, 154–55
Higham, John, 225, 230
Hispanics, definition, 252n
Hochschild, Jennifer, 248–49
Hollinger, David A., 89–90
Hook, Sidney, 31
Horne, Gerald, 249
Horsman, Reginald, 106–7
Huddleston, Senator Walter, 151
Hufstedler, Judge Shirley, 148–49
Huggins, Nathan Irwin, 108

identity politics: essentialism, 49; and ethnolinguistic equality, 162; foundations, 47–51; general, 47–56; and language, 49–50, 224; and material interests, 54–56; and national unity, 176–80; and pluralistic integration proposals, 230–34; primordialism, 49; stakes in, 51–56; and symbolic recognition, 52–54; and U.S. multiculturalism, 232
identity: as constitutive, 48–49; as relational, 48–49
Igbo (Nigeria), 62
Illinois, 29
Imahara, Kathryn, 179
Imhoff, Gary, 123–24, 126–27, 163–64, 167, 190
immigrant incorporation, U.S., 187–91; 196
immigrants: as desiring pluralistic integration, 236–37; and pluralistic integration proposals, 234–37; settlement policy for, 228
Immigration Reform and Control Act (1986), 121
immigration: assimilationist view, 119; recent U.S., 120–22; regions of origin, 121

Improving America's Schools Act (1994), 17
income, U.S. household, 93
India: confederation policy, 64; pluralist policy, 61
Indiana, 29
"Indian Country," 210
Inouye, Senator Daniel, 211–12
"institutional completeness," 217
International Covenant on Civil and Political Rights (1966), 147
internationalized economy, and language policy, 174–76
Ireland, 59
Isaacs, Harold R., 49–50

Jackson, President Andrew, 107
Jefferson, President Thomas, 107
Jim Crow Laws, 158
Johnson, President Lyndon, 12

Kallen, Horace, 111, 225
Karenga, Maulana, 108
Kentucky, 29
King, Martin Luther Jr., 180
Kloss, Heinz, 145, 153
Kuri v. Edelman (1974), 23
Kymlicka, Will, 146, 192–95, 204, 237–38, 239

Laitin, David D., 252n, 254n
Lamm, Richard D., 126–27, 167
language competition, general, 39; U.S., 76–83
language contact: general, 39; U.S., 75–76
language *corpus,* 39
language discrimination, 145–53; against English-speakers, 151–53; assimilationist arguments re, 149–53; pluralist arguments re, 145–49
language diversity: general, 38–39; India, 38; Nigeria, 38; U.S., 38–39, 69–75

language minorities, defined, 21
language minority students: definition, 252n; education for, 11–19
language planning, 40–41
language policy approaches: assimilation, 59–60; confederation, 63–66; domination/exclusion, 58–59; pluralism, 60–63; typology, 57
language rights, in workplace, 24–28
language rights, promotion-oriented, 145; arguments over, 153–59; assimilationist position, 156–59; Canadian B&B Commission's rationale for, 155–56; and ethnolinguistic group survival, 154; pluralist position, 153–56
language rights, tolerance-oriented, 145; assimilationist position, 149–53; and freedom of expression, 147–48; liberalism and, 145–46; and nondiscrimination, 148–49; pluralist position, 145–49
language shift, 1; U.S., 72–75
language *status*, 39
language: as ethnic group boundary marker, 46; as hegemonic, 54; as national boundary marker, 44
Latino National Political Survey (LNPS), 78–83; 253–54n
Latinos, U.S.: definition, 252n; language policy public opinion, 78–83
Latouche, Daniel, 203–204
Lau Remedies, 13
Lau v. Nichols (1974), 2, 12–13, 148, 153
Leadership Conference on Civil Rights, 20
Learn English Advocates Drive (LEAD), 153
liberalism: and cultural pluralism, 192–95; weaknesses of liberal voluntarism, 205–8
limited English proficient (LEP) students, 1
linguistic access, 19–28; to employment rights , 24–28, 227; to public services, 22–24, 227; to voting rights, 19–22, 227
linguistic diversity, U.S., 224
Los Angeles County Board of Supervisors, 172–73
Louisiana Purchase, 101

Macias, Reynaldo, 73–74
maintenance bilingual education, 14, 131–39
Malaysia, 38, 64
Marshall, David F., 171–74
Massachusetts, 14
May, Cordelia Scaife, 34
Méndez v. Westminister School District (1947), 158
Mexican American Legal Defense and Education Fund (MALDEF), 19–20, 125, 246–47
Mexican Americans: compared with Quebecois, 215–19; and confederation alternative, 214–20; conquest and annexation, 101; cultural oppression, 109; as immigrants, 123–24; opinions on language policy, 219; racialized domination/exclusion, 104–5
Meyer v. Nebraska (1923), 147
Miami, Florida, 2, 29, 126–27, 207; two-way bilingual education policy (1998), 245–46
minority, definition, 251n
Mississippi, 29
Molfitt, Phillip, 127
Montana, 29
multiculturalism, as cosmopolitan, 232

Nagel, Joane, 54
"nation of immigrants," U.S. as, 101
nation, definition, 42–43
national unity and language: France, 44; general, 42–45; United Kingdom, 44
nationalism, U.S., 84–86

Native American Languages Act (1990), 35–36, 211–12, 227
Native American languages, endangered, 210
Native Americans: conquest and annexation, 101; cultural oppression, 106–7; racialized domination/exclusion, 103–4; self-determination policy, 210
Navajo-speakers, U.S., 70
Nebraska, 29, 147
net worth, U.S. household, 93
New Hampshire, 29
Nigeria, 64; pluralist policy, 62
nondiscrimination, right to, 148–49
non-governmental organizations (NGOs), 227, 229
North Carolina, 29
North Dakota, 29
Norway, 38

Official English: Arkansas law, 29; Arizona law, 29–30; California law, 3; municipal ordinances, 29; political movement for, 28–35; political opposition to, 32–35; proposed English Language (Constitutional) Amendment, 28; state laws, 28–29
Oh, Angela, 249
Olzak, Susan, 54

Pabon v. Levine (1976), 23
Pakistan, assimilation policy, 59
Paraguay, 38; pluralist policy, 61
Patterson, Orlando, 168–69
Peru, 38; pluralist policy, 61
Phillipines, 38
philology, 106–7
Pioneer Fund, 34
Platt Amendment, 253n
pluralistic integration: appeal to assimilationists, 242–44; appeal to democratic left, 247–49; appeal to political center, 244–47; arguments for egalitarian economic policy proposals, 237–42; arguments for immigrant settlement policy proposals, 234–37; arguments for language-specific proposals, 228–34; clarification of goals, 225–26; egalitarian economic policy proposal, 228; immigrant settlement policy proposals, 228; language-specific policy proposals, 226–27; policy proposal, 225–28; source of concept, 225
pluralists, linguistic: critique by author, 199–209; critique by Quebecois, 202–6; historical perspective, 100–15; introduced, 4–5; position on bilingual education, 14, 131–39; position on language policy and social equality, 130–39; position on national unity, common good and language, 171–76; position on promotion-oriented language rights, 153–56; position on tolerance-oriented language rights, 145–49; strengths of arguments, 198–99
Podhoretz, Norman, 31
policy analysis: value-committed, 6; value-critical, 6–7; value-neutral, 6
Porter, Rosalie Pedalino, 140–41, 167–168
Portes, Alejandro, 207
poverty and welfare receipt rates, U.S., 94
Prendas, Ralph, 169
President's Commission on Foreign Languages and International Studies, 175–76, 229
Proposition 227 (California, 1998), 18–19, 245, 252n
Proposition 63 (California, 1986), 165
public opinion, U.S. language issues, 78–83
public schools, as agents of assimilation, 119
public-private distinction, importance of: assimilationist position, 156–57; author's critique, 191–96

Puerto Rico: commitment to Spanish language, 213–14; commonwealth status, 212; language policy, 213–14; political "fault lines", 212; relation to U.S. government, 212; U.S. efforts at linguistic assimilation, 213

Quebec: confederation policy, 65–66; demographic composition, 216; historical development, 216–17; language policy compared with U.S. Southwest, 215–19; public opinion, 218
Quebecois, critique of pluralism, 202–6
"Quiet Revolution" (Quebec), 203

racial inequality, U.S., 91–95
racialization, U.S., 91; historical, 103–10; ideology, 106–7; and language, 107, 178–79, 189–90; of recent immigrants, 186–91
racialized ethnic groups, 19
Reagan, President Ronald, 15, 21
Reed, Adolph Jr., 249
rights, linguistic access to, 19–28; arguments against, 144–45; arguments for, 139
Rodriguez, Richard, 141–42, 178, 201–2, 256n
Roosevelt, President Theodore, 174

San Diego, 207
San Francisco, 29
Sanchez v. Norton (1974), 23
Schaar, John H., 240
Schauffler, Richard, 207
Schlesinger, Arthur Jr., 116–17
School-to-Work Opportunities Act of 1994, 17
Schwarzenegger, Arnold, 31
Scotland, 59
Serrano, Congressman Jose, 33
Shapiro, Karl, 31
Shumway, Norman, 151
Smith, Anthony D., 43

Smith, Rogers, 43, 244
social conflict, and language policy, 163–74
social equality, and language policy, 130–45, 225–42
South Africa, 38, 64; pluralist policy, 62
South Carolina, 29
South Dakota, 29
Soviet Union. See Union of Soviet Socialist Republics
Spain, 38; assimilation policy, 59–60; confederation policy, 64
Spanish-American War (1898), 101
Spanish-speakers, U.S., 24, 70
state governments, language policies, 28–29; 32
state role, re language, 39–41
Sweden, 38
Switzerland, 38; confederation policy, 64

Tanton, Dr. John, 31, 33–34; 128
Tatalovich, Raymond, 251n
Taylor, Charles, 52, 254n
Tennessee, 29
territorial principle, linguistic, 63, 203, 209. See also confederation, linguistic
Thernstrom, Abigail, 124–26, 140
Title VII, 11–19. See also Bilingual Education Act (1968)
trail of tears, 104
transitional bilingual education, 13–14; 130–31
Treaty of Guadalupe Hidalgo (1848), 101, 114

U.S. Commission on Civil Rights: on bilingual education, 132; on voting rights and language, 20
U.S. English, 30–34
U.S. ex rel. Negron v. New York (1970), 24
U.S. House of Representatives, 3, 30

U.S. Senate Committee on Indian Affairs, 211
U.S. Supreme Court, 2
Uganda, 38
Unger, Roberto, 248
Union of Soviet Socialist Republics, 38; pluralist policy, 61
United Nations Charter (1945), 146
Universal Declaration of Human Rights (1948), 146
Univision, 252n
Unz, Ron, 4
Urciuoli, Bonnie, 190

Virginia, 29
Voting Rights Act of 1965, 153, 227; assimilationist critique of language provisions, 124–26; linguistic access components, 2, 19–22

Waggoner, Dorothy, 71–73
Wales, 59
Weinstein, Brian, 55–56
West, Cornell, 248
World War II, 146
Wright, Guy, 31
Wyoming, 29

Yarborough, Senator Ralph, 12, 131
Yniguez and Gutierrez v. Mofford, Corbin, and Eden (1990), 34–35. See also Arizonans for Official English v. State of Arizona (1997)
Yoruba (Nigeria), 62
Young, Iris Marion, 49, 194, 199
Yugoslavia, confederation policy, 64

Zero Population Growth, 31